Praise for Propaganda and the Public Mind

"In *Propaganda and the Public Mind*, we have unique insight into Noam Chomsky's decades of penetrating analyses ... drawn together in one slender volume by a brilliant radio interviewer, David Barsamian. They make clear that the new electronic media and their corporate culture ignore national boundaries and in that sense exceed in power individual nations of the world whose borders they so easily penetrate."
—Ben Bagdikian, author, *The Media Monopoly*

"To anyone who wonders if ideas, information, and activism can make a profound difference in the twenty-first century, I say: 'Read this book.' *Propaganda and the Public Mind* challenges us to think more independently and more deeply about the human consequences of power and privilege. It also minces no words about the grim results of illusion and inaction. These discussions between Noam Chomsky and David Barsamian will inspire readers to explore wider possibilities.... What we do with it is up to us."
—Norman Solomon, author, *The Habits of Highly Deceptive Media*

Praise for Noam Chomsky

"An exploder of received truths."
—*New York Times*

"Reading Chomsky is like standing in a wind tunnel. With relentless logic, Chomsky bids us to listen closely to what our leaders tell us—and to discern what they are leaving out.... The questions Chomsky raises will eventually have to be answered. Agree with him or not, we lose out by not listening."
—*Business Week*

"One of the radical heroes of our age.... A towering intellect.... Powerful, always provocative."

—*The Guardian*

"Chomsky's work is neither theoretical, nor ideological: it is passionate and righteous. It has some of the qualities of Revelations, the Old Testament prophets and Blake."

—*Times Literary Supplement*

"Noam Chomsky is like a medic attempting to cure a national epidemic of selective amnesia."

—*Village Voice*

Praise for David Barsamian

"David Barsamian is the Studs Terkel of our generation."

—Howard Zinn, author, *A People's History of the United States*

"In conversation [with David Barsamian], Chomsky is more relaxed, tentative, and discursive than he is in his books or his public speaking engagements."

—*Vancouver Sun*

Propaganda and the Public Mind

Conversations with Noam Chomsky

David Barsamian and Noam Chomsky

Pluto Press
London

First published in the United Kingdom 2001 by
Pluto Press
345 Archway Road
London N6 5AA

www.plutobooks.com

British Library Cataloguing in Publication Data
A catalogue record for this book is available from the British Library.

ISBN 0 7453 1789 8 hardback
ISBN 0 7453 1788 X paperback

Printed in Canada

Table of Contents

Noam Chomsky (left) and David Barsamian (right) during an interview in Chomsky's office at MIT in Building 20. Photo by Mark Achbar from the film *Manufacturing Consent: Noam Chomsky and the Media*, produced by Achbar and Peter Wintonick.

Acknowledgments

KGNU, in Boulder, is the nourishing community radio station from whence much of my audio activism springs. Sandy Adler is the transcriber par excellence. Elaine Bernard provides invaluable support. David Peterson is the fact checker extraordinaire. Bev Stohl is a great help on numerous levels. Thanks to Martin Voelker, Lincoln Clarkes, and Mark Achbar for their photographs. Anthony Arnove is a terrific editor. Noam Chomsky is a gem of compassion.

Interview excerpts appeared in *The Nation, The Progressive, Z,* and on Z Net, and have aired on KGNU and "Making Contact." The first interview was recorded in Boulder during Chomsky's 1998 visit. The second, third, and sixth were all recorded at his home in Lexington, Massachusetts. Interviews four and five were done by phone from KGNU, with the East Timor one broadcast live at the height of the post-referendum crisis. The last interview was recorded at Z Media Institute in Woods Hole, Massachusetts.

Noam Chomsky in Canada. Photo by Lincoln Clarkes.

Introduction

I first wrote to Noam Chomsky around 1980. Much to my surprise, he responded. We did our first interview four years later. We've done scores since, resulting in a series of books, as well as radio programs. The interview collections have sold in the hundreds of thousands, which is remarkable since they have had virtually no promotion and have not been reviewed, even in left journals. In working with Chomsky over the years, I've been struck by his consistency, patience, and equanimity. There are no power plays or superior airs. His rich and wry sense of humor often goes unnoticed in the fusillade of facts. In terms of his intellectual chops, he is awesome in his ability to take a wide and disparate amount of information and cobble it into a coherent analysis.

Chomsky is indefatigable. He is, "a rebel," as Bono of U2 calls him, "without a pause." In addition to producing a steady stream of articles and books on politics and linguistics, he maintains a heavy speaking schedule. He is in enormous demand and is often booked years in advance. He draws huge audiences wherever he goes, though not because of a flashy speaking style. As he once told me, "I'm not a charismatic speaker, and if I had the capacity to be one I wouldn't. I'm really not interested in persuading people. What I like to do is help people persuade themselves." And this he has done probably with more diligence over a longer period of time than any other intellectual alive.

To cite just one example of his solidarity, in 1998 I asked him to come to Boulder to speak at KGNU's twentieth anniversary celebration. Notwithstanding being fatigued from recent surgery, he not only came but waived his fee.

Chomsky is a very special person to many people—not just in the United States, but around the world. Frequently he's introduced as someone who speaks truth to power. It's almost a cliché. But that's not really what he's about. He's about speaking truth to us, speaking truth to people. As he reminded us in a classic essay thirty years ago, "It is the responsibility of intellectuals to speak the truth and to expose lies."

Like the Sufi sages of West and South Asia, Noam Chomsky teaches by practice. His practice includes an egalitarian spirit, where the Nobel Prize winner will sit and wait outside his office until the student writing an article for the high school newspaper finishes. His practice includes alerting us to the depredations of language, terms like "free trade" and "national interest." His practice is exemplified in the solidarity and service he extends to people from East Timor to Palestine to Colombia to East Harlem. You need a speaker, you need a signature, you need help, Noam Chomsky is there. His practice is to tell you what he thinks, but not what you should think. His practice is to comfort the afflicted and afflict the comfortable. Rather than simply curse the darkness, his practice is to light a candle for us to see.

Although decidedly secular, he is for many of us our rabbi, our preacher, our rinpoche, our pundit, our imam, our sensei.

— David Barsamian
Boulder, Colorado

Activist Victories

Boulder, Colorado, May 10, 1998

Your busy speaking schedule has taken you recently to Toronto, Winona State University in Winona, Minnesota; Fort Wayne, Indiana; London, England; and today Boulder, Colorado. What's going on at these events? I know you've been getting huge crowds.

You can see that the tour is building up in significance and importance, finally reaching the peak in Boulder. You can't do better than this. [*Laughs.*] It's pretty much what's been going on for a number of years now. There are very large, enthusiastic, and interested audiences that participate actively. They ask serious questions and want to talk about important issues. Topics that I never would have thought of discussing twenty years ago are now perfectly accessible to anyone. I really never think twice about what I'm going to say to a particular audience. London is a different scene, but Fort Wayne was organized by the Northeast Indiana Labor Council, a collection of a couple of dozen unions in the industrial heartland. I don't know the Winona area very well, but I imagine it's mostly farming and small industry. In both cases, you couldn't ask for a more involved, energetic, and thoughtful audience. They want to think hard about what's happening in the world and what they can do about it.

Do you have a sense that you're talking to the choir, or are you reaching the congregation?

These aren't exactly places that are peppered with lefty activists. These are what are called ordinary people.

So, not a lot of Z Magazine *subscribers and readers of Common Courage Press books.*

You meet a few now and then, but they're scattered around. I met one or two people who had been at the Z Media Institute and who were familiar with the magazine, but certainly 99 percent are not.

The Fort Wayne event was singular in one particular respect.

Actually, it was unusual for me. I've spoken to labor groups elsewhere, in Canada and overseas, but it's the first time I can recall being invited by a mainstream labor grouping in the U.S. at a place like that. It is sort of right in the middle of what has been the industrial heartland of the country — in fact, it's considered a pretty right-wing area, but it sure didn't have that feel. After the talk there was a reception. They were raising money for the unions, twenty-five dollars a shot, but a lot of people were there. We stayed around for hours and had a great discussion until early in the morning.

In the May 1998 Z Magazine *you have an article entitled "Domestic Constituencies," where you talk about various free trade agreements and proposals. You comment that "it is always enlightening to seek out what is omitted in propaganda campaigns."* [1] *What did your investigations into the particular propaganda effort around the Multilateral Agreement on Investment reveal?*

The MAI is a major investment treaty. It has been planned and intensively negotiated now for three years, first at the World Trade Organization (WTO), and when they couldn't ram it through there, it moved over to the Organization for Economic Cooperation and Development in Paris. The OECD consists of the twenty-nine rich countries. MAI has been going on there since May 1995. There's been extensive, intimate involvement of the corporate sector. There's a group called the U.S. Council for International Business which is essentially the main lobbying organization for internationally oriented corporations. They actually put out a monograph in January 1996 informing their constituency of the contents of MAI and its importance.[2] Congress hasn't been informed. In this same article, I reviewed the mainstream press. It's been astonishingly silent. It has yet to make the *New York Times*. The *Wall Street Journal* had a report.[3] In early April, the *Washington Post* had its first news article.[4] It reported the failure of the OECD to sign it after three years due in large measure to grassroots pressure. Though the matter was kept virtually secret, nevertheless enough pressure developed through nongovernmental organizations, public interest groups, and grassroots activists so that they felt they had to back down. It is quite an important victory. It shows that things can be done. Canada is the one country where it did break through into the public arena about a year ago. That's still after two years of intense negotiations. It's been on national television and in the mainstream press like the Toronto *Globe and Mail* and journals like *Maclean's*. In Australia it broke through this January and then there was a storm of protest and a lot of discussion. In Europe it was picked up just in the last few months.

But in the U.S., apart from what you might call statistical error, there's been essentially nothing. It's not that it's unknown. All media leaders of course know about it. The whole corporate world knows about it. It was almost certainly the main issue behind giving the president what's called "fast-track" authority to approve trade agreements. There was a lot of furor about fast track, but I couldn't find a single mention of this, although the media must have known that this was a central issue. The *Miami Herald* did have an article last July on the MAI.[5] The fast-track legislation had not yet been introduced in Congress at that point but was being considered. The article pointed out that the U.S. Council for International Business had already approached the White House, asking them to make the MAI a central element of the fast-track negotiations with Congress. That's what they wanted to ram through. It surely was far more important than, say, extending the North American Free Trade Agreement (NAFTA) to South America. But if there was a mention of it, I couldn't find it. It's one of many things that was unreported. There are plenty of others. But, despite the suppression, somehow enough of the public was able to get organized to block it.

That's a very dramatic event — and it is important. *Business Week* had a report last February with the headline, "The Explosive

Trade Deal You've Never Heard Of."[6] And if you are not reading the literature of the U.S. Council for International Business, you didn't hear of it. It is an explosive trade deal, or would be. It's now going to shift to a more secretive framework. It'll go on, and it'll require even more serious activism to try to expose what's happening, to debate it and oppose it if it ought to be opposed, and I think it should. People could decide that for themselves if they had the information.

Why were the negotiations so secretive?

There's a pretty good reason why the information is not being made available. Media and business leaders know perfectly well that the public is going to be strongly opposed. In fact, the public was so strongly opposed to fast track that its supporters couldn't get it through, even though the business world was virtually 100 percent in favor of it, the media were all in favor of it, and the White House was running a big propaganda campaign. Even people in Congress who favored it strongly voted against it because their doors were being rammed down by their constituents. Even without knowing the facts, people have an instinctive and indeed rather healthy reaction of skepticism about these things.

Another thing that wasn't mentioned about fast track and which is worth bearing in mind is that the discussion about it was presented as if it were about free trade. It surely wasn't about free trade. First of all, the agreements that they're talking about are not free trade agreements. They are highly protectionist. They don't fall under free trade — virtually nothing does. But quite apart from that, even the most ardent free trader would have been against fast track if they happen to believe in democracy, because that's what it was about. The question was, "Should the president, the White House, have the right to negotiate trade agreements in secret and then present them to Congress with the privilege of saying 'yes' or 'no' but not discussing them and without the public ever being informed?" That's a question about democracy. It's not a question about trade agreements.

The official White House position was that we have to abide by the principle that the president alone, one person alone, can enter into international trade negotiations. That certainly is no principle.

For example, on human rights issues, it's insisted that Congress have years to tear away at them, cut them back, put in reservations. In fact, that's one of the reasons the U.S. has probably the worst record in the industrial world in ratifying human rights conventions. They almost never get ratified. So on human rights that's certainly not a principle. On trade it may be a principle, but that's because of what they're trying to ram through. They know the public won't like it. The *Wall Street Journal* conceded that, sort of obliquely. In one of their news articles praising fast track as a no-brainer, something so obvious that anybody sensible would want it, they said that nevertheless the critics had what they called an "ultimate weapon": that the public is opposed.[7] So therefore you'd better keep them out of it. That's the implication.

On the MAI, they were afraid that the "ultimate weapon" might be unsheathed, and indeed it was, astonishingly. A lot of people feel that we can't do anything, that prospects are gloomy. I don't think that's true at all. This is a rather dramatic illustration of the opposite. Against tremendous odds, confronting the most concentrated power in the world, the richest, most powerful countries, transnational corporations, international financial institutions, and close to total control of the media. That's a consolidated power of a kind that you can't find in history. Despite that, grassroots activism was able to stop it.

Do you see a possible trend here beginning with the successful UPS strike and the widespread public support for the strikers, then the defeat of fast track, the reversal on MAI, and also the successful Columbus, Ohio, protest against the bombing of Iraq?

The only reservation I have is that I don't think it's new. I think it's been going on for a long time. Right through the 1980s, for example, popular activism was so strong that the Reagan administration was never able to intervene directly in Central America. They were unable to do anything remotely like what Kennedy and Johnson did in Southeast Asia in the 1960s. That's simply because there was far too much public opposition. So they had to do it indirectly, through clandestine terror.

You can see it in reporting that's going on now on the death of Bishop Juan Gerardi in Guatemala. Read that reporting. There's a slight omission. The fact that another leading church figure was murdered in Central America is not big news. That's been happening for a while. But he was killed right as he was about to release a big study done by the church called *Never Again,* which gave a very detailed analysis of the atrocities carried out in Guatemala.[8] It's one of the real horror stories of past years. They calculated that about 200,000 people had been killed, over a million and a half refugees, hundreds of thousands of orphans and widows. They attributed about 80 percent of it to the government and the paramilitaries connected to it, only 10 percent to the guerrillas, the rest unknown.

Who is the government? The government was established, armed, trained, and supported by the United States. The U.S. government couldn't move in directly because of popular opposition, so they used mercenaries. The whole international terror network — Taiwan, Israel, Britain, Saudi Arabia, Argentinian neo-Nazis — was involved in Central America. The worst atrocities in Guatemala, the church report shows, were under the rule of Rios Montt, who was the favorite of Washington. Reagan was praising him all over the place as a real friend of democracy who was getting a "bum rap" from the human rights groups, meanwhile killing tens of thousands of people.[9]

The U.S. was pretty much excluded from the discussion, in some reports wasn't even mentioned at all. But it was behind the scenes. Crucially, it was not directly involved. The place was not being bombed by B-52s. There weren't hundreds of thousands of U.S. troops roaming around. That's because of the brake that was imposed by the popular activism of the 1980s, which was happening all over the country and was not concentrated in urban centers and college campuses. It was taking place in rural areas in the Southwest and Midwest. It was very strong. So there's nothing new about this.

It's right in front of our eyes. The big popular movements — the environmental, feminist, and other movements — are all developments of the past few decades. And they are achieving a lot. Fast track was very dramatic in this respect. As the White House correctly pointed out, that's an option that had been available for presidents all the time. Nobody had ever paid attention, because it was considered right. If the president wants to make important deals in secret and leave Congress and the public out of it, what could be wrong with that? Now people feel there's something wrong with it, and that's a lot of progress. They not only feel that there's something wrong with it, but they feel that strongly enough that they are able to overcome the extraordinarily powerful forces that are trying to ram it through. This is a lot of progress.

One of the chapters in Manufacturing Consent, *which you coauthored with Edward Herman, is entitled "Worthy and Unworthy Victims." The assassination of Juan Gerardi was covered on page 5 of the* New York Times.[10] *What might have been the coverage if he were a Cuban bishop, for example?*

There would have been huge headlines all over the front pages. We need not discuss it. It's obvious.

So that construct still holds.

That's just another example. In fact, in that book that Ed and I wrote, one of the chapters that he did compares a hundred religious martyrs in Central America with one Polish priest killed in Eastern Europe.[11] The killers in Poland were immediately apprehended, sent to long jail sentences, unlike the hundred religious martyrs in Central America, including Archbishop Oscar Romero and four churchwomen from the United States. Ed did a media review that showed that the coverage of the one Polish priest was more than that of 100 religious martyrs, and quite different in character. In that case, the press demanded that it be traced to the highest level. "The Kremlin can't escape blame," and so on. In the case of the archbishop, the nuns, and the laywomen from the United States, as well as lots of other religious martyrs, it was all some local accident. They can't figure out what it is. There was very little coverage and it was relegated to the back pages, with no graphic details. To this day, there has been no serious inquiry here into the death of Archbishop Romero.

When the six Jesuit intellectuals were murdered, it was reported. But ask people what their names were. Ask them to name some dissidents in Eastern Europe. Dissidents in Eastern Europe who suffered, but in the post-Stalin era who suffered nothing like their counterparts in Central America, were heroes. They're well known. Their books are all over the place. They're quoted. They have articles in the *New York Review of Books*. The Central American intellectuals, who suffered far harsher conditions under our supervision, and in this case had their brains blown out, they've been doubly assassinated. First they were assassinated by the same U.S.-trained troops who killed Romero and tens of thousands of others, and then they were assassinated by the intellectual community. What better way of killing intellectuals than suppressing anything they wrote? I've never seen a word of theirs published in mainstream sources here. You'd be hard put to find a reference to it. This terminology, worthy and unworthy victims, which again is Ed's, is quite accurate.

The MAI has been called a political Dracula in that it cannot survive sunlight or any kind of public scrutiny. You cite in that Z Magazine article an interesting quote from Harvard professor Samuel Huntington: "The architects of power in the United States must create a force that can be felt but not seen. Power remains strong when it remains in the dark; exposed to the sunlight it begins to evaporate."[12]

This is a good illustration of that. He's no fool. He understands how power works. He understands the profound importance of keeping the public in the dark, making sure that they don't interfere, that policy will be designed and executed by the authentic centers of power without scrutiny. That's what fast track is about. That's what was illustrated by the MAI.

The point of the MAI is to put up a barrier behind the design and implementation of policy that people will not be able to penetrate. It's to put it behind corporate walls, in effect. Those are impenetrable. Apart from congressional subpoena, you can't find out what's going on inside these tyrannical systems. If they are in a position to make the decisions about social, economic, and political affairs for the world, that's a very efficient tyranny.

There's a nice World Bank phrase for this: People should be able to work in what they call "technocratic insulation."[13] These are the technocrats who know how to run things, the smart guys, and they have to be insulated from scrutiny or interference by the rabble. It's an old idea, not a novel one, but Huntington is describing the forms it has to take in a formally democratic society where you can't send out the death squads.

Whom do you have in mind when you talk about worthy and unworthy constituencies?

In this case, it was made dramatically clear. The *Z* article that you mentioned was called "Domestic Constituencies." That phrase is taken from the one public statement that the White House did make about the MAI. In reaction to the queries from Congress, which were not being answered, and to the public protests which were beginning to surface, they did issue a public statement made by Under Secretary of State Stuart Eizenstat and Deputy U.S. Trade Representative Jeffrey Lang. As far as I'm aware, the public statement was never reported, but it was made. In it the White House spokespersons stated that they wanted to assure the public of their deep commitment to democratic principles. So they said, We are making certain that all of the domestic constituencies that have a vital stake in these issues are being consulted and informed all the way. We wouldn't leave any of them out. They went on to say that we are leading the demand at the OECD because of our profound commitment to democracy. That's approximately the wording.

So, now we can carry out a little exercise in logic. Who are the domestic constituencies? It plainly wasn't Congress. In fact, undoubtedly people in Congress knew, but Congress in general wasn't even informed. Twenty-five representatives wrote a letter to the White House asking, How come you've been negotiating this for three years without telling us? According to the Constitution, international commerce is the province of the Congress. They got the kind of letter that you get if you write a letter to the White House, saying, Dear David, Thank you for your interesting comments. It's written by some computer. That's the kind of letter they got back. So, Congress wasn't a constituency. The public plainly wasn't a constituency. In fact, it was kind of like a negative constituency. The idea was to keep them out of it, keep them off our back.

So, the public isn't a constituency. Congress isn't a constituency. But the U.S. Council for International Business is. They were informed all the way and were intimately involved. The corporate sector was involved. The White House is telling us plainly and clearly who their domestic constituencies are. It's very rare that political leaders are so frank in such a clear and vulgar fashion about exactly the way they perceive the world. It's an accurate perception. But that's not what you're supposed to teach in eighth-grade civics or graduate courses in political science at the University of Colorado. It's just the truth. So it's nice that they said it. I think the media were smart enough to keep it quiet and suppress it. Maybe somebody would think it through.

You've even said that the word "Americans" doesn't refer to Americans.

It's become almost impossible to avoid. Americans should be people from the top to the bottom of the hemisphere, but the U.S. has taken over the word. In Latin America, they use two words, "North American." The word "Americans" is constantly used for the people of the U.S. In part it's because of a linguistic difficulty. It's hard to make an adjective from "United States."

Maybe I should clarify that. You were citing a New York Times *article which said that Americans are basking in the happy glow of an American boom, a fairy-tale U.S. expansion. Which Americans?*

There has been a series of articles about America. For this one, the headline was, "America Is Prosperous and Smug."[14] As I went to England on May 3, the front-page story in the Week in Review in the *Times* was something about "America is fat and happy."[15] It's all about the fairy-tale boom, how Americans are so confident and prosperous and everything is so wonderful. We can ask the same question: Who are they talking about? Is it the roughly two-thirds of Americans whose wages and incomes have either stagnated or declined in the last twenty-five years? Are they the ones who are smug and prosperous and confident or the ones who Alan Greenspan, the chairman of the Federal Reserve Board, is talking about when he attributes the fairy-tale economic boom to what he calls "worker insecurity," since workers are so intimidated that they won't ask for a raise, which is a great thing for the health of the economy because you can drive down wages and make profits high?[16]

Are they the people who are smug and confident and prosperous? Is it the people who are going to the food banks, which are getting increased demand through the fairy-tale boom? No, it's not two-thirds of the population. These articles make it clear who they have in mind. The only example they give of Americans who are happy and prosperous and smug and confident, the one example they keep coming back to, is people who have made money on the stock market. Which is fair. You've got people in the stock market who are doing great. Who are they? It turns out that 1 percent of households own about 50 percent of the stock. One-half percent of households own about 40 percent of the stock. The next half owns the next 10 percent. About 10 percent own 90 percent of the stock. So they're doing fine, so high off the chart that the Census Bureau doesn't count them because they're the top half percent or 1 percent. They're making out like bandits. It drifts down to maybe the top 20 to 25 percent of the population who are getting by or doing all right or maybe even doing well. Then comes maybe the 75 percent who don't count.[17] They're doing worse than before. But when you say Americans are "smug" and "prosperous," you're not referring to them. They're not the people you meet in elegant restaurants and corporate boardrooms, editorial offices, and so on. "Americans" means those people.

There have been a couple of other articles which bring this out in a curious way. I have a feeling reporters, some of them at least, must know what they're doing. Louis Uchitelle of the *New York Times*, who is a very good economics correspondent, has had articles which are framed rather interestingly. He had one called something like "The Rehabilitation of Morning in America."[18] Morning is back again. Reagan. John Wayne riding into the sunset. He talked about how these are great and wonderful times. All through the article he quoted Jerry Jasinowski, the head of the National Association of Manufacturers, who was talking about how good and terrific it is, profits are going through the roof. Then he says something like, But even the millions of Americans who are suffering are now accepting what Mr. Jasinowski calls "the right proportions."[19] That is, their aspirations have diminished. He quotes the head of the University of Michigan research center that monitors public attitudes. He says, It's as if people are saying, We're not quite able to get by, but it could be a lot worse, so we'll live with this. That's America "smug and prosperous." In the old days they used to think they ought to be able to get by, maybe do a little better, but now they've got the right priorities, diminished aspirations. If they can survive, that's good enough. It could be worse. They still have a job today. But they don't count among Americans. They're not the ones who are smug and prosperous. They're the ones who are happy if they can just barely get by.

Do you see a disconnect between the business pages and the front pages? If so, what accounts for it?

I think so. It's always been true. For one thing, the business pages trust their audience. They are speaking to the "Americans," in the narrow sense. They can trust them to understand things properly. Secondly, the Americans they're talking to have to have a fairly accurate picture of what the world is like. They have to make decisions which are going to affect profits and power, and they'd better have a tolerably realistic sense of reality. On the other hand, the general population, from the point of view of media leaders, is better off if it's simply diverted. So there's a tendency, I wouldn't want to say it's too sharp, in the direction you describe. I've never seen it studied, but I think if it were studied you'd find it. For example, some of the best news reporting in the country is done in the *Wall Street Journal.* That's been true for a long time.

The Economist, *the British weekly, in a lead editorial, raised some very critical questions about the actual state of the U.S. economy, suggesting that it was way overextended and that the bubble could burst.[20]*

That's been in the economics journals for a long time. There's what's called "asset inflation" — that is, the value of corporate stock has risen much faster than the economy has. The economy is growing very slowly. This fairy-tale economic boom that they're talking about is actually the slowest since the Second World War. It's even slower than the 1970s and 1980s. It's also the first recovery — there's a business cycle, so there's a recovery — in American history in which there has been no increase in income for most of the population, who are also working much longer hours. On the other hand, stock prices are going up very fast, as is debt.

Is this personal or corporate, or both?

Both. Total debt. Nongovernmental debt. Through the beginnings of records, if you check economic growth and debt relative to the economy, they stay pretty closely correlated. In the mid-1980s they separate very sharply. The growth is very slow and the debt goes up very sharply. These are all signs of real concern. It's been pointed out that although it's claimed there's no inflation, there's a kind of inflation, namely asset inflation, which is not grounded in the productive economy.

What's going on in the stock market is somewhat disconnected from the real economy. Doug Henwood points out in *Wall Street,* a very good book, that when corporations want to generate funds for investment, they rarely turn to the stock market.[21] They generate them internally. In fact, they've been retiring stock faster than they've been issuing it. The stocks have to do with who controls. So mergers, acquisitions, trades, and shifts don't contribute to the economy. They may detract from it.

Mergers and acquisitions have a tendency to lower economic growth. Ed Herman and Richard Du Boff are among the several economists who have studied this issue. They are more about stock prices and the pressure for very short-term profits than the creation of a productive economy. And there are other serious problems. Dean Baker, an economist at the Economic Policy Institute, has written quite well about this. He has pointed out that infrastructure spending has declined quite severely. That means everything from building roads to education to training people. You can't have a healthy economy without solid "human capital," as it is called — an ugly phrase — meaning people with skills, knowledge, training, and creativity, and the facilities needed to do things. Spending on these things is declining. You can see it in everything from potholes in the streets to reading scores. These are the kinds of things *The Economist* has in mind when they say that there's trouble up ahead. It's what they call the "bubble economy."

It seemed almost certain, earlier this year, that the U.S. was going to bomb Iraq. Then an event happens in Columbus, Ohio, that completely derails it.

It was an important event. The Clinton administration had not made any attempt to face the public with its position. They were just sending out lightning bolts from the White House. They apparently felt, or their PR people felt, that they ought to have some sort of public presentation before they bombed another country. So they chose what looked like a very safe place, Columbus, Ohio. It's not somewhere you'd expect a lot of flaming radicals to burn the place down. They prepared in advance. It was carefully controlled. Certain people were allowed in. The questioners were monitored in advance so that only the right kind of people would ask questions.

Despite all of that, people in the town were active. There were meetings. They were distributing leaflets. They were approaching people. There was a fair amount of grassroots organizing going on. And they succeeded in getting some of the official questioners to raise some of their pertinent questions. This was televised. It was shown around the world. I didn't watch it, but I read the transcript afterward. As soon as the first question opened a little breach in the solid flow of propaganda, the whole thing collapsed. Secretary of State Madeleine Albright, Defense Secretary William Cohen, and Sandy Berger, Clinton's national security adviser, couldn't answer a single question. They were stumbling, trying to figure out what to say. The questioners barely had time to say anything, a couple of sentences. But it was enough to make the whole propaganda edifice collapse. The proponents of the bombing were lost.

Cohen afterward made an interesting statement. "Force will be the first recourse," he said in an interview with Chris Black of the *Boston Globe*. "There will be no town meetings, no trial balloons, no lengthy series of warnings and deadlines."[22] It's the Huntington thesis again: Next time we have to make sure that the public isn't even allowed into a canned, prepared program. They are just too dangerous. That event had a big effect. It sparked lots of demonstrations, protests, meetings, and activities all over the country. Things were happening anyway, but this undoubtedly was a big impetus. It had an effect around the world. It's certainly one of the reasons they backed off. I'm not convinced it was the only reason, or even the prime reason, but it was certainly a reason.

There were others. One, which wasn't all that well reported, though it was so important they couldn't miss it altogether, was that there was tremendous regional antagonism. The only country that gave even tepid support, and it was tepid, was Kuwait. Bahrain, which is usually in their pocket, flatly refused to allow U.S. bases to be used. The Gulf principalities, which are practically owned by the U.S., made a very strong statement condemning the plan to bomb. Saudi Arabia is the big prize. It's where most of the oil is. They didn't just say, We're not happy about it. They came out very strongly against it. They also did something which undoubtedly frightened the United States.

Saudi Arabia and Iran have been historic enemies. In fact, technically they're at war. About twenty-five years ago, the Shah occupied some Saudi islands. They're definitely enemies. Secretary of State Albright went to Saudi Arabia right about this time. She was given very standoffish treatment. It was a clear diplomatic signal: We don't want you around. We don't like what you're doing. At the same time, the former president of Iran, Hashemi Rafsanjani, went to Saudi Arabia on a state visit. He was treated royally. He met the king. He was taken around to all the places. That couldn't be missed.

Something even more dramatic happened. The U.S. had organized an economic summit. It was supposed to be associated with the so-called peace process. This was going to be held in Qatar. Almost nobody showed up. Instead, everyone from Egypt to Saudi Arabia went to the Islamic summit in Teheran. These are very striking and significant signals. What they're telling the U.S. is, very clearly, You can't push us too far. Iran for years has been proposing regional security arrangements which would marginalize the U.S. role, and these are moves toward it. How serious the moves are is very hard to say, but it can't be missed in Washington. And undoubtedly that's part of the reason, I suspect most of the reason, why they backed off.

The U.S. had in fact gotten itself into a box. They were being compelled to bomb because they had cut off the other options. They knew there was no strategic point in this. It wasn't going to hurt Saddam Hussein. It would kill a lot of people but probably leave him stronger than before. It would have the effect, and this was pointed out even by the Pentagon, of ending the weapons inspections, which in fact were much more effective in destroying the Iraqi weapons stock than all the bombing. The bombing was strongly opposed in the region, and nobody could predict what kind of effect it would have on the stability of the states that the U.S. supports. Popular uprisings might overthrow them. Here they were being driven toward this policy. I think they probably welcomed the opportunity to back off. They'll maybe try again later, but they were in a pretty bad position.

Let's talk about economic miracles in Southeast Asia. For a long time the Asian tigers were being touted as the economic model of the future. Then came the meltdown. How did the propaganda system rationalize that?

First of all, we have to be a little careful. Asia is not a homogeneous place. For example, Taiwan was barely touched. South Korea has a very solid economy.

The eleventh largest in the world.

These are not pretty societies, I'm not recommending them as a model for anyone, but if you're just talking about economic growth and development, the economic growth and development in South Korea and Taiwan are spectacular. Twenty or thirty years ago South Korea was more like the Philippines. Now it's a far larger economy. The people are much richer. Now it has a fairly solid industrial and economic structure. Taiwan was hardly touched by the meltdown.

The Southeast Asian countries are quite different. Malaysia, although it did have an economic boom, had very high foreign ownership. It was essentially foreign-owned. Indonesia is basically a family-owned business. Nobody knows how much the Suharto family and their cronies own. But the usual estimate is on the order of $30 billion, which is approximately the scale of the IMF rescue package. There's a very trivial way to get rid of their current liquidity problem: let's have the Suharto family pay back what they robbed. Indonesia is potentially a very rich country. It has tremendous resources. Thailand is also extremely shaky. It has enormous poverty. In Israel, many of the guest workers — slave labor, basically — are Thai, for example. They can't survive in Thailand, so they come and do the dirtiest, filthiest work in this rich Western society.

So there was economic development, but on an extremely flimsy basis. These cases are all different. Even the strongest of them, say, South Korea, is dependent. South Korea has not developed its own independent technological growth. It's dependent on Japanese technology. It's an offshoot of Japan in a way. Taiwan has been somewhat more independent. But each case is different.

In the case of South Korea, the problem was connected — closely, many analysts argue, and I think correctly — with the forced liberalization of its financial markets. The United States pressured them very hard to open up their financial markets. A huge amount of speculative capital flow came in and then pulled out and left them holding the bag. Also, from the 1980s on, the industrial conglomerates in South Korea became more independent of state control. Many of them, not all, are pretty corrupt. There's a lot of cronyism. They were making huge borrowings that they couldn't cover. Then all of this collapsed. But over a very successful economy. So the term "tigers" is not misleading.

The same is true of Japan. Japan has had, since the Meiji Restoration, for about 130 years, the highest growth rate in the world. That's even including the total devastation of the Second World War. That's pretty impressive. The growth of the countries in its periphery, primarily South Korea and Taiwan, has been unparalleled in modern economic history.

To get back to your question, the reaction here was, This proves the superiority of the American model: rugged individualism and entrepreneurial capitalism. It means that this state-guided approach of interfering with markets has now collapsed. That's ludicrous. First of all, these were market failures. These were failures due, to a very large extent, to financial liberalization, to opening up financial markets to a free flow of capital. They're basically market failures, not failures of the so-called Japanese development model.

Secondly, the picture of the United States is ridiculous. The Reagan administration was the most anti-market administration in modern American history. They virtually doubled barriers to imports in order to try to save U.S. industry. If they had opened up markets in the 1980s, superior Japanese products would have flooded the automotive industry, steel, and semiconductors. The main industrial base of the U.S. would have been wiped out. So the Reagan administration just barred imports. What's more, it poured public funds into industry.

So, despite all the rhetoric about "free markets," you see regular state intervention in the U.S. economy.

Alan Greenspan just gave a speech in which he talked about the enormous achievements of market capitalism and consumer choice. He gave a list of examples.[23] The Internet was the main one. It was developed by the Pentagon. It was developed for thirty years at public expense, with most of the ideas, initiatives and creativity, the hardware, and the technology. Then it was handed over to private enterprise. Consumer choice was zero. The same is true of the other examples he gives: computers, satellites, transistors. The most ignorant economist in the world must know that the list he gave was textbook examples of development mostly in the public sector then handed over to private power.

The only one that even reaches the level of a joke is transistors. Transistors were developed in a private laboratory, Bell Labs, but it was a monopoly. There was no market and there was no consumer choice. Since it was a government-supported monopoly, they could charge monopoly prices, which is in effect a tax. As long as they had the monopoly, Bell Labs was a very good lab. They did all sorts of things at public expense. As soon as it was deregulated, Bell Labs went down the tubes.

Quite apart from that, Bell Labs was using state-generated wartime technology. Furthermore, they had nobody to sell the transistors to. For about ten years, the only market for high-quality transistors was the government, just like computers. During that period they were able to develop the technology, the scale, the marketing skills so that finally they could break into the market system. But to talk about the U.S. model as being one of rugged individualism and entrepreneurial skills, kept away from state interference — again, it's hard to find words to describe it.

Incidentally, this goes back to the origins of U.S. history. Take the American system of mass production, of manufacturing, the big new system in the nineteenth century. The basic ideas of that were worked out in places like the Springfield Armory, where they needed interchangeable parts and careful quality control. Then it was transferred into the private sector. In fact, the Reagan administration went far beyond just protecting American industry and pouring public funds into advanced technology. It also had to overcome U.S. management failures. In the 1970s, there was a lot of concern that incompetent management meant the United States was falling behind the Japanese particularly, but the Europeans, too. It wasn't developing flexible manufacturing techniques. They were way behind because of management failures.

What happened? The Pentagon stepped into the breach. It understands its place. It started a program called Manufacturing Technology, ManTech. It was a new program to design what they called the "factory of the future," with integrated production, computer control of equipment, flexible technology, and so on. That was then greatly expanded in the Reagan years, because the Reaganites were extreme statists, strongly opposed to market principles, more so than the norm. It was finally handed over to private industry. So that's American rugged individualism and consumer choice in the market as compared with the failure of the state-managed East Asian system. The whole discussion, from one end to the other, has been a tissue of fabrications. It's not a simple story, and if you look at it closely, there are all kinds of complexity; but if that picture had been written in *Pravda*, people would have laughed.

It seems that so much of what you're saying has to deal with asking the right questions. You were quoted in a Newsweek *article I came across from 1993 as saying that you have to be prepared "to ask obvious questions." [24] The subtext here is that children have that knack.*

My intellectual achievement was retarded when I went to high school. I sort of sank into a black hole because I had to go to the high-achieving, academic public high school.

Do people have to "discover their inner child" in order to ask the obvious questions?

Anyone who has had any dealings with children knows that they're curious and creative. They want to explore things and figure out what's happening. A good bit of schooling is an effort to drive this out of them and to fit them into a mold, make them behave, stop thinking, not cause any trouble. It goes right from kindergarten up to what Huntington was talking about, namely, keep the rabble out of their hair. People are supposed to be obedient producers, do what they're told, and the rest of your life is supposed to be passive consuming. Don't think about things. Don't know about things. Don't bother your head with things like the MAI or international affairs. Just do what you're told, pay attention to something else and maximize your consumption. That's the role of the public.

People like Walter Lippmann say that the public must be "spectators," not participants. That's for the "responsible men."[25] They're simply presenting a version of essentially the same theory, which goes back hundreds of years. You can trace it back to the first democratic revolution in modern history in seventeenth-century England. It's all laid out there very clearly.

This year marks the 150th anniversary of The Communist Manifesto. *In an interview you did with Robert McChesney a couple of years ago, you expressed skepticism about Marx and particularly about theories in general.[26] You're not big on theories. Why not?*

I think theories are great. I work on them all the time. But the term "theory" shouldn't be abused. You have a theory when you have some non-obvious principles from which you can draw conclusions that explain in surprising ways some of the phenomena that are worth studying. That's hard to do. It's done in the hard sciences. There are a few other areas where it's done. But for the most part it's impossible. You can understand that. Even in the sciences, when you get to matters of any complexity, theoretical understanding declines quite sharply.

When you get to human affairs, I can't even think of anything that deserves the name "theory." Marx is certainly worth studying. He was a theorist of capitalism. He developed a certain abstract model of capitalism. There's nothing wrong with abstract idealizations. That's the way to study things. He investigated what might happen in that kind of system. How much relationship it had to the real world of that time or this time, one has to ask. He had essentially nothing to say about socialism, a few scattered sentences here and there. He had no theory of revolution or of social change. But you study what he did for its important work, and one should know about it. If you want to call it a theory, OK.

A lot of what people call theories in social sciences — literary theory and others — is obfuscation. I don't know of any understanding that goes deep enough so that you can't present it very simply and in such a way that the principles are pretty much on the surface. We're living in an era when a lot of prestige is given to professional expertise. People have a real responsibility not to claim more than they can offer. If you claim to have a theory that deduces unexpected consequences from nontrivial principles, let's see it.

You don't think highly of the deification of individuals and the construction of cults around people.

That's putting it pretty mildly. I don't think you should deify anybody or anything. In the fields where there really is intellectual substance and progress, everyone knows that this is not how it works. In the hard sciences, for example, the way you make progress is in graduate seminars, where half the ideas are coming from the students. There are people who have interesting ideas, and they're usually partially right and partially wrong. You can try to fix them up, improve and change them, but there's no Einsteinism in physics. You have notions like that only in fields that are, either consciously or unconsciously, covering up a lack of intellectual substance.

What's coming up for you?

The usual mix of stuff. It happens to be a pretty exciting moment in the technical study of language. I've got a lot of things coming along in that.

How's your health holding up?

It's not a terribly important topic. I'll be around for another couple months. [*Laughs.*]

1   Noam Chomsky, "Domestic Constituencies," *Z Magazine* 11: 5 (May 1998), p. 18. On-line at http://www.zmag.org/ZMag/articles/chomskymay98.htm.

2   United States Council for International Business (USCIB), *A Guide to the Multilateral Agreement on Investment* (New York: USCIB, 1996).

3   Glenn Burkins, "Labor Fights Against Fast-Track Trade Measure," *Wall Street Journal,* September 16, 1997, p. A24.

4   Anne Swardson, "Global Investment Accord Put on Hold," *Washington Post,* April 29, 1998, p. C13. See also Fred Hiatt, "Foreign Affairs in Annapolis," *Washington Post,* March 30, 1998, p. A25.

5   Jane Bussey, "New Rules Could Guide International Investment," *Miami Herald,* July 20, 1997. See also the references in Noam Chomsky, "The Ultimate Weapon," in *Profit Over People: Neoliberalism and the Global Order* (New York: Seven Stories Press, 1999), pp. 129–55.

6   Paul Magnusson, with Stephen Baker, "The Explosive Trade Deal You've Never Heard Of," *Business Week* 3564 (February 9, 1998), p. 51.

7   Burkins, "Labor Fights Against Fast-Track Trade Measure," *Wall Street Journal,* September 16, 1997.

8   Archdiocese of Guatemala Human Rights Office, *Guatemala: Never Again!* (Maryknoll, NY: Orbis Books, 1999).

9   Lou Cannon, "Reagan Praises Guatemalan Military Leader," *Washington Post,* December 5, 1982, p. A1.

10   Associated Press, "Guatemalan Questioned in Bishop's Death," *New York Times,* May 1, 1998, p. A5.

11   Edward S. Herman and Noam Chomsky, *Manufacturing Consent: The Political Economy of the Mass Media* (New York: Pantheon Books, 1988; second edition forthcoming), pp. 37–86.

12   Samuel Huntington, *American Politics: The Promise of Disharmony* (Cambridge: Harvard UP, 1981), p. 75.

13   Michael Prowse, "World Bank/IMF Meeting: Theorising on an Eastern Promise: An Attempt to Explain East Asia's Dynamic Growth," *Financial Times,* September 27, 1993, p. 3.

14   David E. Sanger, "America Is Prosperous and Smug, Like Japan Was," *New York Times,* April 12, 1998, p. 4: 1.

15   Sylvia Nasar, "Chaos Theory: Unlearning the Lessons of Econ 101," *New York Times,* May 3, 1998, p. 4: 1.

16   Alan Greenspan, testimony before the Senate Banking Committee, February 1997. Greenspan said the "sustainable economic expansion" was thanks to "atypical restraint on compensation increases [which] appears to be mainly the consequence of greater worker insecurity."

17   See Doug Henwood," "Miscellany," *Left Business Observer* 91 (August 31, 1999), p. 8. See also the Economic Policy Institute's biannual book series, *The State of Working America.*

18 Louis Uchitelle, "Second Thoughts about Being Better Off: The Rehabilitation of Morning in America," *New York Times,* February 23, 1997, p. 4: 1.

19 Quoted in Uchitelle, "Second Thoughts about Being Better Off," *New York Times,* February 23, 1997.

20 See Editorial, "America's Bubble Economy," *The Economist,* April 18, 1998, p. 16; "America Bubbles Over," *The Economist,* April 18, 1998, p. 67; Editorial, "Bubble and Squeak," *The Economist,* May 9, 1998, p. 17; and "Hubble, Bubble, Inflation Trouble?" *The Economist,* May 9, 1998, p. 78.

21 Doug Henwood, *Wall Street: How It Works and For Whom* (New York: Verso, 1998).

22 Chris Black, "Cohen Vows Swift Strike if Iraq Bars Inspections," *Boston Globe,* March 5, 1998, p. A1. See Brett Mahoney and Asha Blake, "Foreign Policy Team Tries to Sell Iraqi Policy," ABC, *World News This Morning,* February 19, 1998.

23 Alan Greenspan, Annual Convention of the American Society of Newspaper Editors, Washington, DC, April 2, 1998. See Chomsky, *Rogue States,* pp. 192–98 and notes.

24 Joshua Cooper Ramo and Debra Rosenberg, "The Puzzle of Genius," *Newsweek,* June 28, 1993, pp. 46ff.

25 Walter Lippmann, *The Essential Lippmann: A Political Philosophy for Liberal Democracy,* ed. Clinton Rossiter and James Lare (New York: Random House, 1963). See Noam Chomsky, *Deterring Democracy,* expanded edition (New York: Hill and Wang, 1992), pp. 367–68.

26 Robert W. McChesney, "On Media, Politics, and the Left, Part 1: An Interview with Noam Chomsky," *Against the Current* 10: 1 (March–April 1995), pp. 27–32, and "On Media, Politics, and Ourselves: Interview with Noam Chomsky, Part 2," *Against the Current* 10: 2 (May–June 1995), pp. 21–25.

2

U.S. to World: Get Out of the Way

Lexington, Massachusetts, February 1, 1999

always get a little nervous when I'm about to interview you. How should I get started? How can I engage you? These interviews are a kind of roulette, where you really don't know where the questions are coming from or what kind of detail you'll need. How do you feel about that?

You've got the upper hand. I'm just your servant. So I have the easy job. I just follow where you lead.

I did notice that you might be losing your grip. That was evidenced by your knowing not only which teams were in the Super Bowl, but also the outcome.

I always read the front page at least of the *New York Times*. It said who won and what the score was, but it's even worse than that. I don't know if I should admit it, but I'm actually going to go to my first professional basketball game in around fifty years. I have a jock grandson who's finally helping me fulfill a secret dream to have an excuse to go to a game because some kid is dragging me. So it's going to happen.

Sounds good, certainly a break from your punishing schedule of speaking commitments, interviews and writing. I'd like to ask you about a Sufi teaching story credited to Rumi, a great thirteenth-century Persian poet. It's called "The Elephant in the Dark." In it several people are blindfolded and asked to examine an elephant by touch alone. One person touches an ear and says, It's a fan. Another touches its tail and says, Oh, it's a rope. Another a leg and says, It's a pillar, and so on. There's something in here about appearance and reality and patterns of delusion and deception.

The world's a complicated place. Anything you look at, whether it's a molecule or international society, there are many different perspectives you can take, and you'll get very different answers depending on which perspective you take. That's a standard problem in the sciences. Why do people do experiments? Doing experiments is a creative act, an effort to try to peel away things that you believe, rightly or wrongly, are irrelevant to determining the fundamental principles by which things are operating and see if you can find something simplified enough that those principles will actually be apparent and then try to rebuild some picture of complex reality from that. But you never get anywhere near it because reality is just too much of a mess. There are too many intervening factors.

Any experiment in the hard sciences is attempting to discover a perspective which will be illuminating. That approach is all the more necessary when you look at things as poorly understood and as complex as human affairs. You have to discover a perspective from which interesting things seem to appear, recognizing that at best you'll capture one significant aspect of a highly complex reality. You hope it's an important one.

What kind of suggestions would you make to individuals who are trying to decode and penetrate conventional wisdom? You could take any current issue — globalization or the crisis in Iraq.

The first thing is to be very skeptical. Take the last topic you mentioned, the crisis in Iraq. One question one should ask is, Why are the U.S. and Britain bombing Iraq and insisting on maintaining sanctions? If you look, you find answers that are given vociferously with near 100 percent agreement. You hear it from Tony Blair, Madeleine Albright, newspaper editors and commentators. That answer is, Saddam Hussein is a complete monster. He even committed the "ultimate" horror, namely, he gassed his own people.[1] We can't let a creature like that survive. I've reviewed a fair amount of the press on this, and this is the near-unanimous justification of the sanctions by commentators, intellectual journals, and so on.

As soon as anything's given with near-unanimity, it should be a signal. Nothing is that clear in the world. So, if it's being given with near-unanimity, you should be asking yourself, Is that correct? There happens to be an easy way to test it in this case, and that's what instantly should come to the mind of anyone who's even thinking, who hasn't had the capacity for thinking driven out of their heads. The obvious question is, How did the U.S. and Britain react when Saddam Hussein committed the "ultimate" horror — the gassing of the Kurdish town of Halabja in March 1988? It's on the record. The second major gassing occurs in August, five days after the cease-fire with the war with Iran, when Iran basically capitulated. How did the United States and Britain react? The answer is straightforward. They reacted by continuing and in fact accelerating their strong support for Saddam Hussein. That tells you something right away: that this can't possibly be the reason. The description is correct. He's a monster who committed one of the "ultimate" horrors — and the U.S. and Britain thought it was fine. They went ahead and supported him. So that cannot be the reason why they are now trying to destroy him. That reasoning takes maybe a minute.

Then the next question you ask yourself is, Since this is so obvious, how come nobody says it? I think you can figure out the answer to that. That's how you should look at things. That's one example. I just mentioned it because it was the last one you brought up. Generally, what you should do when you're looking at any society is begin by asking, How is power distributed? Who makes the main decisions? Who decides what's going to be produced, consumed, and distributed? Who's going to be in the political world? Who makes the decisions that are going to affect people's lives? You can figure that out in most places pretty easily.

Then you should ask whether policies and the shaping of information reflect the distribution of power. That's what any rational person would expect. So that's what's called a null hypothesis. You accept it unless you have evidence to the contrary. Start with a null hypothesis, and ask if it's correct. In fact, you typically find you can explain quite a lot that way, not everything, because the world's too complicated. There are going to be conflicting factors, and you try to sort those out. In fact, that's just treating it as if you were studying molecules in the laboratory. This happens to be human affairs, but there's no reason to be any less rational. When you discover that rationality is essentially not permitted, then you learn more about how the institutional structure works.

In the case of Iraq, elementary rationality is just not permitted. If anyone wants to test this, they can investigate how often that statement, We have to bomb Saddam Hussein because he committed the "ultimate" horror, is followed by the three crucial words, "with our support." That will give you an answer to whether rationality is permitted or not. A striking answer, this recent example, but there are many others. We could pick case after case.

To go back to that Sufi story and to the way that people are blindfolded, compartmentalized, and isolated. They think the tail of the elephant is a rope. There isn't a perception of the whole.

When we look further, we find that this is a major and indeed conscious goal of the industries which are concerned with shaping thoughts and attitudes: the advertising industry, the public relations industry, the responsible intellectuals who talk about how to run the world. Their concern, their commitment, and they say it, is to keep people isolated, as you say, atomized. There's good reason for that. As long as people are alone, they're not going to be able to figure anything much out. If they're together, they'll start having thoughts, interchanging them and learning about them, the same as happens in a scientific laboratory, for that matter. Very rarely is anything done alone. Also, have them focused on something that is not going to affect how power really works. Don't let that in.

Take, say, what's going on in Washington right now, this ridiculous farce of the Clinton impeachment. There are some striking things about it. One thing is that it's an elite obsession, pretty much across the board. So the left-liberal journals are all full of it, and the right-wing journals and the newspapers. On the other hand, most of the population is not interested. It wants the issue to go away and has been saying so for a year. That's kind of surprising, because with the huge amount of publicity you'd think people would get involved. But somehow the public's been very resistant, despite the enormous amount of attention that's been focused on it.

What do you attribute that to?

I think it's related to what we were talking about. We have to immediately ask, Why is that the case? Why is there a class difference, in a sense, between the elite sectors — media elites, political elites, intellectual elites — and most of the rest? We then have to look for a reason for that. I think the reason may have to do with what people are interested in. For example, if you look at the same public opinion studies that tell you that people don't care about this, they also tell you what they do care about. They care about having a job, education, health care, security, making sure the environment isn't destroyed. There's a collection of such issues. The way the questions are asked on polls is extremely narrow. The way the question is usually asked is, Do you prefer the Democrats or the Republicans? Like there couldn't be another option. Which faction of the business party do you prefer, in other words. And on these issues that I just mentioned, they very substantially prefer the Democrats.

What about other issues? There are other issues called "cultural issues": family values, crime, defending ourselves from terrorists, morals in government, whatever that may be. On those issues they tend to prefer the Republicans. Suppose you were a Republican. What would you want people to be paying attention to? It's pretty obvious. So we instantly have an explanation as to why on these strict party-line votes the Republicans want to keep this issue in the focus of attention. Why do the Democrats and left-liberals, in fact radicals, sign petitions saying, We have to defend our president from these charges of sexual McCarthyism? Why do they care? You could think of some reasons for that, too. The Democrats probably have no more interest than the Republicans in having people really focus attention on things like having a job or health care or education. Their positions aren't that different. They can maybe talk a little about it, but what they're going to do is a kind of a moderate Republican approach. So it's just as well if people focus on something else.

Already we have a pretty broad spectrum of interests making sure that people are focusing on these absurdities rather than on the issues that really matter. Because then you get away with a lot. The next step may be dismantling Social Security while people are paying attention to this and not asking the obvious questions that they should be asking. As to why the left gets caught up in it, people who would agree with everything I just said could still get caught up in it. I think that raises further questions, but now it's a small sector of the population we're talking about. A good part of the answer to why it is an elite obsession is plausibly indicated by a simple principle: people are dangerous. If they're able to involve themselves in issues that matter, they may change the distribution of power, to the detriment of those who are rich and privileged.

As far as the Democrats are concerned, suppose Clinton gets impeached. Actually it's a political gain for the Democratic Party. So they don't care. Here again there's something rather similar to the Iraq case. The discussion on National Public Radio, in journals and newspapers, is about how the country is caught in this great moral dilemma over Clinton and Congress's wrestling with this fundamental philosophical issue. Like the case of Iraq, an obvious question comes to mind. If it's a question of principle, how come it's divided on strict party lines? Is there any imaginable issue of principle, whatever it is, that would divide between Democrats and Republicans almost a hundred percent, with barely any deviation? It's immediately obvious that this is impossible. Whatever you think about the two parties, they overlap so much from every point of view that there couldn't possibly be a question of principle that divides them. Therefore you know at once that if there are strict party-line votes, there's no issue of principle. That suffices to eliminate virtually all the discussion about this topic.

If we had anything remotely approaching free and open discussion of these issues, these would be the headlines. They're the obvious answers. Maybe they're wrong, but they're certainly the obvious answers. And if the obvious answers are never discussed, you begin to wonder, but not for very long.

Let's say, if you were to conduct a poll, how many Americans would know that in 1988 the regime of Saddam Hussein, which was allied with the U.S. and the U.K., gassed its own population — in this case, the Kurds — and how many would know about the sex scandal in the White House?

I think plenty of people would know that Saddam Hussein

gassed the Kurds. What they wouldn't know are three crucial words: "with our support." Nor would they know that after the Gulf War, in March 1991, Saddam Hussein returned to our good graces. Immediately after the war was over, there was an uprising in the south of Iraq, right under the eyes of the U.S. military, which dominated the whole region by that point. There was a rebellion. It included Iraqi generals who were rebelling. They didn't ask for U.S. support. The only thing they asked for was access to captured Iraqi military equipment and some protection against Saddam Hussein's counterattack. The United States refused to provide it. They would not provide the rebels with access to captured Iraqi equipment. They would not stop Iraqi helicopters from massacring them. The claim now by Norman Schwarzkopf is that we were "suckered" by the Iraqis.[2] We didn't realize that when they sent those helicopter gunships they were actually going to shoot at people. They told us they weren't going to do it, and we were suckered. Boy, were we dumb. You're supposed to believe that.

The fact of the matter is that the Bush administration stood by while Saddam Hussein carried out a brutal, murderous repression of the uprising in the south. Next thing that Saddam did is turn to the north and do the same thing against a Kurdish uprising. And again, the U.S. didn't lift a finger, until public pressure got so strong that they had to pretend to do something. They didn't even do much because they wanted Saddam Hussein to crush the uprisings and keep the country together. It was pretty public. They said so at the time. They said, We have to preserve stability, to keep an "iron fist" in power.[3] That remains true up till today. General Anthony Zinni, the Marine Corps commander and top-ranking American general in the Middle East, just testified before Congress a couple of days ago and said any replacement of the current regime will probably be worse.[4]

I was looking at your book Pirates and Emperors *recently and just substituting Saddam Hussein for Muammar Qadaffi and Iraq for Libya.[5] I found that I wasn't missing a lot of beats. There are similarities between the mid-1980s and Libya and today with Iraq.*

In fact, it goes much farther back than that. These are continuities in policy, with occasional name changes. It's usually the same record. For example, today happens to be February 1. Let's take a look at today's *New York Times*. The *Times* has a big story on Richard Clarke, the man in charge of counterterrorism, a tough guy who runs an $11-billion-a-year operation to protect the United States from terrorism.[6] The article is interesting. It doesn't give any examples of how he's protecting the U.S. from actual terrorism. But it does give examples of U.S. terrorism, particularly about Libya. It turns out that he was involved in the planning of the actions against Libya in 1986, which interestingly aren't mentioned. There was a major terrorist action involving Libya in 1986 — namely, the United States bombed it, killing a couple of dozen people, including Qadaffi's infant daughter. They bombed two cities on pretexts which, even if they were correct, wouldn't justify it. And there's no reason to believe that they were correct. That's a war crime, actually. That isn't mentioned, although the buildup to it is mentioned, and part of the buildup includes planting false information in the press. So this is counterterrorism. They do mention that this same Clarke was involved in the bombing of Sudan and Afghanistan. That's counterterrorism.

Take Sudan. The United States bombed and destroyed a major pharmaceutical supply house there in 1998. It produced maybe half of Sudan's pharmaceutical supplies. They sort of conceded it afterward that they probably hit the wrong target. But that's counterterrorism. That's not terrorism. If Islamic extremists destroyed half of the U.S. pharmaceutical industry, we'd probably consider it terrorism. But because we did it, this is counterterrorism. In fact, if you look through the article, there is case after case of U.S. terrorism — called counterterrorism — and no examples of protecting the United States from terrorism. Libya in 1986, one of the worst acts of international terrorism, in fact, is given as an example of how we're defending ourselves from terror. That's standard. You can pick any period of years you like and you'll find many examples.

In the same article, Richard Clarke, who is called the "czar" of this anti-terrorism campaign, warns against "cyberwar" and "electronic Pearl Harbors."

I wouldn't say it's impossible, but as compared with the actual bombing of a pharmaceutical plant in the Sudan, how do you rank potential cyberwarfare as a terrorist threat? They're not even in the same universe. The source of cyberterror is very likely to be the advanced countries. It's much more likely to be the U.S. than any other country, because we have the technology and the power.

To get back to Clinton, in his newsletter Left Business Observer, *Doug Henwood writes, "The worst thing about the Lewinsky affair is that it's interfered with the proper hatred of Bill Clinton. He's been indicted … for all the wrong crimes."* [7] *What might your articles of impeachment include?*

Henwood is exactly right. "Impeachable" is kind of like a technical question. I don't know if the crimes are impeachable or not, but there are plenty of crimes. The bombing of Sudan, for example. That's a war crime. The bombing of Afghanistan is a war crime. Bombing Iraq in December. That's a war crime. Enforcing, and by now it's U.S. enforcing, of the sanctions. That's killed a lot of people. That's a major crime. You recall Madeleine Albright's comments about that when she was asked on national television, How do you feel about the reports that half a million Iraqi children have died because of the sanctions? She said that it's a hard choice, but "we think the price is worth it." [8] That's certainly a major crime, I would think, killing a half a million Iraqi children, if that's the number. It's what she accepted.

What about what's called "welfare reform," getting people off the "dole"? Those terms are interesting. Clinton was able to push through a program which eliminated support for poor women with children. Now we have to get them to work. So far they weren't working, like taking care of and raising a child, that's not work. What's "work" is what they do in a Wall Street office, speculating against currencies. That's work, so you get paid a lot of money, but not for raising a child. That's not work, and it has no social value, so therefore there should be no social support for it. And welfare reform has been a great success, a triumph, because fewer people are now on the welfare rolls. Is that good or is it bad? You have to ask those people. But getting them off the rolls in itself is not good, if what happens is what's anticipated — namely that they're getting very low-paying jobs, hence lowering wages for people at the low end of the salary scale, and are forced to essentially abandon their children to entirely inadequate care systems. That's an achievement? I don't say it's impeachable, necessarily, but it's criminal, in a sense.

How about increasing the incarceration rate in the country, which continues to go up, irrespective of crime? That's criminal, if not impeachable. We can get quite a list. Certainly the stuff in Washington doesn't rank anywhere as compared to any of these things. And some of them are real crimes. If some other head of state committed them, we'd insist that he be brought to an international war crimes tribunal.

What about the United Nations Charter and issues involving the planning and waging of aggressive war?

The U.N. Charter is very clear and explicit. It says that either the threat or use of force is illegitimate unless it is self-defense against armed attack. If some country invades you, until the Security Council can act, you're allowed to defend yourself. In other cases, use of force is legitimate if it's specifically authorized by the Security Council after the council has determined that peaceful means won't work. The U.S. has never accepted that principle. But what's interesting about recent years is that the rejection of it is quite public and open and brazen, as brazen as they can make it. In the early years, it was in internal documents. In 1947, right after the Charter was signed, the U.S. National Security Council was also formed. Its first memorandum, NSC1/3, 1947, was concerned with the danger posed by an upcoming election in Italy. They were afraid that in a free, democratic election, the left would win. So the question was, What do we do about this? The answer was, if who they called the communists win in a democratic election, the U.S. should call a national mobilization, get the Sixth Fleet active, support paramilitary activities — in other words, use terror inside Italy to break up the government. That's the threat or use of force, but it's a secret document. Subversion and withholding food supplies and reinstating the fascist police and smashing the labor movement turned out to be sufficient, but otherwise we would have presumably followed that directive. And it continues. I won't run through the record. But in the internal record it runs through the 1950s. It is continually stated, sometimes quite explicitly, that the U.S. will plan to and in fact will use force, even if there is no armed attack. That's stated explicitly. That force may be extreme.

For example, in 1956 — in addition to first use of nuclear weapons, which was always permitted — it was officially determined that first use of bacteriological warfare, which the U.S. already had extensive facilities for, would be permitted. There was a shift in the early 1960s, when the Kennedy administration came in. Then it was semi-open, but in a kind of indirect way. So for example, Adlai Stevenson at the U.N. defended what in fact was the U.S. attack against Vietnam, but nobody called it that. He defended it as defense against "internal aggression."[9]

What's "internal aggression"? Internal aggression means something that isn't armed attack, something happening inside the country that you're going to repress that can't possibly be called aggression. But if our attack on that is "defense," then you've thrown out the U.N. Charter completely. However, you had to think for a minute to see this. In the same year, incidentally, Dean Acheson, a former secretary of state and senior adviser to Kennedy, spoke to the American Society for International Law. He gave a justification for the blockade of Cuba, which of course he realized was illegal. But he said, That's all right, because in cases where U.S. interests are concerned, legal issues don't arise. We're exempt from international law.[10]

By the 1980s, all this became quite open. When Reagan bombed Libya, the official justification given by the State Department was that it was self-defense against future attack.[11] Article 51 of the U.N. Charter says that self-defense against armed attack is legitimate. If Libya invades the United States, you can defend yourself. But this is self-defense against future attack. That's just a slap in the face to the U.N. and everyone in the world, saying, Look, we'll do what we feel like. You can't have self-defense against future attack. But that was the official justification.

That same year, the International Court of Justice, which is sometimes referred to as the World Court, made its first affirmative ruling on these issues. It stated flatly and clearly that the U.S. was carrying out "unlawful use of force" in its attack against Nicaragua and could not claim the right of self-defense against armed attack as it had been.[12] So there's a definitive ruling by the International Court of Justice, saying, This is what international law says. That's the highest authority around. The reaction of the Congress, controlled by Democrats, was to instantly step up the illegal use of force. Congress made another huge grant for contra aid. Across the board, the press, liberal opinion, famous international lawyers, simply said, OK, the court's discredited. It's demonstrated that it's a "hostile forum," as the *New York Times* put it, and therefore it's discredited itself.[13] And that's a way of saying we have the right to use force and violence, and if other people don't understand it, get out of the way.

There was an official explanation by the State Department that didn't get much publicity, but it's worth looking at. Abraham Sofaer, a State Department legal adviser, explained that we could count on most states to vote with us in the early days of the U.N.[14] He didn't say why, but the point was that we held the lash in those days. We had all the wealth and power and they just had to do what we said. But now, with decolonization and a broader representation in the U.N., we can't any longer count on most states to follow our lead. So therefore we cannot allow the World Court or the U.N. to judge anything we do because they may not go along with us. In fact, they probably won't agree with us. It's not that therefore we're wrong. It's that therefore they're wrong. Sofaer said that we must reserve to ourselves the right to determine how to act with regard to matters that are under the domestic jurisdiction of the U.S., as determined by the U.S. The issue that was under the domestic jurisdiction of the U.S. at that time was the U.S. attack against Nicaragua. This is at the time of the World Court decision, explaining why the U.S. wouldn't accept jurisdiction. You couldn't have a clearer statement that international law just doesn't mean a thing.

In the Clinton years, it became totally open. Clinton defended the first bombing of Iraq in mid-1993 as self-defense against armed attack. The armed attack in that case took place a couple of months earlier, when some Iraqis might or might not have been involved — nobody knew — in a failed assassination attempt against former president George Bush. Therefore, two months later, we're defending ourselves against armed attack by firing missiles at Baghdad. We can't even laugh at that. We might check and see what the reaction was. It's just a way of saying we'll do what we like. And it continues up until now.

The U.S. and U.K. also went around the U.N. again recently, when they bombed Iraq in December.

The December bombing was particularly striking. I reviewed a good bit of coverage. It was in flat violation of international law. The reason that they didn't go to the U.N. Security Council is perfectly obvious. The council was not going to permit the attack. The Security Council is another "hostile forum," and it's irrelevant. If the U.S. and Britain want to use force, they will. Furthermore, they did it in as brazen a way as possible to demonstrate their contempt for the U.N. and international law. The timing was picked just when the Security Council was meeting in an emergency session dealing with this crisis. They had not been informed, but they could turn on the radio and say, Just as we were opening our meeting, missiles were falling in Baghdad. That's a way of saying as clearly as possible, You're irrelevant. International law is irrelevant. We are rogue states. We will use force and violence as we choose.

Now we ask, What was the reaction to this? Almost 100 percent approval. In fact, "approval" is the wrong word. It wasn't noticed. There was almost no comment on it that I could find. And the marginal comment there was said it was a technical matter.

We can't be deterred by a technical matter. This is much too important. If we choose to bomb, "We'll set the timetable — not the United Nations and not Saddam Hussein," a senior administration official informed the press, reiterating the standard position that the Security Council cannot have veto power over U.S. policy.[15] That would be ridiculous, as is generally agreed. Except that's what international law requires. The U.N. Charter requires that the Security Council have veto power over threat or use of force. And that is supposed to apply to every other country. Not Britain, because they're our attack dog. And not Israel, because they're an appendage. But countries that aren't appendages of the U.S. are supposed to follow these rules. Not us.

Now it is clear, open, brazen, and with — you can't even say the "approval" of intellectual opinion, because it's so deeply taken for granted it's not even noticed. It's just like the air you breathe. Of course. We're a violent, terrorist state. And that's right and just. That's a big change from, say, 1947, when the contempt for international law was hidden in secret documents which would be released forty years later, to today, when it's flaunted. We have a big flag saying, International law and the U.N. Charter are inappropriate for us because we have the guns and we're going to use them. Period.

What was the reaction outside the United States?

It's not reported here, but the world did notice. In India, for example, the world's biggest democracy, the Indian Council of Jurists is actually bringing a case to the World Court charging the U.S. and U.K. with war crimes. That was announced on December 22. A friend of mine who has database access checked to see if there's been any reference to this. There's nothing to the end of the year, at least — no report, even. The Vatican called it aggression. That got a little mention, at the bottom of a page here and there. In the Arab world, it was widely condemned as aggression. In England, it was not as uniform as here. The *Observer* had a lead editorial condemning it as aggression, but here I couldn't find a break in opinion.[16]

One of the advantages of leaving the United States is to be exposed to different media. I traveled to Thailand in January. The Nation is one of their two English-language newspapers. There was a very critical article by Suravit Jayanama titled, "Containing America in the Post–Cold War Era." The article asked, "While Washington talks about containing Saddam Hussein, what about the need to contain a superpower that zealously acts to protect its own interests?"[17]

That's the attitude in much of the world, and with justice. When the world's only superpower, which has essentially a monopoly of force, announces openly, We will use force and violence as we choose and if you don't like it get out of the way, there's a reason why that should frighten people. Incidentally, the reaction after the Gulf War was the same. It was described in the United States as a triumph of morality and courage. But if you look around the world, it was quite different. I reviewed as much as I could discover of world coverage, and people were very frightened. They said, These guys are out of control. Who are they going to attack next? There is no deterrent left. The United States will do as it pleases, and everybody else had better watch out.

A number of U.N. member states and members of the Security Council opposed the U.S. missile attacks in August 1998 on Afghanistan and Sudan. That number noticeably increased with the December attack on Iraq. What accounts for that?

I think that what accounts for it is concern and fear, which the U.S. is trying to stir up. It's not trying to hide it. This December, one senior European diplomat at the U.N. was quoted as saying that the U.S. has given up on the U.N. It doesn't want to have it anymore. It's now going to conduct its policy through the North Atlantic Treaty Organization and the World Trade Organization, which it feels it can control. That's close to accurate. I think the U.N. will still be used when you can palm off some problem on it. As for NATO and the WTO, they're used only when they follow orders. When the European Union brought a case to the WTO condemning the U.S. embargo of Cuba, the Clinton administration responded by withdrawing WTO jurisdiction, just like Reagan did with the World Court. Actually, the U.S. claimed what they called a "national security exemption."[18] Our national existence is at stake by denial of food to Cuba. They didn't make this too prominent, because it's too ludicrous, but that was apparently the technical reason. So the WTO, yes, as long as they follow orders. If it's an unimportant matter, we may give in to them. NATO, yes, if they do what we tell them. But the U.N. is just not enough under control.

The reaction to the U.N. has been quite interesting over the years. In the early years, the U.S. was very much in favor of the U.N. It was wonderful, because they were doing everything that Washington wanted. With decolonization, that began to change. By the 1960s, relations between the U.N. and Washington were fairly hostile, although the U.N. was still under control. For example, the U.N. never raised the issue of the U.S. war in Vietnam, although most of the countries were passionately opposed, and so was the Secretary General, U Thant. I had a private meeting with him in December 1966 at U.N. headquarters. It would be unfair to report a private conversation, but it was clear he had said the same thing to other people — that he thought this was a real atrocity and it ought to be ended, but the U.N. couldn't do anything about it. It couldn't even discuss it publicly. It was quite different when the Russians invaded Afghanistan. Then the U.N. could take a strong stand and denounce it. But not when the U.S. attacked Vietnam.

By the 1970s and particularly by the 1980s, there was simply an attempt to eliminate the organization. The most striking example was when third world countries, the South, tried to break the Western monopoly over the information systems. There was an attempt through UNESCO, the United Nations Educational, Scientific, and Cultural Organization, to broaden and democratize access to information media and technology. The U.S. reacted with complete hysteria. There followed a very interesting series of incidents in which there was a flood of lies and condemnations of this effort, claiming that it was an attack on freedom of press and state regimentation of news. It was all lies. It was demonstrated to be lies. The lies were repeated after they were refuted, and the refutations were not permitted publication.

There's a good study of this by William Preston, Ed Herman and Herbert Schiller, *Hope and Folly,* which documents the history in detail.[19] I don't think there was a single review of the book. William Preston is a historian of the U.N. He commented on the irony that after the United States condemned UNESCO for attempting to undermine the free marketplace of ideas, the U.S. demonstrated that there is no free marketplace of ideas by refusing even to publish the refutations of the lies. That's exactly what happened. Ed Herman has a detailed accounting, as he usually does, of the media coverage and how it worked — and the refusal to allow refutations to appear and the continual lying after it was known to be false.

What all of this reveals, including the silence over what happened, is a really profound fear that control over doctrine and information might escape the hands of those who are powerful. If it gets into the hands of other people, we're in trouble. And they understand that. UNESCO was practically destroyed because of this. It was tamed. The U.S. is trying to undermine the U.N. That's why it doesn't pay its dues, because it's no longer a useful instrument of power. When it can be used, it will be used. So when the Somalia operation turned into a catastrophe, then it was fine. The U.N. — U.N. incompetence — could take the blame. And maybe sometimes if there's something the U.S. doesn't want to do and the U.N. can be a cover, they'll use it.

You also observed that another similarity with Libya was the prime-time bombing in April 1986.

In the case of Libya, it was really dramatic. It took a lot of self-discipline for the media and commentators never to comment on this. The Libya bombing was precisely at 7 p.m. Eastern Standard Time, and that was no small trick. That happened to be at the time when the three television networks had their evening news. That meant that the Reagan administration was given free time on television. First of all, the television cameras immediately shifted to the exciting events in Tripoli and Benghazi — lights going off, bombs falling, all great stuff. Then you go to Washington and the Reagan administration says what's going on is "self-defense against future attack." They essentially control the story for the first hour. Then of course it's all over.

A couple of questions come to mind. How come the bombing was precisely at 7 p.m., when all three networks begin their evening newscasts? That was no easy job. It was a six-hour flight from England. They couldn't even fly directly because the continental countries refused to allow overflights. They were opposed to the bombing. So they had to fly over the Atlantic and the Mediterranean. They got there precisely at 7 p.m. The first major war crime in history that was timed for prime-time television.

The second question is, Why were the networks even there? Does ABC have a studio in Libya? They were there because they were told, Be ready at 2 a.m. Libyan time. We're going to put on a show for you. So the networks were informed of this exciting event. Nobody was supposed to notice this. You can look back to 1986 and see how much commentary there was about this very subtle fact.

Now let's go to Iraq. That bombing was 5 p.m. Eastern Standard Time, just before the network news programs. Maybe it's an accident, but I think there are grounds for suspicion.

In late January you did a benefit talk for Mobilization for Survival in Cambridge. Someone in the audience asked you what the U.S. should do about Iraq. You had a very interesting response.

I think again whenever something like that comes to mind, the first thing we should do is react with skepticism to what we ourselves are asking. There's a presupposition, namely that we should do something about Saddam Hussein. Is that correct? Suppose for example the question was, What should Iran do about Saddam Hussein? Is that a proper question? You can think of things Iran could do. Maybe they should attack Iraq with nuclear weapons. Is that the right answer? Is that the right question? Iran has much more reason to be concerned with Saddam Hussein than we do. Iran lost hundreds of thousands of its own citizens just a decade ago, when they were attacked by Iraq, and had to capitulate because the U.S. Navy got in on the side of Saddam Hussein. They were victims of gas attacks and chemical warfare attacks, too. So they've got a lot more concern with Saddam Hussein than we do.

Should we ask the question, What should Iran do about Saddam Hussein? As soon as that question is asked, we see that it's an absurdity. Iran shouldn't do anything about Saddam Hussein because they have no authority to do it. If they have no authority, we have vastly less authority. After all, we're his backers and supporters. We weren't attacked by him. We supported his atrocities. So the idea that we have to do something about Saddam Hussein already begs some pretty remarkable questions.

If you ask, What should we do about Saddam Hussein, well, maybe the answer is, the same as what Iran should do, namely follow the law. If Iran feels threatened by Saddam Hussein, and they have every reason to be, approach the U.N. Security Council, and ask them to act in response to this threat. In fact, they don't feel threatened at the moment because Saddam Hussein is so weakened by the U.S. attacks and the sanctions that he doesn't really pose much of a threat by the standards of the region. But if they feel it, that's the way to react.

What should we do about Saddam Hussein? The first thing you should do is remember an old medical adage, "First, do no harm."

After you've gotten that far, you can start asking, Can I do anything good? So let's begin with "First, do no harm." We're doing a lot of harm. We're doing harm by insisting on a policy which is strengthening Saddam Hussein and causing great suffering to Iraqi civilians. That's doing a lot of harm, to the cost of hundreds of thousands, maybe over a million dead. That's harm. So we should stop doing harm and at the same time strengthening Saddam Hussein. More harm was done by the bombing, not only by the damage, but because it ended the inspection regime. The inspection regime wasn't perfect, by any means, but it was pretty successful, far more successful than bombing in reducing Iraq's military force.

By Clinton's own admission.

And furthermore, they knew in advance. They said in advance, If we carry out bombing, it will end the inspections. That was doing harm. In fact, the opposition to a democratic government is doing harm. That was conceded in December 1998 by Secretary of State Madeleine Albright in an interesting comment. She said, "We have come to the determination that the Iraqi people would benefit if they had a government that really represented them."[20] That's what we determined in December 1998. Notice what it tells you. Until December 1998, they didn't realize that maybe the interests of the Iraqi people would be served by a representative government. In other words, they were opposed to it. I don't see any reason to doubt that they are still opposed to it.

Is there anything constructive that the U.S. can do? After all, it has a lot of power. And there may well be. One could think about that. Iraqi opposition groups have made proposals. They should be considered. Whether they should be implemented or not is a decision. But the assumption right off that we have to "go in" and "do something" should be questioned. Who gave us that right?

You, Edward Said, Howard Zinn, and Ed Herman recently issued a statement on Iraq.[21] You say, "The time has come for a call to action to people of conscience.... [W]e must organize and make this issue a priority, just as Americans organized to stop the war in Vietnam.... We need a national campaign to lift the sanctions." I know you're not against sanctions in all instances, for example, you cite South Africa as quite a separate case.

For clarity, the four of us signed that statement. But it was written, organized, and publicized by Robert Jensen, who teaches at the University of Texas. That illustrates something that we know is true all the time: the people who really do the work are rarely known. What is known is somebody who stood up and said something or signed his name. So it's his petition. We signed it.

The burden of proof is always on any imposition of sanctions. Can that burden of proof be overcome? Sometimes. Take South Africa. Two comments about that. One is that the sanctions, as far as anybody could determine, were supported by the overwhelming majority of the population. The black population and in fact part of the white population that was anti-Apartheid favored the sanctions. That's a good argument in favor. If the population is for them, that's an argument, not a proof, that maybe they're a good idea. The second comment is, it would have been a good idea if the U.S. had observed the sanctions, but it didn't. The U.S. undermined them. U.S. trade and interactions with South Africa continued.

Is that "constructive engagement"?

The Reagan administration was opposed to the sanctions. They were forced on it by Congress. The record after that was ambiguous. The U.S. certainly did not closely observe them. In fact, I believe trade actually increased. But it would have been a good idea to observe the sanctions. The same with Rhodesia, which is now Zimbabwe. It would have been an good idea to observe the sanctions. They could have had and did have a constructive effect, and most of the population was in favor of them.

There are other cases like that. Take the military coup in Haiti in September 1991. There was again very good reason to believe, and there was constant testimony, that the overwhelming majority of the population, though it was suffering from sanctions, wanted them imposed. They kept saying so in every way they could get a voice out. I am not saying everybody, but it was certainly a very strong sentiment. In that case, I think sanctions were justified, as in the South

African case, but it would have been a good idea if the U.S. had not undermined the sanctions, as it did.

The sanctions were immediately undermined. They were issued by the Organization of American States right after the military coup. Within a few weeks, the Bush administration stated that U.S. companies would be exempt from these restrictions. That was reported in the *New York Times*. It was described positively as a good step. They said the Bush administration was "fine-tuning" the sanctions for maximal benefit to the Haitian people, namely by exempting U.S. firms from the sanctions regime.[22] Good fine-tuning.

Trade continued with Haiti, not at the full level, but consistently. Under Clinton, I think it went up by about 50 percent. Furthermore, and this is the most crucial part, the core of any sanctions regime needed to be oil. The CIA kept testifying to Congress that oil had been stopped and the sanctions were really working. Everybody in Haiti knew that wasn't true. Oil was flowing in. You could see the rich families building big oil farms. You didn't know exactly where it was coming from, but it was obviously coming in.

The day before the Marine invasion in September 1994, which was going to liberate Haiti, a great victory for democracy, the lead Associated Press story — which means every newsroom sees it — was that the Clinton and Bush administrations had illegally authorized Texaco to supply oil to the military junta.[23] I happened to be monitoring the wires that day, so I saw it. The facts were quietly conceded by the Justice Department. What that means is that we do know where the oil was coming from. Clinton, and Bush before him, had informed Texaco that although there was a presidential directive barring shipment of oil, it wouldn't be enforced, so they could ship the oil if they liked.

So the sanctions regime was undermined by U.S. intervention as part of its tacit support for the military regime until it had terrorized enough people that we could go in and restore the president, Jean-Bertrand Aristide, but under the condition that he follow the program of the defeated U.S. candidate in the 1990 election. But that was a case in which sanctions would have been justified. You can think of other cases. You'd have to look at them case by case. But there is strong prior argument against them, which has to be over-come. There are reasons sometimes to overcome it.

The sanctions regime in Iraq will soon be a decade old. The documentation clearly indicates the staggering impact it's had on ordinary Iraqis.

And there's another side to that. It's also strengthened Saddam Hussein in several respects. For one thing, it weakens the opposition to him. People are just trying to survive. Everyone becomes more desperate and vindictive, sheltering under whatever power there is. Those are natural reactions to total disaster. We should also bear in mind that the bombing itself in 1991 and the sanctions are a form of biological warfare. They are the actual use, not the potential use, of weapons of mass destruction. When you destroy water-purification, sewage, and electricity systems, that's equivalent to spreading bacteria, which will bring about disease. That's biological warfare.

We have every reason to be concerned about the potential for biological warfare in Iraq and a lot of other places including here, but we should also be much more concerned about the actual use of weapons of mass destruction, including biological warfare. The documentation on that is reasonably clear. People can debate how many children have died. Is it really half a million or more or less? But qualitatively it's not questioned, nor is it questioned that it's essentially strengthened Saddam Hussein.

About once a year the New York Times *has an article with a headline like "Many Arabs See Double Standard for Israel."* [24] *Then there's a report quoting various intellectuals and political leaders who say, Well, it could be that the U.S. has a double standard. When you travel around the country and the world and talk about U.S. adherence to U.N. Security Council resolutions, how do people respond?*

I don't quite put it like that. I don't think there's a double standard. I don't think there's inconsistency. I think there's a single standard, and it's followed consistently. There are policies formulated in the perceived interests of domestic U.S. power, the state-corporate nexus. And those policies are followed quite consistently. There are no double standards. They have nothing to do with law or morality or human welfare. They have to do with maximizing certain interests.

We could try to spell out those interests. They're not uniform, but they're pretty well identifiable, and I think they're followed with fair consistency. So when people talk about double standards and inconsistency, as they do all over the world, my response, when I can talk to them, is to say, You're looking at the matter incorrectly. It's very consistent and has been for a long time. The Cold War changed the tactical applications of it, but they were applied before the Cold War and they were applied after the Cold War. Fundamentally it's tactical adjustments, the same with other changes.

Is it perceived throughout the rest of the world? Sure. Take Egypt, which is an ally. Its semi-official newspaper, *Al Ahram,* has a weekly edition in English. I read it. They're very bitter about what they call, incorrectly in my view, the U.S. double standards. The same is true in India, Thailand, and elsewhere. Even in the West, it's called a "strange inconsistency" in U.S. views. In continental Europe, largely opposed to the U.S. stand on West Asia, what we call the Middle East, they talk about this double standard in U.S. policy, which is a serious error, because it fails to recognize that the policy is quite rational — though sometimes people may rationally choose a policy which happens not to work.

U.S. policy is perfectly rational, understandable, consistent, and is explained and applied over time. To call it irrational, a double standard, or inconsistent is to give away much too much. It assumes that there are some crazy people doing things in some random fashion. Not at all. They are perfectly reasonable people doing things according to plans and in terms of interests that they perceive and try to implement. They're not above error. In fact, they make plenty of idiotic errors. There's a lot of stupidity and ignorance. Sometimes under Kissinger it became almost classic. But nevertheless, it's a consistent and understandable policy, and I think it should be seen that way.

The last time you were on National Public Radio's All Things Considered *was during the Gulf War in February 1991. You did a two-minute commentary.*[25]

Two minutes and thirty seconds. I remember very well because, unlike every other country that I know of, they insisted that I give them the text in advance so that they could make sure that it would be OK and that it would be precisely two minutes and thirty seconds. They had to have it taped so that nothing could go wrong. I wouldn't have a chance to say a word other than what they approved. The first time I read it, it happened to take two minutes and thirty-six seconds. So they told me to read it a little faster. The second time, I was able to get it down to two minutes and thirty seconds with exactly the words they had approved.

The thrust of your comments had to do with countries violating Security Council resolutions. You were imagining a U.S. bombing attack on Tel Aviv, Ankara, and Jakarta.

At that time, in 1991, it was right when the Turkish attack on the Kurdish population was beginning to intensify again. I didn't know then, but that was the beginning of several years of highly intensified U.S.-backed attacks on the Kurds in southeastern Turkey, which emptied the countryside. About a million people fled to the city of Diyarbakir, the semi-official Kurdish capital. U.S.-supplied jets were used. Congress found out about it and opposed it because it was illegal. That's Turkey, aside from a whole long list of other atrocities, including the use of torture, human rights violations, and the invasion of Cyprus. Turkey had a horrible record. I said, OK, why not bomb Ankara, the capital of Turkey? We were providing the arms and supplies. In fact, Turkey became the biggest importer of U.S. arms during precisely the period when it was stepping up the attack on the Kurds. As for Jakarta, Suharto's record was at least as impressive as Saddam Hussein's, probably worse.

Not according to the New York Times.

Suharto is "our kind of guy," according to an official in the Clinton administration — a benevolent dictator.[26] He came into power in 1965 with the massacre of half a million people or so, and we don't have to go on with the rest. That year, 1991, a couple of months after my NPR commentary, happened to be the year of the Dili massacre in East Timor, which did bring these issues to some public attention. So, sure, bomb Jakarta.

Israel has been occupying part of south Lebanon in violation of a U.N. Security Council resolution of May 1978, in this case unanimous, ordering Israel out instantly and unconditionally. The U.S. said, Forget it, so they stayed in. They were constantly carrying out terrorist attacks on the rest of Lebanon. Prisoners were being tortured inside Israel. There was harsh repression in the occupied territories, and the stealing of land belonging to Arab citizens inside Israel. We can go on and on. So, fine, bomb Tel Aviv. We could go down the list.

If you look at the list of leading recipients of U.S. aid, virtually every one of them is a major human rights violator. This is pointed out every year by the human rights organizations like Human Rights Watch. They point out that virtually all U.S. aid is illegal under U.S. law. U.S. aid is not permitted to go to countries that systematically torture their citizens. Run down the list of the top recipients. It's true of all of them. In the Western Hemisphere, the leading recipient of military aid through the early 1990s has been Colombia, which also has the worst human rights record.

That was the point of that comment on NPR. And of course, you don't have to bomb these countries. If you want to stop the terror and atrocities that they're carrying out, just stop supporting them. So we're back to, "First, do no harm." There's no need to bomb Jakarta or Ankara. Just stop supporting their atrocities. Then you can ask what more can be done.

The point I was trying to also emphasize was, here was this commentary of two minutes and thirty seconds completely surrounded by a drumbeat of Gulf War propaganda.

It was surprising that NPR allowed even that much deviation, frankly. That's very rare. Usually they insist on total unanimity. But in this case, actually, I suspect, under public pressure, they were willing to allow a minuscule break in the uniformity.

But there was no context for your comments. The average listener would ask, What? Bombing Tel Aviv? I don't get it. And then on to the next news item.

I go back to the comment of the guy who used to be on *Nightline*. *Jeff Greenfield.*

He made a point that was quite accurate. He explained why they wouldn't have me on. He said there were two reasons. First of all, I'm from Neptune. Secondly, I lack concision.[27] I agree with him.

On both counts? Neptune also?

From his point of view. In fact, that's exactly what you were just saying. What I said in the two minutes and thirty seconds that I had on NPR must have sounded to a reasonable listener as if I were from Neptune. There was no context, background, or evidence. My comments were completely different from everything they were hearing. The rational response is, This guy must be from Neptune. This guy's off his rocker. That's correct.

The point about concision is important, too. I'd never heard that word before, but it's a nice term. So you have to frame your comments so they can fit between two commercials or can fit into an outpouring of propaganda that has one line that it keeps to. That means you can't give an explanation of what you're saying. So it leaves you with very simple choices. Either you repeat the same conventional doctrines that everybody else is saying, for which you don't need any proof. If you're marching in a parade, you don't need any evidence. Or else you say something which in fact is true and it will sound like it's from Neptune. Concision requires that there be no backing or evidence. The flood of unanimous doctrine ensures that it will sound as if it's off the wall.

So basically I agree with his comment, and I think they're doing their job very well. That's the way to ensure efficient thought control and to prevent people from thinking, even thinking about extremely simple things, like the ones we were talking about before. Like how can a deep philosophical issue happen to fall on strict party lines vote after vote? Or how can it be that we are bombing the monster because he gassed his own citizens with our support? It's very important to make sure that people can't stop long enough to think about these questions.

Looking at the larger global, geopolitical situation, what do you see developing for U.S. policy vis-à-vis Europe? The Euro, the new single currency, is going to come into use in the next couple of years. Germany is central, with Frankfurt essentially running the Euro and Berlin becoming not only Germany's political capital but also the major transportation hub of Europe. Do you think it's at all desirable that Europe challenge U.S. hegemony?

That depends what "Europe" is. The European Union so far is under the very strict control of central bankers. It's a central banker system, meaning strict monetary policies and efforts to cut away at the social contract, which is far more developed in Europe than it is here. It does challenge the United States in some respects. For example, the Euro could become an alternative global currency, which would have all sorts of complicated effects on U.S. dominance. It would mean that oil prices wouldn't simply be denominated in U.S. dollars. It would probably undermine U.S. power to some extent.

There are differences. Whatever political cast Europe has, it has differences with the U.S. on many issues. The Middle East is an example. "Europe" in this context means Europe minus England. England is still a loyal puppy dog. German-based Europe, which is what it is, has different approaches toward Eastern Europe, the Balkans, West Asia, to the oil producers, and so on. It's important to remember that the United States and Britain are isolated not only on Iraq. They're also isolated on Iran. Cuba is another case. On that, they're totally isolated. In fact, the U.S. is alone on Cuba. Even Britain doesn't go along. Israel says they go along. They have to say it. But they also violate the embargo. On Iran, the U.S. and Britain are essentially alone. Not totally. Israel agrees. Turkey probably agrees. But certainly Europe doesn't, as a body. The more Europe becomes an independent force in world affairs, as it will over time, the more it puts the U.S. in a difficult position.

What force it will be is another question, but some kind of independent force. The U.S. will find it harder to implement its own programs for the West Asian region, which are crucial, because that's where the energy resources are. In my opinion, and this is speculation because we don't have documents, part of the reason why the U.S. is trying to look as violent and vindictive and out of control as possible is to frighten off Europe and others, to say, We know we can't convince you, but get out of our way, because we're violent and dangerous. About a year ago, a planning document of the Strategic

Command called "Essentials of Post–Cold War Deterrence" was released.[28] It's been hard to get hold of, but little pieces have come out. They say that the U.S. should create a national persona of being violent, vindictive, and out of control. That will frighten people.

Sounds likes the Nixon madman theory.

It's sort of a resurrection of the Nixon madman theory. Nobody knows whether that theory actually existed. It was attributed to Nixon by H.R. Haldeman or somebody. This idea is explicit, and is not original to the U.S. There are earlier sources. It says, We can't convince people, and we are powerful. In the domain of force, we're unparalleled. Therefore, it makes sense to have a national persona of being violent, vindictive, irrational, and out of control. We should use our nuclear weapons arsenal for this purpose. Given the array of forces and the degree of isolation of the U.S., especially on West Asian issues, that makes sense. And it might be part of the reason for things like bombing Sudan and Afghanistan, or Iraq in a way which would be the most brazen possible insult to the U.N. Let them know we're out of control and vindictive, and they'd better watch it. That relates both to Iran and Iraq. In the case of Iran, Europe, maybe even England in this case, would like to bring Iran back into the international system.

They recently established diplomatic relations.

It's clear that they want Iran back in the international system. In the Middle East itself, there is now a completely overt alliance between Israel, Turkey, and the Palestinian Authority. They don't sound like equal partners, but you have to remember that the Palestinians have been a big irritant in U.S.-Arab relations. Their plight arouses a lot of concern in the Arab world and the Islamic world, so if that can be kept quiet somehow, it's a big step up for the United States. And that's the role of the Palestinian Authority. They are supposed to harshly and brutally control a little Bantustan under Israeli, meaning U.S., domination. That's supposed to dampen down the Palestinian issue.

Israel and Turkey are the two big military forces. There was a reaction developing to that. Saudi Arabia and Iran have moved a little

closer toward some sort of rapprochement, which is pretty remarkable because they're at war, technically. Iran is occupying Saudi islands in the Gulf. Egypt has gone along, and Syria was drawn in.

The Middle East is a very dangerous area — very volatile, with
shifting alliances, a ton of oil, and heavily armed states. It is the major energy resource of the world and according to all the projections,
its role will be increasing in the coming years.

Europe, even the Arab countries, don't want Iran isolated the
way it has been. Interestingly, even the American oil companies
want to bring Iran back in. But the U.S. administration, so far at
least, refuses to allow it. That's why there is a lot of fuss about the
positioning of the Central Asia oil pipeline. The oil companies and
Europe want it to go through Iran, which is the cheapest, the most
stable, and the best route. The U.S. is refusing, vetoing it so far. They
want it to ultimately end up in Turkey, avoiding Russia. At stake is
the question of who's going to control and make the profits from
the hydrocarbon resources in the Caspian Sea area. They're not on a
par with the Gulf, but they're nevertheless substantial. So there's a
lot of jockeying about that.

To get back to your point, the more Europe is independent, the
more weight it will be able to throw around on this issue.

There are already indications of emerging trade wars with Europe, for ex-
ample, over bananas.

There's a big conflict at the WTO right now between the European Union and the United States. Different corporations are involved. The E.U. has been giving preferences to former European
colonies in the Caribbean. The U.S. wants in this case a "level playing field," because the big producers, the really rich corporations,
happen to be in U.S. hands. So they'd like to have a "level playing
field," which means crushing the Caribbean islands.

You've said many times that you're not Amnesty International. You can't
support every single issue. What are the factors that determine your involvement
in a particular issue? For example, you've been very closely identified with East
Timor. Yet on Tibet, which is an important issue, you haven't said very much.

Part of it is how much you can do about it. It's the same in personal life. If you can't do anything about some problem, it doesn't help a lot to make big statements about it. So we could all get together and condemn Genghis Khan, but there's no moral value. So the first question is, To what extent can we influence things? There's no algorithm for that, but there are some criteria. For example, to the extent that U.S. power is directly involved, we can influence it more than if it's not directly involved. And there are other factors, such as how much publicity the issue is getting. If it's a very popular issue and a lot of people are talking about it, I don't feel that there's much advantage to my talking about it, even if I think it's a really important issue.

Take South Africa. I said very little about Apartheid, although I think that overcoming it was an extremely important thing. The reason is, there were very strong, powerful voices attacking Apartheid. It didn't seem like a useful contribution of my time to say, I agree, which I often did. I'd rather take unpopular issues, ones that are being kept out of the public sphere and on which we can really do a lot and that are intrinsically important. Combine those questions and you can draw some judgments.

There are other things that are just personal. I happen to have been concerned with Israel or what was Palestine ever since childhood. I grew up in an environment that was engaged with these issues. I've lived in Israel, read the Hebrew newspapers, and have a lot of friends there, so naturally I'm involved in that. Aside from personal examples, I think these criteria are important.

In the case of Tibet, I did write about it a little in the 1960s and pointed out that what we ought to bear in mind and ask ourselves, How come Tibet is in China altogether? What about all the outlying provinces? Tibet, Manchuria, Mongolia, why were they ever in China? It turns out the U.S. was in favor of that. Britain was the major global power at the time. But the Western powers and the U.S. supported the incorporation of the outlying provinces into China, primarily because they thought that their friend Chiang Kai-shek was going to run it. So it was under this quasi-fascist regime that the West was backing, and they wanted it to be as big and powerful as possible. There was opposition. For example, Owen Lattimore, a specialist on Mongolia and the outer provinces, strongly opposed it. He was targeted as a communist under Joseph McCarthy. When China formerly incorporated Tibet in 1950, there was no protest in the West, just a continuation of these policies. Furthermore, when you look at the Tibet issue, it's not so straightforward. The Chinese have done atrocious things, but the situation before they took over was not very pretty.

On January 6, in Thailand, I saw a BBC World *story on TV on the Hatfield Report on dioxin in Vietnam. The BBC said dioxin was "a devastating legacy of the Vietnam War," something like 14 percent of South Vietnam was contaminated. Children being born today in Vietnam suffer from cleft palates, mental problems, and limb deformities. But there was only a single story on this in the mainstream U.S. press, in the* Los Angeles Times.[29]

The Hatfield Report is interesting. It's a private Canadian outfit supported I think by Canadian government and other grants. It's doing careful research, and picked a particular valley where it had a good control group. The study found extremely high levels of dioxin. The *Los Angeles Times* article by David Lamb was the only one that appeared at this time. There has been a scattering of articles over the years. I've been collecting them. There was one in the *Wall Street Journal* about a year ago.[30] There are occasional articles in the *New York Times*. They all have the same line, which the David Lamb one does, too. As I recall, maybe in the last paragraph, he says something about how this would be an ideal area for measuring the effects of dioxin. That's the line: our lack of interest in this is a mistake because we could really learn something of use for us.

Here's an ideal testing area. South Vietnam was subjected to chemical warfare, but not North Vietnam. They were spared that particular atrocity, so we have a control population. The people have the same genes, and we have pretty good controls. We can discover something about the effects of chemical warfare — dioxin in particular — and ecological destruction by comparing North Vietnam and South Vietnam. Maybe we could learn something useful from that. Barbara Crossette, the Southeast Asian correspondent for the *Times,* wrote an article in the science section on this topic, saying, Here's a really interesting scientific opportunity.[31]

The idea that we might do something about it, might help those people, doesn't come up. The idea that we might apologize for having left maybe half a million dead or hideously deformed fetuses lined up in Saigon hospitals, that we might apologize for it, or even help the victims, that idea doesn't arise. But we're missing a good opportunity to learn something that might be useful for us. That's the issue. That's pretty remarkable.

It's not the only case, but it's an extremely dramatic example of just what that Thai newspaper you quoted earlier is talking about, the need to contain the U.S. not only because of its power, but because of the extreme viciousness of its intellectual culture. To be able to look at the effects of chemical warfare and say, Maybe we can learn something from it because there's a control population, that's pretty astonishing.

It's very rare that any reporter actually goes to Vietnam to see this firsthand. Sometimes some do. The only case I know of is a very good Israeli reporter, Amnon Kapeliouk. He was also the *Le Monde* correspondent for Israel. He went to Vietnam a couple of years ago and reported in some detail in the Hebrew press in Israel what he saw there.[32] It was pretty horrifying. He said, It reminds me of what we heard during the trials of Adolf Eichmann and John Demjanjuk. That's what Kapeliouk described. He didn't just say, Here would be a nice experiment which maybe we could learn something from, but, Here is a major war crime.

The Hatfield study correctly points out that the chemical warfare in Vietnam was aimed at destroying the food supply. That was a primary target. When Kennedy authorized chemical warfare under Operation Ranch Hand back in 1962, one purpose was to destroy the food supply of those who were carrying out the "internal aggression," namely the domestic population. The ecological damage is enormous. The human damage is extreme. I think Vietnam estimates about half a million people, and that's taken seriously. The results are very clear. There is some concern here because U.S. veterans were exposed to dioxin, too, but of course on a far lower level than Vietnamese.

Through exposure to Agent Orange.

Which has dioxin. And of course the destructive effects on the ecology, the countryside, and most of the population were only there, not here. Some of the commentary is pretty stunning. What I mentioned is an example, but let me mention another case. There was a lead article in the *Wall Street Journal* probably about a year and a half or so ago about one particular province exposed to chemical warfare.[33] That was from the scene. Then it said, Why doesn't the U.S. pay some attention to this? There was a line like this: The U.S., emotionally exhausted after its defeat, couldn't pay attention.

Putting aside that it wasn't a defeat — it was a victory — the moral level that this illustrates is amazing. Here we wiped out a country. We left hundreds of thousands of people either suffering or dying from cancer and other birth deformities, four million corpses, three countries virtually destroyed, but we're so emotionally exhausted we can't pay attention because we suffered so much. You can understand why people outside the U.S. are deeply concerned that you have to contain this superpower.

Lamb writes, "The U.S. has never taken a position on the effects of Agent Orange on the Vietnamese population. And no one in Washington appears eager to take on an issue from a war everyone wants to forget." [34]

Everyone. It's a war in which the U.S. achieved its major war ends. Its major concern was to ensure that Vietnam would not take off on a course of independent development that, horror of horrors, might even be a model for others, what is called a virus. That goal was achieved. When you've destroyed a country, it's not going to follow a course of independence. And it's certainly going to be no model for others. That, incidentally, was realized by the business press back in the early 1970s. The *Far Eastern Economic Review* pointed out, You guys ought to declare victory and go home, because you really have won.[35]

But the U.S. didn't achieve its highest aim. It didn't turn Vietnam into the Philippines, a colony. So that's called a loss. But in fact it achieved its major aims. And now we go home. The attitude has been quite astonishing. Jimmy Carter, for example, in what must count as one of the most incredible comments from any head of state anywhere, told a news conference that we owe no debt to Vietnam because "the destruction was mutual."[36] That passed without comment. It didn't affect his stature as a great moral hero. It got much worse in the 1980s. In fact, the Reagan and Bush administrations probably thought Carter bent over too far in the direction of moral equivalence. He said "mutual." Reagan is not even worth talking about. He read whatever somebody handed him on a note card. But Bush presumably was making up his own lines. His line was, The Vietnamese should understand that we do not ask for "retribution." We just want an honest accounting of the crimes that they committed against us. This appeared in a front-page story in the *New York Times.*[37]

Right next to the story, I don't know if the editor did this on purpose, there was an article puzzling over the fact that the Japanese don't seem to be able to acknowledge their war guilt fully. They use a word, *hansei,* which could translate as "regret" or maybe just "remorse."[38] Then comes a long philological discussion. They apologize for their aggression, but they back off because they say other people committed atrocities, too, and we all know that the French and the British and the Americans never committed any atrocities and it was only the Japanese. So they're not really coming out straight and admitting their war guilt, because they have bad genes.

Right next to that comes a story saying that the Vietnamese know that we don't demand retribution, just that they apologize to us for their crimes and give us an honest accounting.[39] It goes on without batting an eyelash. I've collected similar stories right through late 1998, side by side. So there is this legacy, which maybe we should look at because maybe we can learn something from it. It's an ideal "testing area" or whatever the phrase is.

From 1962 to 1971, the U.S. contaminated vast tracts of South Vietnam with Agent Orange. Might not this be an issue to be discussed when talking about weapons of mass destruction and Iraq?

It's chemical warfare. This story is really worth looking at. Chemical and biological warfare, which is a category, was developed during the Second World War. Bacteriological warfare particularly was developed most extensively by the Japanese. The Japanese had a vicious program run by Shiro Ishii. They did hideous Mengele-style experiments on human subjects, trying to develop forms of bacteriological and other biological warfare. It was apparently very advanced. If you do trials with humans, you learn a lot of things.

The stories are hideous. Right after the war, the unit was picked up by the U.S. They were given immunity against any war crimes trials. The Russians actually had a few of them, and they carried out war crimes trials, but they were denounced by the U.S. as show trials. Meanwhile, the U.S. took them all over, took over everything they knew, folded it into U.S. programs at Fort Detrick and elsewhere for chemical and biological warfare. By 1949, the joint chiefs of staff had already incorporated chemical and biological warfare as a first-strike option. By 1956, first use of chemical and bacteriological warfare became official policy.

Up until very recently, I had always dismissed the claims that the U.S. had used bacteriological warfare in Korea and China. I assumed that was propaganda. It's harder to dismiss now. There's new material coming out. *The United States and Biological Warfare* by Stephan Endicott and Edward Hagerman, based on documentation from both U.S. and Chinese archives, makes — I can't say it's a definitive case — but I'd certainly say one you can't dismiss.[40] There's at least strong circumstantial evidence that the U.S. did in fact follow its doctrine and used bacteriological warfare agents in North Korea and probably China. We can't say for certain. If you had asked me two years ago, I would have said it's nonsense. But I think you can no longer say that. There's evidence for it, and it may be true.

The U.S. tried very hard to conceal all this. Even the taking over of the Japanese unit was denied for years. It was finally published in the *Bulletin of Concerned Asian Scholars,* one of the dissident professional journals that came out of the 1960s.[41] They published an article with a lot of documentation. Finally it was conceded, so that part of it isn't debated anymore.

You mentioned chemical warfare. Vietnam was straight use of chemical warfare, in fact, one of the most extensive uses of chemical warfare. The fact is, it's going on right now. There is what amounts to biological warfare in Iraq. But take, say, Colombia and the Andean region altogether. Part of this quite crazed drug war — and by "crazed," I don't mean irrational — has little to do with drugs. Part of the drug war is the use of a form of biological warfare as an experiment to see if it can be fine-tuned to destroy coca. Nobody knows what the effects will be. It's hard to get the details, but they're introducing biologically engineered fungi which are supposed to go after coca. Who knows what they'll do? There is also a powerful herbicide which the U.S. is using against the explicit recommendations of the manufacturer, Dow, which has stated repeatedly and publicly that this is dangerous and cannot be used, particularly under those conditions. But they're using it. That's an herbicide. This is something different. This is introducing some kind of fungi which are supposed to attack the crops. What else they'll do nobody knows. It's an experiment. It's like the Japanese experiment. It's a field experiment with people who don't matter, just Colombian peasants. So maybe it'll destroy coca. Maybe it'll destroy everything else. We'll find out.

Who's carrying out the spraying? Is it the Drug Enforcement Agency or the Colombian military?

Both. The U.S. is providing them with equipment to carry it out. I don't know if U.S. pilots are actually doing it, but it makes no difference. It's a U.S. and Colombian military operation. And of course you have to ask the question, Why are peasants growing coca? Do they like it? They don't have many options.

Colombia, for example, was a wheat producer thirty or forty years ago. But its wheat production was undermined by the United States under the Food for Peace program back in the 1950s, which flooded Colombia with subsidized agricultural products. So that eliminated one major export.

Coffee is another major export, but for coffee to be of any use to small producers, the price has to be fairly predictable. You can't have vast fluctuations in price and expect a peasant to produce it. A big corporation can absorb one-year declines and wait for next year. But somebody who's trying to feed their children can't do it. So there was an effort to construct a coffee-producers' cartel which would keep the prices more or less controlled, without fluctuating too wildly. The U.S. blocked it in the early 1970s and again in the late 1980s. That drove small producers out of the coffee business.

At this point, you don't have any options. You can go to the cities and live in the slums and get killed as disposable people by the police. Or you can move into marginal areas and grow something that will make a profit. You act like a rational capitalist, like the West is telling you to do. You act like a rational peasant under the conditions that the U.S. has imposed. You grow coca.

The same is true throughout the Andean region. Bolivia is a dramatic case. We're imposing neoliberal policies which try to compel the peasants to go away from producing crops for local consumption to producing crops for agro-export and to do it in the manner of a rational capitalist, maximizing gain, while we cut off options except for the production of coca.

We also have to eliminate the state, get the state out of anybody's business. Meanwhile, we're building up the state, making it more and more powerful — but as a military state, which will destroy the peasants who we are forcing to produce coca. That's in essence U.S. policy toward a good part of the Andean region, and one part of it, apparently, is now the use of biological weapons.

All this is going on right now. It's not easy to get direct evidence about it. So I'm kind of picking it out, making some guesses, but that's certainly what it looks like. It's an experiment, just as the use of chemical warfare in Vietnam was an experiment. That experiment didn't work out too well for a couple of hundred thousand Vietnamese. But the people who are terribly concerned about abortion don't seem to care very much about those fetuses lined up in the bottles in Saigon. It's just an experiment, after all. They're worthless people anyway, so what's the difference?

Another ongoing legacy of U.S. intervention in Indochina, particularly in Laos and Vietnam, is unexploded ordnance and land mines.

Occasionally you'll see a little item saying that seven Vietnamese children were killed when they were playing and touched a land mine, but by far the worst problem is Laos. Laos was saturated with probably hundreds of millions of pieces of ordnance. The U.S. government conceded that most of this bombing had nothing to do with the war in Vietnam. Now it's described as stopping the Ho Chi Minh trail, which would be outrageous anyway, but most of it didn't. Most of it was attacking the Plain of Jars in northern Laos, which was an area where there was a low-level peasant revolution going on. It became the most intensively bombed area in history. It was probably surpassed by the bombing of inner Cambodia. But at that time it was the most intensive bombing in history, aimed at a completely defenseless peasant society.

I know something about this. I was there, a few miles from Vientiane, and was able to interview some of the many refugees. There were tens of thousands of refugees who had just been driven off the Plain of Jars. I went with Fred Branfman, an American Lao-speaking volunteer who was trying to interest people in this issue. I spent a lot of time with him interviewing peasants fresh from the experience. I wrote about it at the time in *At War with Asia*.[42]

These were people who had been living in caves for years. The U.S. was using advanced weaponry, including rockets which penetrated caves. Fred Branfman actually went back to the Plain of Jars a couple of years ago. He visited a cave where a rocket penetrated the entry and killed everybody inside who was trying to find shelter. The Laotians were in caves because they couldn't be outside. They tried to live by farming at night because the bombing cut back at night. The most lethal bombardment was what they called bombies, little colorful things which are not like land mines. Land mines are designed to stop a tank. Bombies were designed to maim and kill people. That was their only purpose.

According to Honeywell, which made them, they have a 20 to 30 percent failure rate, which is a little hard to believe. If that's true, you sort of think that must have been built into the design. Bad as technology can be, it's hard to construct something so bad that twenty to thirty percent of it fails to go off. And it would be an extremely effective antipersonnel weapon if it did fail to go off, because somebody will hit it later, but that's speculation. That means that this region is just littered with maybe hundreds of millions, nobody knows how much, of unexploded ordnance.

The victims are mainly children and farmers. In fact, the one careful province survey that was done found that 55 percent of the victims were children. Kids are playing, see these colorful things, pick them up, and they and anyone else around are dead. Farmers hit them if they're trying to clear the ground. That's going on right now.

We're not talking about ancient history. The Lao government estimates about 20,000 casualties a year, of whom more than half die. Whether that number is right or wrong, nobody knows.

The *Wall Street Journal* did have a good article about it by their veteran Asia correspondent Barry Wain.[43] He reported the numbers and he considered them plausible, said they might be too high, might be too low, but they're not out of range. That article was in the Asia edition of the *Journal*. They never put it in their American edition. It's covered in the British press. There is an occasional article in the U.S. I've collected every one I could find. So it's not unknown.

The first group to try to do something about this issue was the Mennonites. The Mennonite Central Committee has had volunteers working in Laos since 1977 and has been trying to publicize the problem and get people interested in it. They're trying to give people shovels, hardly high-tech equipment. There is a British volunteer mine-detection group — composed of professionals, but not the British government — which has been working there for several years. They have some Laotians working with them. The Americans are notable by their absence, as the British press puts it.

Furthermore, according to the right-wing *Sunday Telegraph,* the British mine-clearance group claims that the Pentagon will not even give them technical information that would allow them to defuse the bombs.[44] There's some technique you can use to make sure they don't go off, but they won't give them that information. So the British mine clearers themselves are at risk because this is secret information. The U.S. is not there clearing the bomblets and won't give the British who are doing it information about how to do it safely. The U.S. is now, after a lot of pressure, training some Laotians. All of this is happening right now, right in front of our eyes.

There's another case, even closer. During Hurricane Mitch in Nicaragua and Honduras, especially on the Nicaraguan side, mudslides displaced lots of land mines. They estimate about 75,000. There had been a mine clearing effort, but now they don't know where the mines are because they have been washed all over the countryside. Those mines didn't come from Jupiter or Neptune, where I came from. We know where they came from, and we know who's not there getting rid of them. There was a Reuters report, which as far as I know was published only in the Quaker press here, that a French de-mining team is going.[45] But I haven't seen anything further on that. So there's another similar case.

The Laotian case is much worse. Those are not mines. They're much more dangerous than mines, and they are much denser. There's probably nothing in the world that compares with the density of the unexploded ordnance in Laos. There are plenty of mines in Afghanistan. The Russians gave maps as to where the land mines were. I'm fairly sure of that. I don't think that's ever come up in the United States.

This is fairly esoteric information. Let's say someone just read this. What kind of solutions would you suggest?

In this case, the solutions are very straightforward. For a fraction of the expense that the U.S. taxpayer put into destroying Laos, you could clear the unexploded ordnance. So the first step would be to do what we claim the Japanese can't do: take responsibility. Maybe that would be a start. So let's overcome this strange defect and accept responsibility. That defect is not in the American public. It's in American educated elites. They can find this out. If they don't know it already, they can easily find it out. It's not like learning quantum physics. It takes no time to find it out. They can use their position to make sure everybody knows about it.

When the editors of the *New York Times* and the rest take responsibility — which they condemn the Japanese for not taking — that will be step one. Step two will be to put in the resources that are required to overcome this U.S. atrocity and stop killing Laotian children. It's not a big step. It's not like bombing somebody. It would cost a lot less than bombing Iraq or the Sudan. So there are some easy answers. Very easy answers.

Since the collapse of Mexico and more acutely since the fall of the Thai baht in July 1997, there seems to be an ongoing crisis in global capitalism. We've seen markets careening from Thailand to Russia to Japan and most recently to Brazil. What's your understanding of what's happening?

We should begin by recognizing that for a good part of the population of the world, and probably the vast majority, it's been a crisis for a long time. It's now called a crisis because it's starting to affect the interests of rich and powerful people. So now it's a crisis. Up until then it was just starving people. They're not a crisis. But now even rich investors might get harmed, so yeah, it's a crisis.

What has happened, point number one is, nobody really understands. The Bank for International Settlements, which is sometimes called the central bank of central bankers, has an annual report. Its last annual report said that we have to approach these questions with "humility," because nobody has a clue as to what's going on.[46] Jeffrey Sachs, an economist at Harvard, said in a recent article that we have to recognize that the international economy is "dimly understood."[47] In fact, every international economist who is even semihonest tells you, We don't really understand what's going on, but we have some ideas. So anything that's said — certainly anything that I say — you want to add many grains of salt to, because nobody really understands.

However, some things are moderately clear and there's a fair consensus. Through the Bretton Woods era — roughly from the end of the Second World War up to the early 1970s — exchange rates were pretty close to fixed and capital was more or less controlled. So there weren't extreme capital flows. That was changed in the early 1970s by decision. Capital flow was liberalized. There have been associated events, maybe consequences, maybe not. The humility comes back. Associated with this period of liberalization of capital has been a number of things. One of them has been a considerable decline in economic growth and productivity. That's true of the rich countries like the United States.

There has also been an attack on the welfare state. There has also been a sharp increase in inequality. That's more extreme in the U.S. and in England to some extent than other places. For the U.S., the richest country in the world, the most recently available statistics as of January are that for the majority of the population incomes have stagnated or declined during this period, while work hours have increased considerably. So the typical American family by reasonable measures is working about a month a year more than they were twenty years ago to keep a real income of about the same level or less. The U.S. is now first among the rich countries in hours of work, and also first in poverty, child poverty, hunger and other things. This is a uniquely rich country. So these are social policies, not because of not having the resources for it.

In the poor countries, it has been a disaster. The Latin American debt of the 1980s led to a decade of negative development. You look at the debt in Latin America, and it's roughly matched by the amount of capital flow — meaning that rich Brazilians were sending their money to New York and Swiss banks because there were no controls on capital. And that's called debt. Poor Brazilians then have to pay the debt. That's the crisis. But it wasn't called a crisis then because the rich people were still doing fine.

In Southeast Asia, what had happened was a tremendous flow of short-term speculative capital, which then quickly flowed out as soon as the first sign of trouble came. That's typical of financial markets. The standard line in the professional international economics literature is that financial markets are governed by panics, mania, and hysteria. They're completely irrational, and totally unpredictable. Nobody knows how they're going to work. And financial markets have grown in an extraordinary fashion since the early 1970s.

To come back to what is a reasonable consensus, with all due humility, it's generally assumed that the liberalization of capital flow is a major factor in the sudden collapse of the Southeast Asian economies and more strikingly of South Korea, which was a strong economy. So it wasn't the East Asian model of development that failed, but rather the moving away from it that failed. That's actually the judgment of Joseph Stiglitz, the chief economist of the World Bank, not a marginal figure. It's probably correct.

Brazil is pretty much the same. The problem in Brazil right now is that they cannot stop the flight of capital. Capital is flowing out at a mad rate. The government keeps raising the interest rate to try to keep the capital inside, and speculators are betting that they're not going to be able to get it high enough. There is a way to stop it. The flow of capital is not like the flow of water, not like a tidal wave. It's under human control. But you have to decide to stop it. Brazil alone couldn't decide. Capital controls have to be at both ends.

During the Bretton Woods era, the period of rapid growth of the world economy, when capital controls still worked, controls existed at both ends. So the recipient countries, the country from which the capital was flying, agreed to block capital flight. If there are a couple of rich countries like the United States that won't play the game, then the game's over. But these are social policies that are under potential control.

There have been technical proposals around for twenty-five years, like the Tobin tax, that might slow down speculative capital flows. And other things are possible. But the business sector doesn't want it. Up until now they haven't wanted it because they're gaining from it, especially financial capital. They're gaining a huge amount of profit from it. So they've been perfectly happy to see the slowdown of the economy. Of course they love the inequality since it's pouring wealth to the rich sector. They haven't seen it as a crisis because it's benefiting them, not harming them. Now it's a crisis, and now there's general talk for the first time of instituting some sort of new financial architecture. They're talking about some form of regulation of completely irrational financial markets right now, at the World Economic Forum in Davos, Switzerland. Jagdish Bhagwati, a free-trade true believer and economist at Columbia University, has been writing about how we have to understand elementary economics. He claims free trade is great for manufacturing but it's a disaster for finance. Financial markets just don't work like markets in goods. There's good reason to believe that. Economists like John Maynard Keynes and Hyman Minsky have studied this. It's a well-known area of economics, and the experience of the last twenty-five years seems to bear it out.

It's also worth remembering that one of the reasons why back in 1944 the Bretton Woods system did insist on regulation of financial flows was because they wanted to preserve the welfare state. They understood what should be a near truism, that if you free up financial flows, it's a very powerful weapon against social spending. Any country that uses resources for things like, say, education or health, or what is considered irrational by investors, is instantly punished by flight of capital. We've seen that. Keynes and others were correct in making that assessment. That's at least part of the background, maybe a large part of it, for the East Asian and the Southeast Asian crises, which are not quite the same.

East Asia and Southeast Asia are different. Russia is going the same way, but for different reasons. In Russia, we have to ask ourselves what the Cold War was all about. I think what's happening is that Russia is going back to what it was before the Cold War. The U.S. won, just as it won in Nicaragua and Grenada and Guatemala. In the case of Russia it was a bigger fight. Now Russia is returning to being essentially a third world colony of the West, which is what it was pre-1917. This is being done with the cooperation, in fact the enthusiastic cooperation, of the Communist Party bosses. They made the decision, not implausible from their point of view, that they would do better playing the role of third world elites than of running their own dungeon. So they're enriching themselves. It's a market economy.

People talk about how awful it is, there must be something special about Russia. But it's pretty much like every other third world country. If you impose market economies on the backward countries, that's what they're going to look like. Demographic catastrophe, starvation, tremendous wealth, criminal syndicates operating all over the place, Communist Party bureaucrats happily overseeing it. What do you expect?

In the particular case of Russia, there are also some specific issues. The IMF imposed policies on them that turned out to be completely disastrous. Look into the details. They lived up to those policies, and it's fine for the rich. They're doing OK. There are a lot of people driving Rolls Royces and Mercedes.

Brazil has the eighth largest economy in the world. The U.S. arranged an IMF rescue package of $41 billion in late 1998. Is the U.S. worried that the crisis in Brazil could spread through the southern cone and up through Latin America, perhaps unleashing an immigration stampede?

Immigration from Brazil isn't a big worry, I don't think.

But from Mexico and Central America it is.

Mexico and Central America, yes, but I don't think that's a big worry. The real problem, I think, is that the problems in Brazil might cut into profits. The international economic system is patched together with Scotch tape. There was a study by the IMF. This is from memory, so I can't vouch for all the details. But from 1980 to 1995, the IMF found that something like a quarter of its 180 or so members had serious banking crises, sometimes several, and two-thirds had one or another financial crisis.[48] That's a lot.

There's debate about this. It seems that since the liberalization of financial markets, they have been extremely volatile, unpredictable, irrational, and prone to crisis. Nobody knows when they're going to blow up. A leading international economists, Paul Krugman, had an article in *Foreign Affairs* in which he basically says, We don't understand what's happening. It's like the Depression.[49] Maybe it'll somehow be patched together, but nobody can say and nobody knows what to do.

There's one possibility that Krugman rules out, and that is capital controls. He rules it out on theoretical grounds. He says capital controls leads to inefficient use of resources, and we can't have that. That's certainly true in a certain abstract model of the economy, the neoclassical model. Whether that model has anything to do with the real world is another question. The evidence doesn't seem to support it. During the period in which some degree of capital controls were in place, there was substantial growth. The period of elimination of capital controls was one of slow growth and these crises we're talking about. Maybe that's an accident, maybe not.

Also one has to ask the question, What is meant by "efficient use of resources"? That sounds like a nice, technical notion, but it's not. When you unpack it, it's a highly ideological notion. So you can efficiently use resources if it increases gross national product. But increasing gross national product may harm everybody. That's efficient by some ideological measure, but not by other measures.

Let me just give you one example to illustrate. A study by public interest groups released one or two years ago tried to estimate the effect of the decline of spending on maintaining highways.[50] There's been a considerable decline since the Reagan era, so a certain amount of money has been saved by not repairing highways. They tried to estimate the cost. I forget the exact number, but the cost was considerably higher than the saving. However, the cost is cost to individuals. If your car hits a pothole, it's a cost to you. To the economy, it's a gain. That improves the efficiency of the economy.

Because if your car hits a pothole, you go to the garage and you pay someone to fix it, or maybe you buy a new car, and something more is produced.

So it's made the economy more efficient in two ways. You've cut down the size of government, and everybody knows that government drags down the economy, so you've improved it that way. And you've increased profits and employment and production. Of course, for you as a person, there was a loss. But for the economy, there was a gain, according to the highly ideological way in which efficiency is measured. This is a tiny case. It extends across the board. So when one hears words like "efficiency" used, maybe don't reach for your revolver, but at least reach for your gray cells. Ask, What exactly does that mean? That's an ideological measure.

The Brazilian archbishop Dom Hélder Câmara once said, "When I fed the poor, they called me a saint. When I asked why are they poor, they called me a communist."[51] *Did you know him?*

I didn't know him, but about two years ago I happened to be in Recife, which was his base. He was one of the leading figures in liberation theology. He made a real difference in Brazil and in the world, and in particular in Recife. The church traditionally had been the church of the rich. He turned it into a church of the poor. He got his priests and nuns to work in the poor areas. Church buildings were given over to educational and health institutions. It made a big change. Recife was one of the leading centers of liberation theology. It was devastated, mainly by violence, but also by the Vatican.

The Vatican was strongly opposed to Dom Hélder Câmara. The Vatican doesn't have guns, but it had its own force. The Pope was able to undermine liberation theology, get rid of the progressive bishops, and put in very reactionary ones. The effect is that there is nothing left in Recife. Except for people roughly my age, people don't even know about this history anymore. Liberation theology was dismantled.

There's been a lot of commentary in the last couple of weeks about the Pope's visit to Mexico. I've collected these articles, too. The standard one says that liberation theology is extinct. Now there is what they call "post-liberation theology." There's a question about just how liberation theology became extinct. Liberation theology was one of the reasons for the regime of terror and repression that spread over the continent, with national security states and state terror — always with U.S. backing. It was an awful period, a real plague in Latin America. The Vatican played its role.

Symbolic of that is the fact that the new archbishop in El Salvador is a right-wing Spanish priest who's also a brigadier in the Salvadoran army. This is the army that murdered Archbishop Romero and the Jesuit intellectuals, along with a few other exploits. That's symbolic, and they understand it. The new post-liberation theology is semitolerable to elites. The tepid version that gets reported, and it's not totally false, is that the post-liberation theology pleads with the rich to be nicer to the poor. The new idea is, you evangelize the rich so that they have a social conscience and they'll drop some more crumbs down on the poor. They'll accept their social responsibility. The bad kind of liberation theology, which has in some mysterious way become extinct, called on priests to do what Dom Hélder Câmara was doing: organize base communities of poor people who might organize to take their fate into their own hands. That's not right, according to the preferred morality. You're supposed to at most plead with the ruler to be a benefactor.

If you want another example of that, take today's article on the World Economic Forum in Davos, Switzerland, in the *New York Times*. It talks about how the rich have to have more of a sense of social responsibility.[52] It's not that poor people ought to organize and take what's their right. Not that we should have a democratic society in which people organize and take over and make their own decisions. But we rich folk better be a little more benevolent. The proles might get out of hand. That's post-liberation theology, or at least the version of it that reaches the press.

Actually, if you look at the Pope's statements, it's not quite like that. The Pope made a major speech on January 1, as he always does, and it was devoted to this issue. It received minimal coverage. The *Washington Post* had a report in which they didn't comment on its content. The *Times* had a report in which the last sentence sort of hinted at its content.[53] But the content was interesting. It described the major crimes of today, which are Marxism, fascism, and materialist consumption, on a par with the first two. Not only did it have the line that was allowed to seep through, pleading with the rich to be more benevolent. It also said that nations and peoples have the right to make the decisions that determine the nature of their own lives. That somehow has disappeared. But that was the message of liberation theology, the kind that the Vatican tried to crush and that the United States much more dramatically did crush. And Dom Hélder Câmara is an example. He wasn't killed, but what he tried to do was killed.

The Pope also said, "The human race is facing forms of slavery which are new and more subtle than in the past. And for far too many people freedom remains a word without meaning." At the University of Cape Town, you said: "Freedom without opportunity is a devil's gift." [54]

I agree with him. But to me, the important part of the January 1 statement was the line I quoted before, that nations and peoples are losing the right to determine the course of their own lives. They are losing what the real liberation theology tried to create. He talks about their losing it by the mechanisms of the market, which is not false. But they've also lost it because of direct violence and Vatican interference. That's also true. Mainly direct violence. The U.S. was basically fighting a war against the church in the 1980s. It was one of the main themes of the Central American atrocities. And something similar happened in Brazil. In Brazil, it didn't get completely wiped out. I don't want to overstate it. At the National Bishops Conference, which I visited, a sector of progressive bishops still functions. And there are major popular movements in Brazil — the most important in the world that I know of — like the Landless Workers' Movement, which is an extremely important and spontaneous popular movement. And it receives support, as do the indigenous movements and others, from sectors of the church. So it hasn't been completely wiped out by any means. But it was saddening to visit Recife and see what Dom Hélder's legacy was.

I note a bit of change in at least one of your public speaking strategies. At the Cambridge talk I mentioned earlier, you were challenged by someone in the audience who wanted you to enlist in the struggle to "smash capitalism." Usually in the past you would give a detailed, cogent response, but you handled this one differently.

It was a very good meeting, very constructive, and was really going places. Groups were forming to organize things. There was the usual fringe of sectarian left parasites whose main function for years has been to disrupt popular movements. One line was, I've got to get up and organize the working class to smash capitalism. Nothing else does any good. I think I said something like, I agree. I think it would be a great idea to get the working class to smash capitalism, but obviously this isn't the place to do it, so what you ought to be doing is going to the nearest factory — I'll be happy to pay your carfare. It's not a new strategy. I never had an old one.

Using humor to deflect arguments like that is sometimes very effective.

It wasn't intentional. It was spontaneous.

It got the guy to shut up.

Maybe it works.

1   Editorial, "A Just Attack," *Boston Globe,* December 17, 1998, p. A30. See Noam Chomsky, "US Iraq Policy: Motives and Consequences," in *Iraq Under Siege: The Deadly Impact of Sanctions and War,* ed. Anthony Arnove (Cambridge: South End Press; London: Pluto Press, 2000), pp. 47–56.

2   David Frost, interview with General H. Norman Schwarzkopf, "Sizing Up Iraq," *USA Today,* March 27, 1991, p. 11A. See also Russell Watson et al., "The Gulf: After the War," *Newsweek,* April 8, 1991, pp. 18ff.

3   Thomas L. Friedman, "A Rising Sense That Iraq's Hussein Must Go," *New York Times,* July 7, 1991, p. 4: 1.

4   Associated Press, "US General Criticizes Policy on Destabilizing Hussein," *Boston Globe,* January 29, 1999, p. A17, and Philip Shenon, "U.S. General Warns of Dangers of Trying to Topple Iraqi," *New York Times,* January 29, 1999, p. A3.

5   Noam Chomsky, *Pirates and Emperors: International Terrorism in the Real World,* expanded edition (Montreal: Black Rose Books, 1991), pp. 113–49.

6   Tim Weiner, "The Man Who Protects America from Terrorism," *New York Times,* February 1, 1999, p. A3.

7   Doug Henwood, "Antisocial Insecurity," *Left Business Observer* 87 (December 31, 1998), p. 1.

8   Leslie Stahl, "Punishing Saddam," produced by Catherine Olian, CBS, *60 Minutes,* May 12, 1996.

9   Adlai Stevenson, speech before the United Nations Security Council, May 21, 1964. See Edward S. Herman and Noam Chomsky, *Manufacturing Consent: The Political Economy of the Mass Media* (New York: Pantheon Books, 1988; second edition forthcoming), pp. 182–84.

10 Proceedings of the American Society of International Law 13, 14 (1963), cited in Louis Henkin, *How Nations Behave: Law and Foreign Policy* (New York: Council on Foreign Relations/Columbia UP, 1979), pp. 333–34.

11 "Council at U.N. Meets on U.S.-Libya Clashes," *New York Times,* March 27, 1986, p. A9, and John M. Goshko, "Administration Acts on 'Self-Defense' Principle Espoused by Shultz," *Washington Post,* April 15, 1986, p. A20.

12 *Case Concerning Military and Paramilitary Activities in and Against Nicaragua* ("Nicaragua v. United States of America"), International Court of Justice, June 27, 1986. See Loren Jenkins, "World Court Says U.S. Violates International Law by Aiding Contras," *Washington Post,* June 28, 1986, p. A1, and Associated Press, "Court Decries U.S. Actions on Nicaragua," *Toronto Star,* June 27, 1986, p. A1.

13 Editorial, "America's Guilt — Or Default," *New York Times,* July 1, 1986, p. A22.

14 Abraham Sofaer, *The United States and the World Court,* U.S. Department of State, Bureau of Public Affairs, Current Policy Series, number 769 (December 1985).

15 Steven Lee Myers and Barbara Crossette, "Iraq Is Accused of New Rebuffs to U.N. Team," *New York Times,* December 16, 1998, p. A1.

16 Editorial, "Babes and Bloodlust," *Observer,* January 3, 1999, p. 23.

17 Editorial, "Containing America in the Post–Cold War Era," *The Nation* (Thailand), January 10, 1999.

18 Richard Lawrence, "US Will Snub WTO Panel on Anti-Cuba Law," *Journal of Commerce,* February 21, 1997, p. 1A.

19 William Preston, Jr., Edward S. Herman, and Herbert I. Schiller, *Hope and Folly: The United States and Unesco, 1945–1985* (Minneapolis: University of Minnesota Press, 1989).

20 Serge Schmemann, "The Critics Now Ask: After Missiles, What?" *New York Times,* December 18, 1998, p. A23.

21 Noam Chomsky, Edward S. Herman, Edward Said, and Howard Zinn, "A Call to Action on Sanctions and the U.S. War Against the People of Iraq." On-line at http://www.zmag.org/CrisesCurEvts/Iraq/callaction.htm. See also, Noam Chomsky et al., "Sanctions Are a Weapon of Mass Destruction," in Arnove ed., *Iraq Under Siege,* pp. 181–83. Initial statement drafted by Robert Jensen.

22 Barbara Crossette, "U.S. Plans to Sharpen Focus of Its Sanctions Against Haiti," *New York Times,* February 5, 1992, p. A8.

23 John Solomon, "Agency Head Failed to Stop Texaco Leak, Citing Bush Treasury Secretary," Associated Press, September 18, 1994. For further details, see Noam Chomsky, "Democracy Restored," *Z Magazine* 7: 11 (November 1994), pp. 49–61.

24 See, for example, Stephen Kinzer, "Many Arabs See Double Standard for Israel," *New York Times,* November 27, 1998, p. A15.

25 Noam Chomsky, commentary, National Public Radio, *All Things Considered,* February 22, 1991.

26 David E. Sanger, "Real Politics: Why Suharto Is in and Castro Is Out," *New York Times,* October 31, 1995, p. A3.

27 Mark Achbar, ed., *Manufacturing Consent: Noam Chomsky and the Media* (Montreal: Black Rose Books, 1994), pp. 146–49.

28 John Diamond, Associated Press, "U.S. Should Appear 'Irrational, Vindictive,'" *Ottawa Citizen,* March 2, 1998, p. A7.

29 David Lamb, "Vietnam Study Finds Dioxin in Food Chain," *Los Angeles Times,* October 31, 1998, p. A5. See also David Lamb, "Vietnam Ends Silence on Issue of Wartime Exposure to Agent Orange," *Los Angeles Times,* September 26, 1998, p. A14.

30 Peter Waldman, "Body Count: In Vietnam, the Agony of Birth Defects Calls an Old War to Mind," *Wall Street Journal,* February 12, 1997, p. A1.

31 Barbara Crossette, "Study of Dioxin's Effect in Vietnam Is Hampered by Diplomatic Freeze," *New York Times,* August 18, 1992, p. C4.

32 Amnon Kapeliouk, *Yediot Ahronot,* April 1, 7, and 15, 1988.

33 Waldman, "Body Count," *Wall Street Journal,* February 12, 1997.

34 Lamb, "Vietnam Study Finds Dioxin in Food Chain," *Los Angeles Times,* October 31, 1998.

35 Derek Davies, "The Region," *Far Eastern Economic Review Yearbook* 1971, p. 38; 1972, pp. 37–40.

36 *New York Times,* March 25, 1977. See also Noam Chomsky, *For Reasons of State* (New York: Vintage, 1973), pp. 31–66.

37 Barbara Crossette, "Hanoi Said to Vow to Give M.I.A. Data," *New York Times,* October 24, 1992, p. 1: 1. See Noam Chomsky, *Rogue States: The Rule of Force in World Affairs* (Cambridge: South End Press, 2000), pp. 170–72.

38 David E. Sanger, "Japan's Emperor Tells China Only of His 'Sadness' on War," *New York Times,* October 24, 1992, p. 1: 1.

39 See Crossette, "Hanoi Said to Vow to Give M.I.A. Data," *New York Times,* October 24, 1992, and Jane Gross, "Hanoi Photos Leave Families of U.S. M.I.A.'s Astir," *New York Times,* October 24, 1992, p. 1: 2.

40 Stephen Endicott and Edward Hagerman, *The United States and Biological Warfare: Secrets from the Early Cold War and Korea* (Bloomington: Indiana UP, 1999).

41 John W. Powell, "Japan's Germ Warfare: The U.S. Cover-Up of a War Crime," *Bulletin of Concerned Asian Scholars* 12: 4 (October–December 1980), pp. 2–17.

42 Noam Chomsky, *At War with Asia* (New York: Vintage, 1970), pp. 188–258.

43 Barry Wain, "The Deadly Legacy of War in Laos," *Asian Wall Street Journal,* January 24, 1997, p. 10. See also Simon Ingram, "Laos Struggles to Clear Leftover US Bombs," *Christian Science Monitor,* January 4, 2001, p. 1.

44 Keith Graves, "US Secrecy Puts Bomb Disposal Team in Danger," *Sunday Telegraph,* January 4, 1998, p. 20. See also W.F. Deedes, "Nation Tied to the Land Learns to Live with Deadly Harvest," *Daily Telegraph,* November 14, 1997, p. 14.

45 Reuters, "French to Clear Unearthed Mines," *Peacework* 291 (December 1998–January 1999), p. 7.

46 Bank for International Settlements, *68th Annual Report,* June 8, 1998, Basle, Switzerland. Cited in Chakravarthi Raghavan, "Globalization Not Without Risks, Says BIS," *Third World Economics* (June 16–July 15, 1998).

47 Jeffrey Sachs, "International Economics: Unlocking the Mysteries of Globalization," *Foreign Policy* 110 (Spring 1998), pp. 97–112. See also Robin Hahnel, *Panic Rules! Everything You Need to Know About the Global Economy* (Cambridge: South End Press, 1999).

48 David Felix, "Asia and the Crisis of Financial Liberalization," in Dean Baker, Gerald A. Epstein, and Robert Pollin, eds., *Globalization and Progressive Economic Policy* (Cambridge: Cambridge UP, 1998).

49 Paul Krugman, "The Return of Depression Economics," *Foreign Affairs* 78: 1 (January–February 1999), pp. 56–74.

50 Randolph E. Schmid, "U.S. Drivers Absorb Cost of Bad Roads in Cities," Associated Press, *Boston Globe,* September 17, 1997.

51 Dom Hélder Câmara, *Revolution Through Peace,* trans. Amparo McLean (New

York: Harper and Row, 1971).

52   Alan Cowell, "Annan Fears Backlash Over Global Crisis," *New York Times,* February 1, 1999, p. A14.

53   Sarah Delaney, "Peace Can Be Won Through Respect for Human Rights, Pope Says," *Washington Post,* January 2, 1999, p. A20, and John Tagliabue, "Looking Back at 20th Century, Pope Says Respecting Human Dignity Is the Key to World Peace," *New York Times,* January 2, 1999, p. A4.

54   Noam Chomsky, "Market Democracy in a Neoliberal Order: Doctrines and Reality," Davie Lecture, University of Cape Town, May 1997. On-line at http://www.zmag.org/ZMag/articles/chomksydavie.htm. See also Noam Chomsky, *Profit over People: Neoliberalism and Global Order* (New York: Seven Stories Press, 1999), pp. 89–118.

3

For Reasons of State

Cambridge, Massachusetts, February 2, 1999

In your writings you rarely refer to literature. There is one major exception. In Necessary Illusions *you cite "The Grand Inquisitor" chapter in the* Brothers Karamazov.[1] *What was Dostoyevsky writing about that caught your attention?*

That's a particularly striking passage. He's talking about manufacture of consent. It's a very dramatic and accurate presentation of the way mystery, ceremony, fear, and even joy are manipulated so as to make people feel that they must be subordinate to others. It's a denunciation of Christ, because Christ was trying to give people freedom from these constraints. Christ didn't understand that this was what people wanted. They need to be subordinated to mystery and magic and control. So Christ is really a criminal. That's the burden of the argument.

And that the Church must correct the evil work of Christ, as it were. You understood that to be the state.

For Dostoyevsky it just meant power. He was writing in Russia, remember. So it's a combination of the church and the czar, both very closely related.

You say, "[F]ew reach the level of sophistication of the Grand Inquisitor."

The Grand Inquisitor is articulating the view that freedom is dangerous and people need, and indeed at some level even want, subordination, mystery, authority, and so on. That's a sophisticated version of manufacture of consent.

I came across this quote from George Orwell which perhaps relates to the manufacture of consent. He says, "Circus dogs jump when the trainer cracks his whip, but the really well-trained dog is the one that turns his somersault when there is no whip."[2]

I suspect he was talking about intellectuals. The intellectual class is supposed to be so well trained and so well indoctrinated that they don't need a whip. They just react spontaneously in the ways that will serve external power interests, without awareness, thinking they're doing, honest, dedicated work. That's a real trained dog. I bet if you look back at the context it's something like that.

Are there other examples of literature in your work?

There are several. One I actually remember. That was a passage from Ignazio Silone from his novel *Fontamara*.[3] At the top of the world is the local landlord and below that are his dogs and below that is nothing and below that is nothing and then below all of that are the peasants. I took it from the Italian original, and when I checked the English translation, it turned out it was mistranslated. I had to use my own translation.

Let's talk about war crimes and war criminals. Let's start with General Augusto Pinochet in Chile. Do you think that he should be brought before some kind of international tribunal or a Spanish court for crimes?

He should be brought before a tribunal. It can't be done in Chile, where it should be done, because the military is still very much in control. You sense that as soon as you go there. Human Rights Watch writes about the papier-mâché quality of democracy in Chile, the lack of freedom of expression, despite the overt forms of democracy.[4] It can't be done in Chile. So it should be done elsewhere. The Spanish courts are a possibility, as is an international tribunal.

I should say, however, that one can understand the reaction of a good part of Latin America, including sectors of the Latin American left, that this has an imperialist taint to it. For example, they're going after Pinochet but they're not going after Kissinger. In fact, if you did go after Kissinger, Chile would be the least of his crimes. The point is that, as through much of the justice system, the weaker and more vulnerable are subject to it — not the powerful. The answer to an unequal justice system is not, of course, no justice. It's to make it more equal.

What about a war crimes tribunal for the Khmer Rouge in Cambodia?

Just a few weeks ago Hun Sen, the Cambodian president, whose background was in the Khmer Rouge up until 1977, accepted the idea of a war crimes trial for the Khmer Rouge. That would mean him, too, as long as it was a trial for crimes. That means it would cover 1969 through the period when the Khmer Rouge ended, say, ten years. What is called the "decade of genocide" in the one independent governmental study of this period, *Kampuchea: Decade of Genocide* — if you want to use the word genocide — went from 1969 to 1979.[5] The first six years of that was U.S.-sponsored, and it was not a joke.

Just recently, a friend in Phnom Penh sent me a report that came out in the Cambodian press about François Ponchaud, a French priest who wrote one of the first books on Khmer Rouge atrocities in Cambodia, where he had been a missionary. He was asked what he thought about war crimes trials for the Khmer Rouge, and he said that he thought that it was quite appropriate, but they should also go after the Americans.[6] So, yes, honest trials should go after the people who have committed crimes. That includes the people who directed one of the most intense bombings in history against a largely defenseless peasant society in Cambodia in the early 1970s.

We don't know a lot about it. One reason is there was very little interest. There were over a million refugees driven into Phnom Penh, but there was very little reporting about what life was like in the countryside. The reason is, the press wouldn't interview the refugees. In *Manufacturing Consent*, Ed Herman and I went through all of the *New York Times* reporting, right through the peak period of U.S. bombing.[7] Sydney Schanberg was the regular correspondent. Malcolm Browne was in and out. Later there were plenty of interviews from the Thai border, where you could find out about Khmer Rouge crimes. So it's OK to go to the Thai border, wandering through the jungle to get reports of Khmer Rouge crimes, but it's a different story when you have to cross the street from your hotel to find out about crimes that the U.S. is committing.

There's one exception to this. If you saw the film *The Killing Fields,* it begins with the one exception, an American bombing of a village and the horror stories that followed. There was coverage in that case. That happens to be a case where they hit the wrong village. So you could frame it as a mistake. How about the cases where they hit the right village, with unknown numbers of casualties in the tens if not hundreds of thousands, generating a huge refugee flow, well over one million people? That's not the right history.

Michael Vickery is one of the few serious Cambodia historians. He pointed out once that Pol Pot's forcible evacuation of Phnom Penh is regarded as a major atrocity, as indeed it was. But he also pointed out that the driving of those same people into Phnom Penh by intensive bombing is not called an atrocity.[8] Food for thought.

More reportage from the New York Times, *January 1999. Seth Mydans wrote a series of articles on Cambodia triggered by the surrender of two notorious Khmer Rouge leaders. Mydans apparently left out some significant information in his reports.[9]*

You have to remind me of the reports. They always leave out the same information, so I assume it was left out here.

It stops in 1979.

It probably begins in 1975. And there's something that happened before 1975, and there's something that happened after 1979. Before 1975, in fact from early 1969, the U.S. was bombing Cambodia and supporting a brutal war there that went on until April 1975. We may bear in mind that at the time the Khmer Rouge took over Phnom Penh, deaths in the city alone were estimated by Western doctors there to be running at about a hundred thousand a year from the war. That's in Phnom Penh. Nobody knows what was going on in the countryside.

A high American official, probably Kissinger, although the person has never been identified, predicted one million deaths under any circumstances because of the effects of the bombing. In 1979, the U.S. and Britain essentially picked up support for the Khmer Rouge, which had been driven out of Cambodia by the Vietnamese. The Khmer Rouge received not-so-tacit support from the United States and Britain.

In 1982 a representative of the State Department was asked in congressional hearings why the U.S. was supporting what they called "Democratic Kampuchea," which is the Khmer Rouge, but not supporting the resistance group FRETILIN, the Revolutionary Front for an Independent East Timor. His answer was something like, There is no doubt that Democratic Kampuchea, the Pol Pot group, is more representative of their people than FRETILIN is of the East Timorese. He also mentioned their "continuity" with the Pol Pot regime.[10] So therefore we have to continue the support of Democratic Kampuchea.

The pretense was they were supporting the non-Communist opposition, but that was such a thin pretense that nobody took it seriously. The journalist John Pilger in particular has dug up a lot of information, especially on direct British support for the Khmer Rouge.[11] The U.S. supported them through China and Thailand, and diplomatically. So that's what you're referring to. That was left out in the post-1979 period. A large part of the trouble of the country today is the result of the attacks that were made by the Khmer Rouge, operating from Thai bases and from western Cambodia with the backing of the West.

Ken Silverstein and Alexander Cockburn report in their newsletter, CounterPunch, *that there was a joint U.S.-Thai operation known as Task Force 80 operating along the Cambodian-Thai border. It was an effort, they write, "to restore the battered Khmer Rouge" and to revive their prospects.*[12]

There certainly was such an operation. I didn't know that it had that name. But yes, from 1979, that's exactly what the U.S. was doing. It was doing it through food aid, through aid that was allegedly going to refugees, military training, and diplomatic support. They insisted that the Khmer Rouge keep its seat at the U.N. A lot of this has been brought out. Pilger has probably done more on this topic than anyone.

Let's talk about Israel and what's been described by the Times *as its "internal conflict." It is the question of, Who is a Jew? It springs probably from the Orthodox rabbinate monopoly over conversion and other rites such as marriage and burial. Today's* Times *reports that a group of American Reform rabbis were praying at the Wailing Wall. They were booed and taunted by some Orthodox yeshiva students and told to "go back to Germany" to be exterminated, one of the students explained later.[13] What's going on there?*

It's a very fanatic and pretty large fundamentalist group. What's going on has its roots in a compact that was made in the early days of the state. The leadership at the time, David Ben-Gurion and others, was secular. They called themselves socialists, whatever that means. They made a deal with the religious Jews that they would give them certain degrees of control over social and cultural life in return for their support in the state-building project.

Many of these religious Jews are not Zionists. A lot of them are anti-Zionist. They think that the state is a sacrilege. You're not supposed to have a state until the Messiah comes. But they were happy to take many gifts from the government, including very high funding for Orthodox schools, control over a good part of civil life, like marriages, and in return they would be loyal servants of the state — not too loyal, like they don't generally serve in the military — and they are very well paid for it.

It goes on through the present. That's the reason for the specifically Orthodox control over a good part of civil life. There's a lot of bitterness and anger now about it, and a real, sharp split in the society. There are plenty of publications coming out about the way in which the Orthodox have extorted money for their own benefit, as well as maintaining controls over others. By now they're kind of like a swing vote between the two major political groupings. So each of them, Labor and Likud, offers them lots of benefits to join in. They play the game very cynically. I don't have the exact figures, but one of the results is that the expenditures for religious schooling are way beyond secular schooling. They have many other kinds of benefits from the state. And of course they try to rip off what they can.

The rabbinate, it varies, but some of them are pretty astonishing. From their point of view, most of the American Jewish community, mostly Conservative and Reform, are worse than Christians, which is bad enough. They're traitors. They're pretending to be Jews, but they're really not Jews, because they don't follow the Orthodox rules, and that's even worse than being an outright Christian. If you go back to traditional Jewish culture in either Eastern Europe or North Africa, being a Christian, a non-Jew, was a different species, below the level of Jews. For example, Jewish doctors are not supposed to treat non-Jews unless Jews can gain by it. So Maimonides could be the doctor of the Sultan because Jews would gain by it, but not otherwise.

Is this canonical or a cultural tradition?

It's in the Halakah, the rabbinic tradition. There's plenty of stuff like this. They were on the one hand an oppressed minority, but on the other hand very racist. The racism carried over when they became a non-oppressed minority.

What's been the response among American Jews, who as you say are mostly Reform or Conservative, over this particular issue? Largely they have been very supportive of the Israeli state.

There's been a lot of protest. Israel was one of the few countries, for a long time, I don't know if it's still true, in which you couldn't publish Jewish prayer books, meaning the prayer books used by the majority of the Jewish community here, and in which an American rabbi, Reform or Conservative, couldn't perform a marriage or arrange a divorce or a conversion. To some extent these things are changing, but there was tremendous protest here about it, and threats that what's called "support for Israel" would decline unless Israel recognized the interests of the diaspora communities. That's a constant battle that's become much sharper now. It's not just Orthodox and Conservative Jews. In this report today they mentioned that women were praying at the Wall, and that's considered an abomination by the Orthodox.[14]

There are religious councils in the towns and cities in Israel which have a fair amount of authority because of the domain of civil life that they control. There's a big battle about whether to allow women in. Very recently there was one or maybe more cases where women were allowed in. But that's a big struggle. Now the Orthodox are quite huge. They have a very high birth rate. They and the Palestinians have a much higher birth rate than secular Jews, who are kind of like Europeans, who tend to have low birth rates. The demographic projections indicate that in the not-too-far-distant future it may be substantially a population of Palestinians and Orthodox Jews, fundamentalist Orthodox Jews, many of whom don't work in the civil society. They're under the control of fanatical rabbis. They live their lives studying Talmud.

Eqbal Ahmad, of Pakistan, said that states which are founded as national homelands, based on religion or ethnicity, such as Israel and Pakistan, which was founded as the homeland of Indian Muslims, were prone to these kinds of sectarian divisions.[15]

I don't think you could have predicted it in 1948. I didn't. The religious elements then were a small sector. They became a much larger sector with the immigration from the Arab countries and North Africa. There are a lot of complications here. The Arab Jews, the Oriental Jews, as they're called, were treated extremely badly within Israeli society. I think that's part of the reason why they gravitated toward the religious communities that were separated from the state. They were very bitter. That broke out into public in the late 1970s, when they voted Menachem Begin in, which shocked everyone. Though he was Polish, they regarded him as Moroccan, not without reason.

There are similarities between the feudal-like Jewish society of Morocco and its counterpart in Eastern Europe, which is where Begin's origins are. There was a modern, Westernized sector of Jews in Morocco, too, but they mostly went to France. As many of the Moroccan Jews claim, the Moroccan Jews who went to France became doctors and so on, and the ones who went to Israel became construction workers. There's a lot of bitterness about this.

There was an Associated Press report in mid-January of 1999. In response to criticism that Israel security services use torture and excessive force when inter-

rogating Palestinians, a government attorney, Yehuda Schaeffer, said, "In this as in other matters we are still a light unto the nations," referring to the century-old utopian Zionist slogan.[16]

This has been a scandal even inside Israel. In fact, Israel does use torture, according to international standards. They're constantly condemned for this by human rights groups. Furthermore, they use it consistently. Arab prisoners who are often kept in administrative detention without charge are routinely tortured under interrogation. You can read about this in reports by Human Rights Watch, Amnesty International, and the Israeli human rights group B'Tselem.

About ten years ago, this issue broke through to the public. A Druze had been convicted for some crime. It turned out that he was innocent of the crime for which he had been convicted and he had confessed to it. Immediately one asked, How come he confessed? It turned out he had been tortured. For years, Palestinian prisoners claimed that their confessions had been obtained under torture. The courts, all the way up to the High Court, uniformly rejected this charge. They just dismissed it as false.

After this Druze case, they had to recognize that at least in this one instance the confession was obtained under torture. Then came an inquiry. It turned out that they had been routinely using torture to interrogate. That was considered a huge scandal — not so much because they had used torture, but because the intelligence services hadn't told the court. It was kind of like Watergate. It wasn't bombing Cambodia that was a crime, but not telling Congress about it, that's the real crime.

Here, too, the High Court condemned the fact that the intelligence services were misleading them, which was a joke. Everybody outside, except for the justices of the High Court, knew that the confessions were being obtained under torture. Moshe Etzioni, one of the High Court justices, was in London in 1977 or so. He had an interview with Amnesty International, which asked why the Israelis were getting such a tremendously high confession rate. Everybody knows what that means. He said, Arabs tend to confess. "It's part of their nature."[17]

There was no doubt that Israel was using torture, but the courts, including the High Court, decided to believe the intelligence services, despite what any evidence was. So their claim that they had been misled is a little misleading. They chose to be misled.

At that point, the Landau Commission was formed. It had secret meetings and came out with partially public and partially secret recommendations about the use of torture. They didn't call it "torture," but "force" or "pressure," or some euphemism. It said you shouldn't use this except when — and then comes a secret protocol. It describes the methods you're allowed to use. Nobody knows what's in it, but you can tell what those methods are by what has happened to prisoners.

There are good ways of studying this. You can take independent testimony from prisoners who don't know each other but have been in the same place and see if they describe exactly the same thing. The human rights groups have been doing this for years. Probably Israeli torture has been more systematically and carefully investigated than maybe any other. The reason is, you have to have higher standards in the investigation. If you discuss torture in Pakistan, you don't need very high standards. Some prisoner tells you he was tortured, OK, headline. You say the same thing about Israel, you've got to meet the standards of physics. So when the Swiss League of Human Rights, Amnesty International, or the London Insight team for the *Sunday Times* did studies of torture in Israel, they were extremely careful. But they still couldn't get these studies reported in the United States.

This was in the 1970s. Maybe a mention. I remember cases in which the press published Israeli denials, but not the original report, things like that. For that reason, because of the absurdly high standards that are required, the studies are quite careful. I think it's a common thing, essentially accepted by the human rights community and reported in their publications, that torture is routine and it continues after the Landau Commission report in specific ways.

This trial that you're talking about, which did get up to the High Court, had to do with a case about the use of torture. The High Court has to determine, they can see what's in the Landau secret protocol, whether these methods were legitimate. That's what the debate is about. It's in that context that the government attorney made the statement you quoted, which was, I should say, considered scandalous in Israel.

What do you say to those who hear your critique of Israel and its use of torture and excessive force, and ask, Well, what about Syria? Why aren't you talking about Libya or Iraq? Aren't things much worse there?

Sure. I mentioned Pakistan. Those countries are much worse. I would agree. I'm not really making a critique. I'm just quoting Human Rights Watch and Amnesty International. These are very conservative comments. I would take the same point of view they do, that we should keep to explicit U.S. law, which bars aid to countries which systematically use torture. So I don't think we should be sending aid to Iraq. In fact, I protested strongly when we were doing exactly that in the 1980s. We shouldn't send aid to Syria or Israel.

Of course, it's academic in the case of Iraq and Syria. But if you look at U.S. aid, and I've often pointed this out, as has Human Rights Watch and others, all the leading recipients are states that use torture systematically. The leading recipients of U.S. aid are usually Israel, Egypt, Turkey, Pakistan, and Colombia. And that aid is illegal.

Just another point about torture. It's not only abroad that the U.S. is supporting torture. It's also happening inside, and that's of even more significance to us. Amnesty International just published a long report on this, for example.[18]

As things are evolving, one could make an educated guess that some kind of Palestinian entity is going to have statehood fairly soon. It will be a truncated Bantustan-like state. What does that imply for long-term peace and stability in the region?

How will a Palestinian state evolve? It's hard to predict these things. The U.S.-Israeli plan, and that's the Labor Party in Israel, I'm talking about the doves, was to establish a kind of South African solution. I've written about this in detail for years.[19] Since 1971, as one of Kissinger's contributions to human welfare, the U.S. has been internationally isolated in opposing two things: Israeli withdrawal from the occupied territories, and recognition of Palestinian national rights.

One of the achievements of the Gulf War was that the U.S. was able to ram through its own rejectionist program, first at the Madrid conference and then at the Oslo negotiations. It's what's called the "peace process" in the United States, because the U.S. is behind it. That makes it the peace process. This is based on two basic principles that the U.S. has held in virtual international isolation since the 1970s. The first principle is, there will be no Israeli withdrawal to the internationally recognized June 1967 borders. The withdrawal will be only partial, as the U.S. and Israel determine, contrary to the interpretation of U.N. Resolution 242 held by almost the entire world, and indeed by the U.S. itself until Kissinger took over planning in 1971. The second principle is, there can be no recognition of Palestinian national rights.

Up until very recently, leading Israeli doves like Shimon Peres adamantly opposed a Palestinian state. That's a very stupid position. There is no reason, from their own point of view, for their being to the racist side of Apartheid in South Africa, which is the realistic model. In South Africa in the early 1960s, when the homelands, the Bantustans, were set up, they were called states. Transkei, which was the first, was a state. Nobody recognized it, but it was a state. South Africa even subsidized the Bantustans.

When I was in Israel recently, giving talks on the thirtieth anniversary of the occupation, I quoted a passage about the Bantustans from a standard academic history of South Africa.[20] You didn't have to comment. Everybody who had their eyes open could recognize it. There were many people who just refuse to see what's happening, including most of the doves. But if you pay attention to what's happening, that's the description. So it is absurd for Israel to be to the racist side of South Africa under Apartheid. I assume that sooner or later they will agree to call these things states.

The Likud information minister, David Bar-Illan, wrote somewhere, They can call it what they like. They can call it "fried chicken" if they like. Or they can call it a state. We don't care.[21] That's the reasonable approach. Let them call it fried chicken. Let them call it a state. As long as we take the resources, the usable land and water, and ensure that whatever scattered regions we leave under their control are run by a very brutal Palestinian security force that we will control. In fact, the CIA is now involved in controlling the Palestinian security forces, too — openly. That's fine. They can call themselves fried chicken or a state if they want. That's the reasonable position, and even Shimon Peres has come over to it. The man of peace has finally decided that yes, they can call it a state.

What are the long-term possibilities? It depends. What were the long-term possibilities for Transkei? If the U.S. had initiated the Bantustan settlement and had strongly supported it, the long-term prospects would have been very good for the survival of the Bantustans — not, of course, for the majority of inhabitants. In fact, the U.S. didn't initiate them. It certainly tolerated them, but it didn't strongly support them. The resistance movements in South Africa basically never paid any attention to them. Look at the resistance histories and some mention them, but they weren't even going to discuss this. They wanted liberation in South Africa, not a little more subsidy for Transkei. It wasn't an issue.

But in this region, in Israel-Palestine, it's quite different. The Bantustan settlement is initiated by the U.S. It's an outgrowth of the U.S. position held in isolation for twenty-five years. If the U.S. supports it, so does almost everyone else. The U.S. is a big boy in the world and in that area particularly, and certainly a Palestinian state, if it's set up with proper Israeli controls and under the rule of tough enough guys inside, the U.S. will not only support it but probably give direct aid and assistance to it, as will Europe. Maybe it will keep the Palestinians under control. We can't tell. It's hard to know.

There are real signs in the territories of opposition to the agreements as they are playing out.

Just a couple of days ago, I saw a poll taken by some group in Israel on attitudes of Palestinians in the territories. One thing that they measured was support for violent acts against Israel. It was going up. The last poll it was higher than 50 percent, and it's going steadily up. That's a consequence of the conditions.

Since the Oslo accords were implemented, the quality of life in the territories, which was bad enough before, has sharply declined. Furthermore, it's declined in the way that is characteristic of the third world. In Gaza, the great majority of the population has trouble finding food to eat and water to drink. Worse than that, they can look at the grand villas with wonderful views of the sea being built by the gangsters of the Palestinian Authority.

The Wye accords, the latest agreement, are unusual. Maybe it's a historic first in international treaties. They essentially call for human rights violations. One of the conditions in the Wye accords is that the Palestinian Authority is supposed to carry out repression of the population to ensure that there's no opposition to the agreements that are being imposed. That's pretty broad.

Nobody who cares doubts what the nature of that repression is. It's very brutal: torture, killing, imprisonment without trial. That's what the Palestinian Authority is supposed to do under the supervision of their CIA and Israeli intelligence mentors. The Wye accords don't say it in those words, but that's what they amount to. They call for that kind of control. Israel now claims that the Palestinians aren't living up to this obligation, so that's why it's delaying negotiations.

Whether that will work or not, who knows? Again, if Israel has any intelligence, it will really follow the model of the white racists in Apartheid South Africa, who did subsidize the Bantustans. Israel doesn't. Israel gives almost no support to the territories it has occupied. In fact, that's a scandal that's happened under Israeli occupation. It's willing to have Europe pump in money to the Palestinian Authority, most of it ripped off by Arafat and his friends and stuck in Israeli banks. They're willing to have that, and then they can complain about the corruption and the brutality. But they're not doing anything for the territories.

Israeli industrialists have been pointing out for years, even before the Oslo accords, that this is stupid. What they ought to do is set up something like the maquiladoras, or what South Africa did around the Bantustans. Put up industrial parks where you can get super-cheap labor under miserable conditions. You don't have to worry about work standards or anything else. Then you won't get the Palestinians coming into Israel to do the dirty work. They'll be over there. But we'll make huge profits and we'll control the exports — kind of a maquiladora setup. That would make a lot more sense.

So far, they've been too racist to do that. But if they move to the standard colonial pattern — like the United States in Central America, or the South Africa model in the Bantustans — if they elevate themselves to that level, they'll allow for the kind of dependent development in the territories that takes place in Haiti, in northern Mexico, or El Salvador.

Do you see any traces of that old Zionist dream and something that you shared, of a binational federated state where Israeli Jews and Palestinian Arabs could share the land of Palestine?

Interestingly, that's finally beginning to come back. When I was writing about it thirty years ago, I was practically read out of the civilized world. In Israel they published a talk I gave about this in one of the most extreme dovish, left-wing journals, *New Outlook*.[22] But there was a bitter attack on it. How could anyone dare say this? I had delegations of Israel intellectuals, well-known doves, come to my house to denounce me.

In the U.S. you couldn't even talk about it. Now it's beginning to be heard. Meron Benvenisti, who's a dissident, but well within the Israeli spectrum, in a recent book makes some kind of such a proposal.[23] How seriously I don't know, but he certainly talks about it. You read about it in Israeli intellectual journals. There are such proposals made. Again, how seriously, nobody knows. It's still a fringe.

Within the Palestinian Arab community it's getting presented much more vocally. Azmi Bishara, who's an Israeli Arab philosopher and now a member of the Knesset, has been writing and speaking about it in public.[24] Bishara's articles get published in *Ha'aretz*, which is kind of like Israel's *New York Times*. It's sharply criticized, but it's there. What he's saying, essentially, is, and I think he's right, that there's no point in struggling for two states. That's gone, over the hill. The problem now is to fight for civil and human rights within Israel itself — because they don't exist for the Arab population in many fundamental respects — and then within the whole area. That ends up being a secular democratic state of some kind, or maybe a binational state or a federated state. Just recently, the *New York Times Magazine* even allowed an article by Edward Said on this issue.[25]

Let's move on to some domestic issues, specifically Social Security. In 1935, in response to what was then one of the greatest market failures of all time, the Great Depression, Social Security was created. It's been one of the most popular and successful government programs ever. Today, the media frame this issue as, It's broken. We've got to fix it. Bob Edwards on NPR talked about Clinton's plan to "rescue Social Security." Peter Jennings, on ABC World News, discussed the president's ambitious plan to "save" it.[26] First of all, is it broken? Does it need to be fixed?

Even before getting to that, How come people are talking about it? Just a few years ago, this was called the third rail of American politics. You couldn't touch it. It's a popular program, and such a successful one, with all its defects, that the Reaganites, who were trying to get rid of everything, didn't dare touch it. Within a very few years, the ideological system has been able to shift the frame of reference so that now the question is, How do you save it? That's quite an achievement for propaganda. Now just about every report takes it as a fact that the system's in real danger and we have to do something. Then the debates are, How do you fix it, since it's broken? That transition, over a very few years, is a quite remarkable triumph of propaganda. We shouldn't undervalue it. It's impressive.

So what are the facts? The facts are that there are Social Security trustees, and they make projections. The projections are for seventy-five years. To start with, that's ridiculous. When economists try to predict what's going to happen next year, they do about as well as throwing a dart at a board. The *Wall Street Journal* every year takes the master financial analysts, asks them to predict what's going to happen, and compares their picks with a random guess using a dartboard. It usually turns out the dartboard is about as good. It's not that the people on Wall Street are stupid. It's just too hard to predict. To try to predict what growth and income levels will be two years from now is virtually impossible. Forty years from now, it's playing games.

However, some things are fairly clear. The Social Security trustees have predicted, and now this is just given as fact, it's like the time that the sun will rise, that in 2013 such-and-such a tragedy will take place, the surplus will be gone, and in 2032 they'll only be paying 75 percent of what's due workers.

Where do these numbers come from? The basis for them is the prediction of the trustees that the economy is going to grow at a rate of 1.7 percent over this period. That's conceivable, but it's well below anything that's ever happened, except for the decade of the 1930s or occasional periods of depression. In the postwar period, even from the 1970s to 1990s, which had lower growth rates than the 1950s and 1960s, growth has been way above that. So they're predicting a decline to a growth rate that's well below the historic average and even below the anemic level of the 1970s to 1990s. That's conceivable, but there's no basis for that prediction.

At the same time, they're saying that we have to put the money into stocks, because look how well stocks are doing. At this point, that's not a matter of absurd predictions. It's a matter of virtual self-contradiction. The stock market cannot grow over a long period in a manner that's uncorrelated with the economy. Maybe for a short period it will grow faster, but over time, it's going to more or less track the economy. It has to. So if indeed the economy is going to undergo a historically unprecedented slowdown as far into the future as we can see, then the stock market is going to undergo a sharp slowdown, too. You can't have it both ways.

This is not a particularly radical criticism. You can read it in *Business Week*. It's been pointed out over and over. First of all, it's difficult to make predictions with any confidence based on the number of variables involved over very long stretches of time. But in this case the predictions are made on the basis of assumptions that are very strange. In fact, if you change the assumptions slightly, and say it will be a little less of a slowdown, all the projections change.

So the idea that there's a crisis coming is, first of all, extremely dubious. In fact, it's pure ideology. And if you accept that ideology, you can't accept the other part of it, that it will be a big saving to put it in the stock market.

There's a minimally more subtle point which was pointed out years ago. Frank Ackerman, a radical economist, in his book *Hazardous to Our Wealth,* which South End published in 1984, before Social Security was ever even an issue, said, There's a fallacy in all this talk.[27] The problem is supposed to be the huge number of baby boomers. So by 2012 they're going to retire. What's going to happen? He made a very simple point. He said, Yes, it's true that there will be more retired people after that period. But the economy has already dealt with that problem. Those people were cared for when they were children. When you're six years old, you're not at a job paying wages. If the economy was able to deal with these people when they were children, it's able to deal with them when they retire.

In fact, it's now a much richer economy, despite the fact that the growth rate has been unusually slow. It's still a considerably more wealthy economy than it was in the 1960s. And in 2012 it will be a still richer economy, even if you accept the ridiculous projections of the trustees. So if it was economically possible to deal with these people when they were children, it's surely economically possible to deal with them as retirees.

The pundits claim that the Social Security system is reaching a breaking point because of demographic changes.

When you look at the demographic calculations that are given, what's usually given to show that we have a crisis is what's called the "dependency ratio." That's the proportion of adults over twenty who are wage earners as compared to the whole population over twenty. It's true that this ratio is going to decline. So the percentage of people over twenty who are working will decline. Everybody agrees on that. As there are more retirees the dependency ratio is going to get worse.

On the other hand, if you look at another figure, the total dependency ratio, namely the number of people from zero on, the percentage of those who are working, that number is not going to change very much. Under every projection it's going to be better than it was between 1960 and 1975. So as far as you can project demographically, let's say into the middle of the next century, the total dependency ratio is going to be better than it was in the 1960s and early 1970s. The reason? That was the period of the baby boom. So the demographic projections, if made realistic, don't show any crisis.

Of course, there's an accounting problem. How do you shift the money from funding of children to funding of retirees? But that's an accounting problem. The economy doesn't have a problem with that. Ackerman is quite right. Take care of them when they're children and take care of them when they're adults. The economist Richard Du Boff in technical papers and elsewhere has pointed out very forcefully and well that in that period, 1960 to 1975, there was a very sharp increase in expenditures for education.[28]

That's one aspect, only one, of course, of taking care of children. There are other aspects that aren't measured because those are household expenditures. What does a household expend for taking care of children? You can make up some numbers, but that's not government expenditures. But if you look just at the numbers, they went up very sharply in this baby boom period for things like education and child care. The projected increase to pay for retirees, even if you take the worst projections, turns out to be less than that. So the economy has already dealt with it, even the public economy, but just in a different pocket — and that was a poorer society. Once again, we see that the crisis is being manufactured.

The Social Security trust fund itself has pointed out in the very same reports, as Du Boff has stressed, that one of the problems the system is facing is that the total percentage of wage income that is taxed for Social Security is declining. The reason is, there's a cap at $72,600. Because of the radical redistribution of income of past years, a lot of the income is going to very rich people, and they don't pay Social Security taxes beyond the cap. So the burden on poorer people is increasing.

There's an easy answer to that: raise the cap, or get rid of it. Why should Bill Gates pay only on the first $72,600? So a simple solution: raise the cap, or eliminate it. Then you overcome this problem, which is one of the major problems of the Social Security trust fund as pointed out by the trustees, the same ones who are saying it's in crisis. And there are plenty of other answers, like more progressive taxation.

So the first question, Is it broke? Only on the basis of extremely weird assumptions. If you take any realistic assumption, it's well under control as far ahead as anybody can see.

Some on Wall Street are proposing that a way of raising more revenue for Social Security would be to invest the trust fund in the stock market.

Here you really have to think. If some of the funds are invested in the stock market, there's only one thing that anybody can say with confidence: it's going to be a bonanza for Wall Street. Ask yourself who's funding the propaganda and who's pushing it, and you discover, to your amazement, financial capital. The one thing that's certain is, they'll make plenty of money on it. As to other effects, you hear a lot of talk about how the stock market is more profitable than government securities. There's something to that, but at this point you're outside of economics, despite the pretense of economists like Milton Friedman.

These are not economic judgments. These are ethical judgments. It's true that if you put money in a risky stock, you may make much higher profits. But you're facing the risk. How do you evaluate that? There's no way to do that. It's an ethical judgment. An individual may decide to choose it for themselves, and for a rich individual, you can choose it and it's not going to matter much. If you lose some money, you get by. For a person who's on the margin of survival, that's a very serious judgment.

How do you estimate that risk? You can't go to an economics textbook and find out how to estimate that risk. Social Security is social security. It spreads the risk over the population. It's somewhat progressive, though its funding is actually regressive. Its funding is more of a burden on the poor than the rich because of the cap and because it's flat. But the distribution is progressive, so more goes to poor people than rich people, proportional to their incomes.

Absolute quantities don't mean anything. That's spreading the risk over the whole population. That's social solidarity. The Social Security Act said, We're going to care. It's like public education. You say, We care what happens to other people. We care if somebody else's kid goes to school. We care if some other elderly person starves. We don't want that to happen. The idea of putting it in the stock market, though it's framed in all sorts of fraudulent gobbledygook, is to break down that sense of social solidarity and say, You care only about yourself. If that guy down the street when he gets to be seventy starves to death, that's not your problem. It's his problem. He invested badly, or he had bad luck. That's very good for rich people. But for everyone else, it depends on how you evaluate the risk. We want the society to care for its elderly, and in fact it's been very effective in that respect.

A big antipoverty program.

It's the hugest antipoverty program. Starvation among the elderly has dropped considerably. Furthermore, there's another point, which again Du Boff and others have made, and that is that Social Security is not just for retired workers. It's for their dependents, for disabled workers, for spouses, and so on. That's a big chunk of it. That's going to go, too. There's no insurance for that, unless you buy very expensive insurance policies which are not for poor people.

One should also take a good look at other elements of the fix. Mark Weisbrot of Preamble Center has been writing about these issues for years.[29] One of the things that's being done, for example, is to raise the age level at which you start collecting benefits from sixty-five to sixty-nine. Take a look at survival rates. Here is some demographic information we have. If you look at projected survival rates, that's class-related. By and large, the wealthier you are, the longer you're going to live. If you're a production worker, you've had a tough life. You probably haven't had great nutrition. If you're a black production worker, it's even worse. That means your chance of survival is less after whatever age your retirement is than it is for a rich white person. That means that the poorer people are going to get fewer benefits. The more you add to the age at which benefits come, the more you take away from poor people in terms of total benefits — because they aren't going to live that much longer — and the more you give to rich people, who are going to live longer.

Another change that has been proposed is to increase the period of payments that serves as the base for the Social Security payment. What's the effect of that? It's essentially to harm women and others who don't spend a large part of their life in the full-time workforce. They'll spread out the base over the period when they're not working, so they'll have no income in that period.

Just about every proposal that's been made is regressive. It slams the poor and benefits the rich, or else it privatizes risk, which is OK for rich people but not for the general public and furthermore is a blow against the very idea that we should be together on this, that these are things to do for one another.

Put all this together, and I think it's clear what's going on. You're going to raise some technical questions here and there, but the general picture is clear. And what is remarkable is the way this has been sold by the wealthy and the powerful. That includes all the people you mentioned and all the institutions they work for. They have managed to ram this thing through within a very small period of time, turning highly questionable projections into absolute fact, imposing virtually self-contradictory assumptions, and suppressing everything relevant.

You do get part of the story straight in the business press. There are a few mainstream professional economists, not the ones I've quoted, who are telling the truth. But it's drowned in a chorus of deceit. And unless something is done about it, this very effective program will be destroyed. There's plenty wrong with Social Security, like the fact that it's regressively funded, which should be changed. But the problems are not the ones that are being discussed.

Alan Greenspan was critical of Clinton's plan to invest in the stock market. He said he was fearful that the assets might be used for political ends.[30]

Greenspan wants the program to be even worse. I think Clinton's plan is a bad one. For one thing, it's based on faulty assumptions. But at least it has the property that risk is spread in some way. Greenspan doesn't want that. He wants private plans, so the whole thing is completely privatized and just a bonanza for Wall Street and fine for rich people, because if something goes wrong they'll make out anyhow. But his ethical judgment, though he won't say it, comes down to, It's right to let people take the risk that they will starve to death when they're seventy years old. That's OK. They can take that risk, he's saying. But that's not an economic judgment.

In Japan, the government invested some of its retirement funds in the early 1990s in the Tokyo stock market. The market has since crashed, resulting in cuts in benefits and higher taxes.

However it's done, if you key retirement to the stock market, what happens to you depends on when you retire. Because the stock market is fluctuating all the time. It may go up over time, but what it's done over a hundred years doesn't help you if you retire at a point when the stock market is declining. In Japan it happens to be a very rapid collapse, but there have been many periods of collapse here, too. I don't have the numbers at hand, but the studies that take twenty-year periods find many cases in the twentieth century in which you would have been smashed if you had to get your retirement benefits from the stock market. And those are the real problems that people face.

Again we come back to the problem of how to handle that risk. I want to stress again, no economist has an answer to that, because it's not a problem of economics. The problem of how you evaluate the risk of personal disaster is not a question of economics. It's a judgment that you make on other grounds. The economists can give you some numbers. They can say, Here's the probability this will happen. There's the probability that will happen. But the choice of how to assess the risk that somebody and his disabled spouse or survivors will starve is not a matter of economic theory.

Another contentious issue is public education. Has the same kind of media ideological campaign been conducted in that area?

Very much so. There's a campaign under way to essentially destroy the public education system, the system which is based on the principle that you care if some other child who you don't know gets an education. That's the public education system. There's an attempt to destroy that, along with every aspect of human life and attitudes and thought that involve social solidarity. It's being done in all sorts of ways. One is simply by underfunding. So if you can make the public schools really rotten, people will look for an alternative.

Any service that's going to be privatized, the first thing you do is make it malfunction so people can say, We want to get rid of it. It's not running. Let's give it to Lockheed. So first you make a system malfunction. Then you get popular support for handing it over to the corporate sector.

So public education is being very seriously malfunded. Teachers aren't paid enough. Resources are bad. In general there's a serious decline in funding for infrastructure. That's a late Carter, Reaganite program, and the school system is one of them. In fact, public concern about schools is increasing.

There's also a lot of hype. During the Reagan years, around 1984, some famous study came out announcing that we had a huge educational crisis. Our schools aren't working. We can't compete.[31] It was taken apart by specialists and it was shown pretty quickly that it was mostly fakery. But the point is to make people afraid that there's an educational crisis coming. The second thing is, Make that crisis come by underfunding, Not enough school construction, low salaries and so on. Then propose alternatives, which sound at the beginning like good ideas: charter schools, magnet schools, vouchers, who could be against that? You gradually chip away, making the public system less and less functional, less and less popular because it's nonfunctional, producing propaganda about how awful it is, offering alternatives which begin small and end up where the big investment firms are expecting it to.

A couple of years ago Elaine Bernard from the Harvard Trade Union Program sent me a brochure from Lehman Brothers. It was sent out to their clientele. It was about the great investment opportunity for the future and how you should really get in now on the ground floor. We'll help you get in on EMOs, Educational Maintenance Organizations. That's the educational analogue of HMOs. So we've taken over the health system, we're privatizing the prisons and the welfare system. We're going to run everything. The next big target of public money that we can go after in the parasitic fashion of the rich is the education system. So we'll get EMOs. Public money will come in. You guys will invest and make a lot of money.

This is already beginning. There have been efforts to privatize part of education. That means that you take first-grade kids, expose them to advertising, of course, because that's where all the money comes from, design programs, and have a private corporation, an EMO, run them. This was a couple of years ago, and they're letting their prize investors in on this future plum, but I think that's the direction that financial capital wants to move in.

Thirty-nine million elderly or disabled Americans are enrolled in Medicare. A recent federal advisory commission recommended that private health insurers be given a much bigger role in running Medicare. Ted Kennedy said that this was a threat to privatize Medicare.

That's the same thing. Privatization, when it takes place, will be like anything else in the private sector. A private institution has one goal: maximize profit, minimize human conditions. Because that maximizes profit. That's what they're after. They couldn't be after anything else. If the system is even minimally competitive, they must do that. It's the nature of the system.

There will be, of course, regulations, same with the investment firms that take retirement funds. Sure, there will be regulations. But there are so many ways around regulations, especially if you're rich and powerful and have a lot of lawyers. That's not a big problem. It's just like there are regulations around worker safety.

Kennedy's correct. This is a part of the effort to make the system malfunction so that there will be pressure to privatize. Once it becomes privatized, it will surely be designed to minimize costs. That's what privatization means. And that means you go after the patients who are least risky and are not going to cost you much. You get rid of the rest. The 80-20 rule again, just as they teach in business schools: 80 percent of customers aren't worth the bother, so get rid of them, and provide services for the 20 percent who are rich enough to yield profits. This is the nature of private economy. And of course you get a public subsidy. There will be plenty of taxpayer funding coming in to put a floor under your profit.

The number of Americans without health insurance rose sharply in the last year to more than 43 million. That's 16 percent of the total population. One-fourth of them are children. Steffie Woolhandler of Physicians for a National Health Program says, "What's startling is the magnitude of the increase when the economy is booming."[32]

The extent to which the economy is booming is debatable. It's booming for a small sector of the population. But the general point is accurate. It will be a scandal, no matter what the facts. But with an economy that's kind of functioning, it's not in a recession, it's even more of a scandal.

The idea that people should not have access to health care in the richest country in the world is so outrageous you don't know how to talk about it. And it's not just lack of access. Talk to anybody who's working in the health care system, or if you happen to have been unlucky enough to have been in a hospital, you'll know it yourself: the level of care is declining.

Nurses have a horrible job. They're incredibly overworked, even in the fanciest, most expensive hospitals. More and more care is being transferred over to basically paramedics. I could tell you personal experiences, having just been in one of the richest private hospitals in the world. Health care professionals can tell you all about this. Nurses are protesting, and rightly. They're being terribly overburdened. People with limited competence and training are doing things that they shouldn't be doing. With all of this, we still have unusually high health expenses, much higher than any other industrial country relative to the size of the economy.

Talking to people, I find an enormous amount of discontent with the HMOs, specifically on the issue of choice and limitations. You can only go to a specific doctor in a specific area.

Sometimes that also means for a pregnancy you have to go to a hospital twenty miles away and not the one that's two miles away. The HMOs are businesses. They're going to maximize profit. If it turns out that they can do it the way you maximize profit in a factory, by standardization and regulation and interchangeable parts, and treating people like interchangeable parts in a machine, of course they'll do that.

Also, the HMOs have quite high costs, naturally. They're private businesses. A lot of the money goes into things like advertising, overhead, and layer after layer of micromanagement. You have to manage the doctors. If a doctor wants to do something, he's got to get approval from what the right likes to call "pointy-headed bureaucrats," though the term is used only for government. Doctors have to go to the pointy-headed bureaucrats who don't know what the case is and can't see the patient, but they've got to approve it.

Also, this is adding costs that are unmeasured. A lot of the costs are transferred to the public. Economists don't measure that. For example, if a doctor has to spend twenty hours a week extra doing paperwork, that's not called a cost. If a patient has to sit longer in an office, that's not called a cost. If you have to travel across town, that's not a cost. All those costs are transferred to the public and magnified by the number of users, which is huge.

This is true of the whole economy. Let's say you call up to get an airline ticket. The airlines are automated, which saves them a lot of money. Economists can tell you it's very efficient. On the other hand, when you call, it's costing you money because you're sitting there for half an hour while you're hearing the messages, Thank you for calling, We appreciate your call, We love you, Just hang on, The next customer service representative will … and then comes the music. That whole time is a cost to you. But it's not a cost that anybody is measuring.

That cost is multiplied by the number of users. It's quite a sum. You take the cost to the individual, multiply it by the number of people using that service, compare that with the efficiency of automation, you might well discover that automation is a total loss to the economy. But it's a gain the way it's calculated. The same is true of health services. The costs are transferred to doctors, to nurses, to patients and others in ways that are unmeasured.

Given the centrality of these issues, Social Security, public education, Medicare, health care, in terms of how they touch people's lives — these are not abstract things happening in faraway Bangladesh or Afghanistan — it would seem that these would be lightning rods to organize around and create popular movements.

It should be a bonanza for organizers. But there are plenty of things that should be. I remember at the time of the bicentennial of the signing of the Declaration of Independence, there were polls taken about people's attitudes. In one amusing poll, they gave people slogans of various sorts and asked them to say whether those statements were in the Constitution or not. Nobody knows what's in the Constitution. Maybe you studied it in eighth-grade civics, but you forgot. So when people answer that question, Is it in the Constitution, what they're effectively answering is, Is this such an obvious truth that it must be in the Constitution? One of the statements was,

"From each according to his ability, to each according to his needs." About half the population thought that was in the Constitution.[33] Speak of an organizer's paradise. If those sentiments aren't developed and used, then organizers are failing.

Talk about what's been called the seismic shift from print to cyberspace. What kind of effect is that going to have on the future of research? What will the archives of the future look like?

Nobody really knows. Part of the reason is that nobody knows the longevity of the methods of storage that are now being used. There have been some technical conferences of librarians and others to discuss how long electronic storage will last. You can be pretty sure that seventeenth-century books will last, because they were made of good paper. Take a look at them. I do often. They're in real good shape and are fun to read. Then look at a twentieth-century book. It's much less likely that it's going to be around long. The paper's much cheaper. It's going to deteriorate and disintegrate. Things are being put over into electronic storage, and here there's just not a lot of experience. So it's a good question what the shape of the archives will be.

As for scholarly research, it's a sort of mixed story. On the whole it's beneficial. You can get access to technical material and you can communicate around the world very quickly. If I'm teaching a class tomorrow and I'd like to have an example in Swedish, I can e-mail a friend in Stockholm and ask, Can you say this in Swedish? If I know somebody who wrote a paper on such-and-such, I can get it. I can get reprints of material very easily.

On the other hand, there's an overload problem. The real problem in the sciences and elsewhere is not shortage of information. It's sensible analysis of the information. When you get overload, that cuts back the possibilities of sensible analysis. Just the amount of e-mail communication is a terrific burden, and a growing one, for business, too. There are some studies in business of how many hours a day everybody spends just answering e-mail. It's going up very fast, enough so that it may well be cutting down productivity.

There's been a debate in the economics profession for some years over the fact that there's been very extensive capital expenditures on computers, and there's almost no detectable increase in productivity. Some people say, It will take longer to come. Wait twenty years. Maybe. But there are other possibilities, which have been discussed. That is that it doesn't really contribute to productivity. It's mixed. It may not even contribute to efficiency, in the technical sense, for the reasons that we were discussing before. A lot of it transfers cost. But the burden of dealing with this flood of information has a mixed character.

Another thing which I see myself is that it's just too damn easy. Anybody who has some harebrained idea for three seconds can punch a key, and all of a sudden there's something that half the people in the world see. It's a sense of power. The half of the people of the world who are receiving it have to do something with it. You should see some of the stuff I get.

Also, people get addicted. There are people who are simply addicted to the Web. They spend time surfing the Web. People who wouldn't care where France is are getting the latest newspapers from Tibet. It is an addiction which could be harmful.

So, it's contributing to the atomization that people experience?

The interconnection among people that the Internet establishes is very positive in many ways, for organizing and just for human life. But it has its downside, too. I've spoken to friends whose teenage children go up to their rooms after dinner and start their social life with virtual characters, chat friends, and who make up fake personas and maybe are living in some other country. This is their social circle. They are with their friends on-line who are pretending to be such-and-such and they're pretending to be so-and-so. The psychic effect of this is something I wouldn't like to think about.

We're human beings. Face-to-face contact means a lot. Not having an affair with some sixty-year-old guy who's pretending to be a fourteen-year-old girl in some other country. There's an awful lot of this stuff going on. It's extremely hard to say what the net effect of the whole thing is.

However, this is all small potatoes. The real problem is totally different. The corporations have, only in the last few years, discovered that this public creation can be a tremendous tool for profit, for basically a home marketing service. And marketing means not just perfume, but also attitudes, beliefs, consumerism, and so on. And they want to take control of it. Whether that's technically possible is not so certain. But it's being worked on.

The point of control that looks most vulnerable is access. Anybody can put up a Web page, if they want to bother. But to access the Web means you go through a megacorporation which controls access. The question is, Can they figure out ways, as they surely are trying to do, to design the access so that for all but the most dedicated users you will be led through a path that takes you to where they want you to go, not where you want to go? How much that will work, one doesn't know, but we can have very little doubt about what they're trying to do. They also want to cut back the use of the system for constructive purposes, like, say, to organize against the Multilateral Agreement on Investment. The last thing that business wants is to have a system around which allows people in Canada and France to work together in combating the MAI.

One of the cases where the Internet was quite effectively used was within Indonesia among students and dissidents, who used it to communicate and organize their efforts to overthrow the Suharto dictatorship. The Indonesian dictatorship didn't like it, and their supporters in the United States, Britain, France, and Germany — namely, major corporate power — didn't like it either. The system is one that they've profited from greatly. The idea of a democratic revolution against it is not something that they're very excited about. So they're trying to cut back that kind of usage. Whether this will work or not is an open question. It will work unless there's a lot of struggle against it.

Will there be a Chomsky e-mail collection at some point?

You'll have to ask Mike Albert over at *Z Magazine* about that. I erase a good bit, but he may keep a lot of it.

You talked about the demands on your time, for example, the hours you're spending on e-mail. How do you organize your time? With the constant and ever-increasing demands on your time, how do you do it?

Badly. There's no way to do it. There are physical limitations.

The day's twenty-four hours long. If you do one thing, you're not doing something else.

But if you're spending a couple of hours responding to e-mail, you're not writing an article on linguistics or a political article for Z.

That's a decision I made forty years ago. You cannot overcome the fact that time is finite. So you make your choices. Maybe badly, maybe well, but there's no algorithm, no procedure to give you the right answer.

Do you have a time that you particularly like to work? Are you a morning or late-night person?

Virtually all the time.

The last time we did an interview was in May in Boulder.[34] I asked you about your health because you were just coming off an operation for prostate cancer. You were kind of jocular in your answer. You said you'd be around for a couple more months. You've actually made it almost nine months now. How is your health?

Pretty good prediction. Last fall I started picking up on the talks I had to postpone. I have a very intense schedule, a lot of things had to be delayed. It was total chaos because it's always right at the brim anyway. The last several months, on top of the usual schedule, have been very busy. There's been lots of foreign travel. It's working OK. I guess there's still a few more months.

1   Noam Chomsky, *Necessary Illusions: Thought Control in Democratic Societies* (Boston: South End Press, 1989), p. 18. Fyodor Dostoyevsky, *The Brothers Karamazov,* trans. Constance Garnett (New York: Random House, 1950).

2   Quoted in Michael Sheldon, *Orwell: The Authorized Biography* (New York: HarperCollins, 1991), p. 367.

3   Noam Chomsky, *Turning the Tide: U.S. Intervention in Central America and the Struggle for Peace* (Boston: South End Press, 1985), p. 9. Ignazio Silone, *Fontamara,* trans. Gwenda David and Eric Mosbacher (London: Redwords, 1994), p. 32.

4   See Human Rights Watch, *Limits of Tolerance: Freedom of Expression and the Public Debate in Chile* (Washington, DC: Human Rights Watch, 1998). On-line at http://www.hrw.org/reports98/chile/.

5   Kimmo Kiljunen, ed., *Kampuchea: Decade of Genocide: Report of the Finnish Inquiry Commission* (London: Zed, 1984).

6   Richard S. Ehrlich, "Ponchaud's Warning on Cambodia's Future," *Cambodia Today,* July 14, 1997.

7   Edward S. Herman and Noam Chomsky, *Manufacturing Consent: The Political Economy of the Mass Media* (New York: Pantheon Books, 1988; second edition forthcoming), pp. 260–96.

8   Michael Vickery, *Cambodia: 1975–1982* (Boston: South End Press, 1984), p. 17.

9   Seth Mydans, "A Tale of a Cambodian Woman: Assigning the Guilt for Genocide," *New York Times,* January 21, 1999, p. A1.

10 John Holdridge, hearing before the Subcommittee on Asian and Pacific Affairs of the Committee on Foreign Affairs, House of Representatives, 97th Congress, Second Session, September 14, 1982, p. 71.

11 See John Pilger's articles, "The Monster We Created," *Observer,* April 19, 1998, p. 19; "In the Service of a Murderer," *Guardian,* October 16, 1990; and *New Statesman,* November 2, 1984.

12 Alexander Cockburn and Ken Silverstein, "Was Carter Worse?" *CounterPunch* 6: 1 (January 1–15, 1999), p. 2.

13 Deborah Sontag, "Orthodox Confront U.S. Reform Rabbis at Western Wall," *New York Times,* February 2, 1999, p. A3.

14 Sontag, "Orthodox Confront U.S. Reform Rabbis at Western Wall," *New York Times,* February 2, 1999.

15 See David Barsamian, *Eqbal Ahmad: Confronting Empire* (Cambridge: South End Press, 2000).

16 Jack Katzenell, "State Says Israel 'Has Nothing to be Ashamed Of' on Torture Issue," Associated Press, January 13, 1999.

17 Amnesty International, *Newsletter* (September 1977). See Noam Chomsky, *Towards a New Cold War: Essays on the Current Crisis and How We Got There* (New York: Pantheon, 1981), p. 454 n5.

18 See Amnesty International's reports on torture in the United States on-line at http://www.amnesty-usa.org/.

19 Noam Chomsky, *Fateful Triangle: The United States, Israel, and the Palestinians,* expanded edition (Cambridge: South End Press Classics, 1999).

20 Chomsky, *Fateful Triangle,* p. 560. Bill Freund, *The Making of Contemporary Africa: The Development of African Society Since 1800,* second edition (Boulder: Lynne Rienner, 1998), p. 270.

21 David Bar-Illan, interview with Victor Cygielman, *Palestine-Israel Journal* 3: 3–4 (Summer–Autumn 1996), p. 14.

22 Noam Chomsky, "Nationalism and Conflict in Palestine," *New Outlook* (Israel) (November–December 1969). Reprinted in Noam Chomsky, *Peace in the Middle East? Reflections on Justice and Nationhood* (New York: Vintage Books, 1974), pp. 49–92.

23 Meron Benvenisti, *Intimate Enemies: Jews and Arabs in a Shared Land* (Berkeley: University of California Press, 1995).

24 See Azmi Bishara, "Where Suicide Bombs Come From," *New York Times,* February 17, 1995, p. A31.

25 Edward W. Said, "The One-State Solution," *New York Times Magazine,* January 10, 1999, p. 6: 36ff. Or see Edward W. Said, "Truth and Reconciliation," in *The End of the Peace Process: Oslo and After* (New York: Pantheon Books, 2000), pp. 312–21.

26 Bob Edwards, interview with James Glassman, NPR, *Morning Edition,* January 21, 1999. Peter Jennings, "No Easy Way to Save Social Security," ABC, *World News Tonight,* December 8, 1998.

27 Frank Ackerman, *Hazardous to Our Wealth: Economic Policies in the 1980s* (Boston: South End Press, 1984).

28 Richard B. Du Boff, "Social Security Is Not in 'Crisis,' " National Jobs for All Coalition *Uncommon Sense* 21 (February 1999).

29 See Dean Baker and Mark Weisbrot, *Social Security: The Phony Crisis* (Chicago: University of Chicago Press, 1999). See also http://www.cepr.net/ for additional publications.

30 David E. Rosenbaum, "Social Security on Wall Street," *New York Times,* February 7, 1999, p. 4: 3.

31 National Commission on Excellence in Education, *A Nation at Risk: The Full Account* (Cambridge: USA Research, 1984). See David C. Berliner and Bruce J. Biddle, *The Manufactured Crisis: Myths, Fraud, and the Attack on America's Public Schools* (Reading, MA: Addison-Wesley, 1995).

32 Robert Pear, "Americans Lacking Health Insurance Put at 16 Percent," *New York Times,* September 26, 1998, p. A1.

33 *Boston Globe Magazine,* September 13, 1987, cited by Jules Lobel in Jules Lobel, ed., *A Less Than Perfect Union: Alternative Perspectives on the U.S. Constitution* (New York: Monthly Review Press, 1988), p. 3.

34 See Chapter 1.

4

East Timor on the Brink

KGNU, Boulder, Colorado, September 8, 1999

T*he situation in East Timor has gone from bad to worse. You have written an article for MoJo Wire on why Americans should care about East Timor.*[1]

The primary reason is that there's a lot that we can do about it. The second reason is it's a huge catastrophe. Actually, it's considerably worse than when I wrote about this a couple of weeks ago. And there is a bit of history involved. The U.S. has been directly and crucially involved in supporting the Indonesian invasion, arming it, carrying it through the worst atrocities, which were in the late 1970s under the Carter administration and pretty much right up till today.

But putting aside history, we can do a lot. This is a place where the United States has plenty of leverage and can act to stop something which, if the U.S. doesn't act, might turn into a Rwanda, and that's not an exaggeration.

In your essay you say that "President Clinton needs no instructions on how to proceed." Then you go on to describe some events that happened in late 1997 and in the spring of 1998. What exactly went on?

What went on is that General Suharto had been the darling of the U.S. and the West generally ever since he took power in 1965, carrying out a huge mass murder. The CIA compared it to the slaughters of Hitler and Stalin and Mao, described it as one of the

great mass murders of the twentieth century. It was very much applauded here. He wiped out the main, the only popular-based political movement, a party of the left, killed hundreds of thousands of
peasants, opened up the country to Western investment, virtual robbery, and that was greeted very warmly. And so it remained, through
atrocity after atrocity, including the invasion of East Timor, which
was supported very decisively by the United States up until 1997.

In 1997, Suharto made his first mistake. He was beginning to
lose control. If your friendly dictator loses control, he's not much
use. The other was, he developed an unsuspected soft spot. The International Monetary Fund, meaning the U.S., was imposing quite
harsh economic programs that were punishing the general population for the robbery carried out by a tiny Indonesian elite, and
Suharto, for whatever reason, maybe fearing internal turmoil, was
dragging his feet on implementing them.

Then came a series of rather dramatic events. They weren't
much reported here, but they were noticed in Indonesia, widely, in
fact. In February 1998, the head of the IMF, Michel Camdessus,
flew into Jakarta and effectively ordered Suharto to sign onto the
IMF rules. There was a picture taken which was widely circulated in
Indonesia and Australia showing a kind of humble Suharto sitting at
a table with a pen and an imperious-looking Camdessus standing
over him with his arms folded and some kind of caption saying,
Typical colonial stance. Shortly after that, in May 1998, Madeleine
Albright said that Washington had decided that the time had come
for what she called "a democratic transition," meaning, Step down.[2]
Four hours later, Suharto stepped down. This isn't just cause and effect. There are many other factors. It's not just pushing buttons. But
it does symbolize the nature of the relationship.

There's very good reason to believe that if the Clinton administration took a strong stand, made it very clear to the Indonesian generals that this particular game is over, it would be over. I doubt very
much that they will do so, though there is talk about an intervention
force, which the U.S. is refusing to make any commitment to, and
about sanctions, which the U.S. is also dragging its feet on. And
there are other, even weaker, measures that could be very effective,
such as, for example, threatening the Indonesian generals with war

crimes trials, which is a serious threat for them. It means they would be locked up in their own countries for a long time.

It already happened to one of the Indonesian generals, the architect of the massacre in Dili, East Timor. He was driven out of the United States by a court case that he lost, and had to flee. Those are things that the generals care about. They're easy. But I frankly don't think that any of these things are necessary. We don't know that they're necessary, and we won't know until the Clinton administration does something simpler, namely, take a strong stand, saying approximately what they said to Suharto in May 1998. I rather suspect that this would work. Although by now it may be too late. The time to do this was February or March, certainly not later than April, when the killings were already picking up substantially. There were serious massacres, like killing sixty people hiding in a church in Liquiça, for example.

That happened in April.

There were a lot more. That was a particularly awful one. The Clinton administration again dragged its feet on even allowing unarmed U.N. observers. They finally let in a couple of hundred observers as part of the United Nations Mission in East Timor (UNAMET) observer team that was there. I should say that the remnants of that team is now, as of a couple hours ago, locked up in a compound being attacked by Indonesian troops and militia groups, and is running out of food and water.

One of the people holed up in there apparently is the journalist Allan Nairn, who escaped. Dili, the capital city, is apparently wiped out, according to the few people who are left. A lot of it is burned down. The population is driven out. Nairn was trying to keep looking in to see what was going on in the city and was finally trapped by Indonesian soldiers. He somehow made it to the U.N. compound and is at least alive. That's what's happening right now, after the referendum. The referendum was an overwhelming victory for independence and a remarkably courageous act on the part of the Timorese. To vote for independence in the midst of terrible terror with an occupying army organizing it, that takes a lot of guts.

Almost 99 percent of eligible voters turned out, and close to 80 percent voted for independence.

There were tens of thousands of people who came out of hiding to vote and fled back into hiding. Right after, the rampage which is devastating the country started. This morning, the U.N. reported that there are now 200,000 Timorese refugees. Very reliable church sources in Dili have reported about 3,000 to 5,000 people killed in the first half of the year — and more in the last couple of days. Those numbers are going up.[3]

Those numbers alone are approximately twice as bad as Kosovo in the entire year before the bombing. That was at a time when there was a big guerrilla movement going on which had occupied 40 percent of the country. Here it's just plain massacre in a country of less than half the size of Kosovo. So the scale is huge, and it's increasing. We don't know how bad it is because the first thing that the Indonesians did was to drive all observers out of the country. So virtually all the journalists were forced to flee. Some, like Nairn and a couple of Australians, stayed.

The United Nations has been compelled to withdraw virtually everyone. If they can get those people out of the compound in Dili, I presume they'll get them out, too. That means that terror can go on unobserved.

Nobody has any idea what's going on in the countryside. Telephone service has been cut off. The university has been burned down. Bishop Belo's residence has been burned down. He had to flee. He was taken out by the Australian military. The descriptions that are coming through, mainly from Australia by Australian reporters and diplomats, are pretty horrendous. Dili, the one place anybody knows anything about, has apparently been virtually cleansed. That's the term used by a few U.N. officials. Also, there's been tremendous looting and robbery. Apparently they're trying to destroy the place.

The Indonesian apologetic for what they're doing in East Timor is that if East Timor becomes independent it will set a precedent for other regions seeking independence, like West Papua and Aceh.

Let's remember that East Timor is not part of Indonesia. East Timor was invaded and conquered by Indonesia. That has never been recognized by the U.N., never even been recognized by the U.S. It's been recognized by the U.S. press for a long time. Up until very recently, the reports used to be "Dili, Indonesia." But it's no more a part of Indonesia than occupied France was part of Germany during the Second World War.

Seth Mydans, who writes for the New York Times, *describes Timorese independence advocates as "separatists." Is he off the mark?* [4]

That's like saying the French resistance were separatists under the Nazis. Indonesia was ordered to withdraw instantly from East Timor by the Security Council back in 1975. The U.S. didn't even veto the resolution, though it undermined it. The World Court has declared that the population retains the right of self-determination. Australia did grant *de jure* recognition of East Timor's annexation, but they've essentially withdrawn it. That's it. The Indonesians have no right whatsoever to be in East Timor, except for the right of force and the fact that the United States has supported their presence. Otherwise they'd be out.

What happened has been very graphically and lucidly described by Daniel Patrick Moynihan. He was the U.S. ambassador to the United Nations at the time of the Indonesian invasion in 1975. He wrote his memoirs a couple of years later and was very frank. He said, The State Department wanted things to turn out as they did. It was my responsibility to render the U.N. "utterly ineffective" in anything it might do, "and I carried it forward with no inconsiderable success." [5] Then he goes on to say what happened afterward. The next couple of weeks about 60,000 people were killed, roughly the proportion of the population of Russia killed by the Germans. That's him, not me. Then he turned to some other subject. That's pretty accurate, and it continued.

Richard Holbrooke just presented his credentials to the U.N. as ambassador yesterday. The press, in reporting this, did talk about his diplomatic successes at Dayton. They didn't look at his diplomatic career in connection with another item that's on the front pages, namely East Timor. He was Undersecretary of State for Asian Affairs for the Carter administration, and he was a leading apologist for the Indonesian invasion.

What ties does the U.S. military have to General Wiranto and the Indonesian military? Was there a yellow light for the Indonesian military to carry out operations in coordination with the militias in East Timor?

The Indonesian military was for a long period essentially a U.S.-run military force. The officers were trained here. They had joint exercises. They had mostly U.S. arms. That's changed. By now I think Australia is probably much more involved in training and joint exercises. But the U.S. had joint exercises very recently, including with Kopassus, the commando forces that have a horrible record and are modeled on the Green Berets. They have been implicated in most of the current massacres.

Britain has been a major arms supplier. The White House has been blocked by Congress from sending most arms and carrying out direct training. The Clinton administration has evaded those restrictions in the past, found ways around them and continued under another hat.

Whether that's still continuing is very hard to say, because nobody is looking at it, as far as I know. These things usually come out a couple of years later. But whatever the arrangements may be, there is no doubt that the U.S. military has plenty of leverage, and the White House, too, if they want to use it. The Indonesians care quite a lot about what stand the U.S. takes with regard to what they do.

I should say that they are not powerless, however. One of the reasons why the U.S. is maybe hanging back — apart from the fact that Indonesia is a loyal, rich client and there are plenty of U.S. corporations operating there and they don't care one way or another about the Timorese — there's another problem looming right now. It doesn't get reported much. A couple of days ago, the Chinese president, Jiang Zemin, was in Thailand. He made a very strong speech which got a lot of attention in Southeast Asia in which he condemned U.S. "gunboat diplomacy" and economic neocolonialism.[6] He talked, not in detail, about security arrangements between China and ASEAN, the Association of Southeast Asian Nations. According to the limited press coverage from Southeast Asia, the

Thai elites welcomed this because they are glad to see a counterforce to the U.S., which they and much of the world are very much afraid of now. China is clearly offering some kind of security arrangement in which it will be the center. That means also an economic bloc with the Southeast Asian countries or part of them, maybe Japan ultimately brought in, and North Asia, that would exclude or at least marginalize the United States.

You have to remember that the major concern of the U.S. in that region of the world since the Second World War has been to prevent that from happening. That has been the driving concern behind the remilitarization of U.S. allies, including Japan, the Indochina war, U.S. clandestine operations in 1958 that aimed to break up Indonesia — which at that time was neutralist — and right on to the present. They didn't care much about Russia. They didn't have a Cold War connection. But it was a concern that the countries of the region might accommodate China, as it was put in internal documents, and create a kind of an Asian bloc in which the United States would not have privileged access and control. I can't imagine that Washington policy makers aren't aware of this. Indonesian generals may be thinking of it, too, thinking that it offers them a certain degree of leverage against even mild U.S. pressures.

What can people concerned about East Timor do?

There is one last chance to save the Timorese from utter disaster. I stress "utter." They've already suffered enormous disaster. In a very short time span, in the next couple of days, probably, unless the U.S. government takes a decisive, open stand, this thing may be past rescue. It's only going to happen in one way, if there's a lot of public pressure on the White House. Otherwise it won't happen. This has been a horror story for twenty-five years. It's now very likely culminating, and there isn't much time to do anything about it.

1   Noam Chomsky, "Why Americans Should Care About East Timor," MoJo
    Wire, August 26, 1999. On-line at http://www.motherjones.com/
    east_timor/comment/chomsky.html.

2   Philip Shenon, "Clinton Welcomes Suharto's Exit But Says Indonesia Still
    Needs 'A Real Democratic Change,' " *New York Times,* May 21, 1998, p. A8,
    and Andrew Higgins and Mark Tran, "US Pulls Plug on Suharto After
    Army Clears Streets," *Guardian,* May 21, 1998, p. 2.

3   Arnold S. Kohen, "Beyond the Vote: The World Must Remain Vigilant
    Over East Timor," *Washington Post,* September 5, 1999, p. B1, and Philip
    Shenon, "Timorese Bishop Is Calling for War Crimes Tribunal," *New York
    Times,* September 13, 1999, p. A6. See also Noam Chomsky, *Rogue States: The
    Rule of Force in World Affairs* (Cambridge: South End Press, 2000), pp. 51–61,
    and Noam Chomsky, *A New Generation Draws the Line: Kosovo, East Timor,
    and the Standards of the West* (New York: Verso, 2001), pp. 48–93.

4   Seth Mydans, "The Timor Enigma," *New York Times,* September 8, 1999, p.
    A12.

5   Daniel Patrick Moynihan, with Suzanne Weaver, *A Dangerous Place* (Boston:
    Little, Brown, 1978), p. 247.

6   Ted Bardacke and James Kynge, "China Lashes Out at US 'Gunboat
    Diplomacy,' " *Financial Times,* September 4, 1999, p. 4.

The Meaning of Seattle

KGNU, Boulder, Colorado, February 23, 2000

et's talk about what occurred in Seattle in late November and early December around the World Trade Organization's ministerial meeting. What meaning do you derive from what happened there?

I think it was a very significant event and potentially extremely important. It reflected a very broad feeling which has been pretty clear for years and has been growing and developing in intensity around a good part of the world. It is opposed to the corporate-led globalization that's been imposed under primarily U.S. leadership, but the other major industrial countries, too. It is harming a great many people, undermining sovereignty and democratic rights and leading to plenty of resistance.

What was interesting in Seattle was several things. First of all, the events reflected very extensive programs of education and organizing, and it shows what can be achieved by that. It wasn't just that people suddenly showed up. Secondly, the participation was extremely broad and varied. There were constituencies brought together that have rarely interconnected in the past. That was true internationally: third world, indigenous, peasant, labor leaders, and others participated. And it was true here in the United States: environmentalists, labor, and other groups, which had separate interests but a shared understanding, worked together.

It's been pretty evident before. That's the same kind of coalition of forces that blocked the MAI a year earlier and that had strongly opposed other so-called agreements like NAFTA or the WTO agreements, which are not agreements, at least if the population counts. Most of the population has been opposed to them. It has reached a point of a kind of dramatic confrontation. Also it will presumably continue and I think could take very constructive forms.

Are there any lessons from Seattle?

One lesson is that education and organizing over a long term, carefully done, can really pay off. Another is that a substantial part of the domestic and global population — I would guess probably a majority of those thinking about the issues — range from being disturbed by contemporary developments to being strongly opposed to them. People are opposed to the sharp attack on democratic rights, on the freedom to make your own decisions, and on the general subordination of all concerns to the specific interests, to the primacy of maximizing profit and domination by a very small sector of the world's population. Global inequality has reached unprecedented heights.

The United Nations Conference on Trade and Development has been meeting in Bangkok. Andrew Simms, writing in the Guardian Weekly, *says, "Given the right power and resources it could help overcome failings in the international system" and has "the confidence of developing countries."* [1]

That's a bit of an exaggeration. UNCTAD, first of all, is basically a research organization. It has no enforcement powers. It does reflect to some extent the interests of the so-called developing countries, the poorer countries. That's the reason why it's so marginalized. For example, there was very little reporting of the UNCTAD conference in the U.S. apart from the business press here and there. It has third world participation. And when UNCTAD does reflect the concerns of the great majority of the world's people, it is generally ignored.

One example with substantial contemporary repercussions is the UNCTAD initiative thirty years ago to stabilize commodity prices so that poor peasant farmers would be able to survive. Agribusiness can handle a collapse in prices for a year; a poor farmer can't tell his kids to wait until next year to eat. The proposals conformed to policies routinely adopted in the rich countries, but were blocked by the rich, following the advice of "sound liberal economists," as the political economist Susan Strange puts it — advice that is followed when it contributes to profit and power, and ignored otherwise.[2]

One consequence is the shift from production of "legitimate crops" such as coffee to coca, marijuana, and opium, which are not subject to ruinous price fluctuations. The U.S. reaction is to impose even harsher punishments on the poor, abroad and at home. It's not the only case. UNESCO was undermined for rather similar reasons. But to speak of "confidence of developing countries" would be overstating it.

Have a look at third world–based publications, say from the Third World Network in Malaysia. One of its important publications is *Third World Economics*. A recent issue has run several very critical reports of the UNCTAD conference because of its subordination to the agenda of the powerful.[3] It's true that UNCTAD is more independent and reflects the interests of the developing countries more than, say, the WTO, which is run by the industrial states. So yes, it's different. But one shouldn't exaggerate.

The issue of inequality, not only in the U.S. but around the world, as you just mentioned, is hard to ignore. Even the Financial Times *recently commented that "At the beginning of the 19th century, the ratio of real incomes per head between the world's richest and poorest countries was three to one. By 1900, it was 10 to one. By the year 2000, it had risen to 60 to one."*[4]

And that is extremely misleading. It vastly understates what's going on. The real and striking difference is not the difference among countries but the difference within the global population, which is a different measure. That's risen very sharply, which means that within countries the divisions have sharply risen. I think it's now gone from about something like 80 to 1 to about 120 to 1, just in the last ten years or so. Those are rough figures. I'm not sure of the exact numbers. But it's risen very sharply. The top 1 percent of the population of the world now probably has about the income of roughly the bottom 60 percent. That's close to 3 billion people.

These outcomes are the results of very specific decisions, institutional arrangements, and plans which can be expected to have these effects. And they have these effects. There are principles of economics that tell you that over time things ought to even out. That's true of some abstract models. The world is very different.

Thomas Friedman, writing in the New York Times, *called the demonstrators at Seattle "a Noah's ark of flat-earth advocates."* [5]

From his point of view, that's probably correct. From the point of view of slave owners, people opposed to slavery probably looked that way. If you want some numbers, I just found some. The latest issue of Doug Henwood's invaluable *Left Business Observer* gives the global facts. The inequality index, the Gini index, as it's called, has reached the highest levels on record. [6] That's world population. One might argue that this doesn't matter much if everyone is gaining, even unequally. That is a terrible argument, but we don't have to pay attention to it, because the premise is incorrect.

Going back to Thomas Friedman, for the 1 percent of the population that he's thinking about and representing, the people who are opposing this are flat-earthers.

Would it be fair to say that in the actions in the streets in Seattle, mixed in with the tear gas was also a whiff of democracy?

I would take it to be. A functioning democracy is not supposed to happen in the streets. It's supposed to happen in decision making. This is a reflection of the undermining of democracy and the popular reaction to it, not for the first time. There's been a long struggle, over centuries, in fact, to try to extend the realm of democratic freedoms, and it's won plenty of victories. A lot of them have been won exactly this way, not by gifts but by confrontation and struggle. If the popular reaction in this case takes a really organized, constructive form, it can undermine and reverse the highly undemocratic thrust of the international economic arrangements that are being foisted on the world. And they are very undemocratic.

Naturally one thinks about the attack on domestic sovereignty, but most of the world is much worse. Over half the population of the world literally does not have even theoretical control over their own national economic policies. They're in receivership. Their economic policies are run by bureaucrats in Washington as a result of the so-called debt crisis, which is an ideological construction, not an economic one. That's over half the population of the world lacking even minimal sovereignty.

Why do you say the debt crisis is an ideological construction?

There's a capitalist principle which nobody wants to pay any attention to, which says that if I borrow money from you, it's my responsibility to pay it back and it's your risk if I don't pay it back. That's the capitalist principle. But nobody even conceives of that possibility.

Suppose we were to follow that. Take Indonesia, for example. Right now its economy is crushed by the fact that the debt is something like 140 percent of GDP. Trace that debt back. It turns out that the borrowers were something like a hundred to two hundred people around the military dictatorship that we supported and their cronies. The lenders were international banks. A lot of that debt has been by now socialized through the IMF, which means taxpayers in the North who fund the IMF are responsible.

What happened to the money? They enriched themselves. There was some capital export and some development. But the people who borrowed the money aren't held responsible for it. It's the people of Indonesia who have to pay it off. And that means living under crushing austerity programs, severe poverty, and suffering. In fact it's a hopeless task to pay off the debt that they didn't borrow.

What about the lenders? The lenders are protected from risk. That's one of the main functions of the IMF, to provide free risk insurance to people who lend and invest in risky loans. They earn high yields because there's a lot of risk, but they don't have to take the risk, because it's socialized. It's transferred in various ways to Northern taxpayers through the IMF and other devices, like Brady bonds. The whole system is one in which the borrowers are released from the responsibility. That's transferred to the impoverished mass of the population in their own countries. And the lenders are protected from risk. These are ideological choices, not economic ones.

In fact, it even goes beyond that. There's a principle of international law that was devised by the U.S. over a hundred years ago when it "liberated" Cuba, which means conquered Cuba to prevent it from liberating itself from Spain in 1898. At that time, when the U.S. took over Cuba, it canceled its debt to Spain on the quite reasonable grounds that this debt was invalid since it had been imposed on the people of Cuba without their consent. That principle was later recognized in international law, again under U.S. initiative, as the principle of what's called "odious debt."[7] Debt is not valid if it's essentially imposed by force.

The third world debt is odious debt. That's even been recognized by the U.S. representative at the IMF, Karin Lissakers, an international economist, who pointed out a couple of years ago that if we were to apply the principles of odious debt, most of the third world debt would simply disappear.[8] These are all ideological decisions. They're not economic facts. It is an economic fact that money was lent and somebody owes it, but who owes it and who takes the risk, those are power decisions, not economic facts.

To return briefly to the events at Seattle, Newsweek *had a cover story on December 13 called "The Battle of Seattle." They devoted some pages to the anti-WTO protests. There was a sidebar in one of the articles called "The New Anarchism."* [9] *Among those mentioned as being somehow representative of this new anarchism are Rage Against the Machine and Chumbawamba. I don't suppose you know who they are.*

I'm not that far out of it.

The list continues with the writer John Zerzan and Theodore Kaczynski, the notorious Unabomber, and then you. How did you figure into that constellation? Did Newsweek *contact you?*

Sure. We had a long interview. [*Laughs.*] I can sort of conjure up something that might have been going on in their editorial offices, but your guess is as good as mine. The term anarchist has always had a very weird meaning in elite circles. For example, there was a small article in the *Boston Globe* the other day about how all these anarchists are organizing these protests.[10] Who are the anarchists? Ralph Nader's Public Citizen, labor organizations, and others.

There will be some people around who will call themselves anarchists, whatever that means. But from the elite point of view, you want to focus on something that you can denounce in some fashion as irrational. That's the analogue to Thomas Friedman calling them flat-earthers.

Vivian Stromberg of Madre, the New York–based NGO, says there are lots of motions in the country but no movement.[11]

I don't agree. For example, what happened in Seattle was certainly movement. Just a couple of days ago students were arrested in protests over the failure of universities to adopt strong anti-sweatshop conditions that many student organizations are proposing. There are lots of other things going on which look like movement to me. While we're on the Seattle matter, in many ways what happened in Montreal a few weeks ago is even more dramatic.

That was the Biosafety Protocol meeting.

That wasn't much discussed here, because the main protesters were European. The issue that came up was clear and important. A kind of ambiguous compromise was reached, but the lineup was very sharp. The *New York Times* report stated it pretty accurately.[12] The United States was virtually alone most of the time in the negotiations leading to the compromise. The U.S. was joined by a couple of other countries which would also expect to profit from biotechnology exports.

The United States is against most of the world over a very significant issue, what's called the "precautionary principle." That means, is there a right for people to say, I don't want to be a subject in some experiment you're carrying out? At the personal level, that is permissible. For example, if somebody comes into your office from the university biology department and says, You're going to be a subject in an experiment that I'm carrying out. I'm going to stick electrodes into your brain and measure this, that, and the other thing, then you're permitted to say, I'm sorry, I don't want to be a subject. They are not allowed to come back to you and say, You have to be, unless you can provide scientific evidence that this is going to harm you. They're not allowed to do that. But the U.S. is insisting on exactly that internationally.

In the negotiations at Montreal, the United States, which is the center of the big biotech industries and genetic engineering, was demanding that the issue be determined under WTO rules. According to those rules, the experimental subjects have to provide scientific evidence that it's going to harm them, or else the transcendent value of corporate rights prevails and they can do what they want. That's what Ed Herman calls "producer sovereignty."[13]

Europe and most of the rest of the world insisted on the precautionary principle, that is, the right of people to say, I don't want to be an experimental subject. I don't have scientific proof that it's going to harm me, but I don't want to be subjected to that. I want to wait until it's understood. That's a very clear indication of what's at stake, an attack on the rights of people to make their own decisions over things even as simple as whether you're going to be an experimental subject, let alone controlling your own resources or setting conditions on foreign investment or transferring your economy into the hands of foreign investment firms and banks.

Those are the issues that are really at stake. It's a major assault against popular sovereignty in favor of the concentration of power in the hands of a kind of state-corporate nexus, a few megacorporations and the few states that primarily cater to their interests. The issue in Montreal in many ways was sharper and clearer than it was in Seattle. It came out with great clarity.

Food safety, irradiation, and genetic engineering seems to touch a deep chord in people and also to cross traditional what's called left-right, liberal-conservative lines. For example, French farmers, who are fairly conservative, are up in arms around these issues.

It's been interesting to watch this. In the U.S., there's been relatively little discussion and concern about it. In Europe, India, Latin America and elsewhere, there's been great concern and a lot of very activist popular protest. The French farmers are one case. The same is true in England and elsewhere, quite extensively. There's a lot of concern about being forced to become experimental subjects for interventions in the food system, both in production and consumption, that have unknown consequences. That did cross the Atlantic in a way that I don't entirely understand. At some point last fall the concerns became manifested over here as well, to the extent that something quite unusual happened.

Monsanto, the major corporation that's pushing biotechnology and genetically engineered crops, their stock started to fall notably. They had to make a public apology and, at least theoretically, maybe in fact, cancel some of their more extreme projects, like terminator genes — genes that would make seeds infertile so that, say, poor farmers in India would have to keep purchasing Monsanto seeds and fertilizers at an exorbitant cost. That's quite unusual, for a corporation to be forced into that position. It reflected in part the enormous protests overseas, primarily Europe, which is what mattered because of their clout, but also a growing protest here.

On the other hand, we should also take account of the fact that it's essentially a class issue in the United States. Among richer, more educated sectors, there are tendencies which amount to protecting themselves from being experimental subjects, by buying high-priced organic food, for example.

Do you think the food safety issue might be one around which the left can reach a broader constituency?

I don't see it as a particularly left issue. In fact, left issues are just popular issues. If the left means anything, it means it's concerned for the needs, welfare, and rights of the general population. So the left ought to be the overwhelming majority of the population, and in some respects I think it is. There are other related matters that are very hard to keep in the background. They're coming to the fore all over the place, dramatically in the poorer countries again, but it's showing up here, too.

Take the price of pharmaceuticals, for example. They are exorbitant. Pharmaceuticals in the United States are 25 percent higher than in Canada and probably twice as expensive as they are in Italy because of monopolistic practices that are strongly supported by the U.S. government and were built into the WTO rules. These are highly protectionist devices called "intellectual property rights," which essentially guarantee profits to the huge megacorporations that produce pharmaceuticals by allowing them to charge what amount to monopoly prices for a long period and keep less expensive generic versions off the market. This is being very strongly resisted in Africa, in Thailand, and elsewhere.

In Africa, the spread of AIDS is extremely dangerous and may lead to a major health catastrophe. Here, when Clinton or Gore makes a speech, they talk about the need for Africans to change their behavior. Well, OK, maybe Africans should change their behavior. But the crucial element is our behavior of guaranteeing that the producers, mainly, though not entirely, U.S.-based, be able to charge prices so high that nobody can afford them.

According to the latest reports, about 600,000 infants a year are having HIV transmitted to them from the mother, which means they'll probably die of AIDS. That's something that can be stopped by the use of drugs that would cost about a couple of dollars a day. But the drug companies will not permit them to be sold under what's called compulsory licensing, that is, allowing the countries to produce them themselves at a much cheaper rate than the drug companies charge under the monopolistic conditions. There may soon be 40 million orphans just from AIDS alone in Africa.

Similar things are going on in Thailand. And they're protesting. They have their own pharmaceutical industries in Thailand and parts of Africa, particularly trying to gain the right to produce generic drugs which would be far cheaper than the ones sold by the major pharmaceutical corporations. This is a major health crisis.

The same is true in other domains: malaria, tuberculosis. There are preventable diseases that are killing huge numbers of people because the means of prevention are kept so expensive that people can't use them. That's not as much of a problem in the rich countries. Here there's a problem of getting the pharmaceutical companies to permit Medicare to provide prescriptions for the elderly. That's a problem, and it's a real one. But in the poor countries, and not so poor, like Thailand, for example, Africa, South Asia, we're talking about the deaths of millions of people in a few years.

Why do drug companies get this enormous protection and in effect monopolistic rights? They claim that they need it because of the costs of research and development. But that's mostly a scam. A substantial part of the costs of research and development is paid by the public. Up until the early 1990s, it was about 50 percent, now maybe it's 40 percent. Those numbers much underestimate the actual public cost because they don't take into account the fundamental biology on which it's all based, and that's almost all publicly supported.

Dean Baker, a very good economist who has studied this carefully, asked the obvious question. He said, OK, suppose the public pays all the costs: double the public cost, and then insist that the drug simply go on the market. His estimates are a colossal welfare saving from this.[14] We're not talking about abstract issues. We're talking about the lives and deaths of tens of millions of people just in the next few years.

Returning to the U.S., talk more about the student sweatshop movement. Is it different from earlier movements that you're familiar with?

It's different and similar. In some ways it's like the movement against Apartheid, except in this case it's striking at the core of the relations of exploitation that are used to reach these incredible figures of inequality that we were talking about. It's very serious. It's another example of how different constituencies are working together. Much of this was initiated by Charlie Kernaghan of the National Labor Committee in New York and other groups within the labor movement.

It's now become a significant student issue in many areas. Many student groups are pressing this very hard, so much so that the U.S. government had to, in order to counter it, initiate a kind of code. They brought together labor and student leaders to form some kind of government-sponsored coalition, which many student groups are opposing because they think it doesn't go anywhere near far enough. Those are the issues that are now very much contested. Last I heard, I don't know the details, there was a big demonstration in Wisconsin with students arrested.

Aren't the students asking the capitalists to be less mean?

They're not calling for a dismantling of the system of exploitation. Maybe they should be. What they're asking for are the kinds of labor rights that are theoretically guaranteed. If you look at the con-

ventions of the International Labor Organization, the ILO, which is
responsible for these things, they bar most of the practices, probably
all of them, that the students are opposing.

The U.S. does not adhere to those conventions. Last I looked,
the U.S. had ratified hardly any of the ILO conventions. I think it
had the worst record in the world outside of maybe Lithuania or El
Salvador. Not that other countries live up to the conventions, but
they have their name on them at least. The U.S. doesn't accept them
on principle.

*Comment on an African American proverb that perhaps illustrates what
we're talking about: "The master's tools will never be used to dismantle the master's house."*

If this is intended to mean, don't try to improve conditions for
suffering people, I don't agree. It's true that centralized power,
whether in a corporation or a government, is not willingly going to
commit suicide. But that doesn't mean you shouldn't chip away at it,
for many reasons. For one thing, it benefits suffering people. That's
something that always should be done, no matter what broader con-
siderations are.

But even from the point of view of dismantling the master's
house, if people can learn what power they have when they work together, and if they can see dramatically at just what point they're going to be stopped, by force, perhaps, that teaches very valuable
lessons in how to go on. The alternative to that is to sit in academic
seminars and talk about how awful the system is.

*Tell me what's happening on your campus, at MIT. Is there any organiz-
ing around the sweatshop movement?*

Yes, and on a lot of issues. There are very active undergraduate
social justice groups doing things all the time, more so than in quite a
few years.

What accounts for that?

What accounts for it is the objective reality. It's the same feel-
ings and understanding and perception that led people to the streets
in Seattle. Take the U.S. The U.S. is not suffering like the third

world. In Latin America, after by now twenty years of so-called reforms, they haven't moved. The president of the World Bank has just reported that they're where they were twenty years ago. Even in economic growth. This is unheard of. The whole so-called developing world, I don't like the term, but it's the one that's used for the South, is pulling out of the 1990s with a slower rate of growth than in the 1970s. And welfare gaps are increasing enormously. That's in the rest of the world.

There's also an unprecedented development in the United States. Growth of the economy, productivity, and capital investment in the last twenty-five years has been relatively slow compared with the preceding twenty-five years. Many economists call it a "leaden age" as compared with the preceding "golden age." There has been growth, but it's slower than before and it's accrued to a very small part of the population. For most non-supervisory workers, which is the majority of the workforce, wages are maybe 10 percent or more below what they were twenty-five years ago. That's in absolute terms. In relative terms, they are much farther below.

There has been productivity growth and economic growth during that period, but it is not going to the mass of the population. Median incomes — meaning half are below and half are above the figure — are now barely getting back to what they were ten years ago and are well below what they were ten and fifteen years before that. This is in a period of reasonably good economic growth. They call it amazing, but only the last two or three years of growth has been about what it was in the 1950s or 1960s, which is high by historical standards. It's still left out most of the population.

The international economic arrangements, the so-called free trade agreements, are basically designed to maintain that inequality. They undergird what's called a "flexible labor market," meaning that people have no security. The growing worker insecurity that Alan Greenspan has said is one of the major factors in the fairy-tale economy. If people are afraid, they don't have job security. If they have a fear of job loss, which is one of the consequences of the mislabeled free trade agreements, and there's a flexible labor market, meaning you don't have security, people are not going to ask for better conditions and benefits.

The World Bank has been very clear about the matter. They recognize that labor market flexibility has acquired a bad name as a euphemism for pushing wages down and workers out. That's exactly what it does. It acquired that bad name for a good reason. That's what labor market flexibility is. They say it's essential for all regions of the world. It's the "most important" reform. I'm quoting from a World Bank development report.[15] It calls for lifting constraints on labor mobility and on wage flexibility.

What does that mean? It doesn't mean that workers should be free to go anywhere they want — that Mexican workers come to New York. What it means is they can be kicked out of their jobs. They want to lift constraints on kicking people out of their jobs.

People are aware of this at some level. You can hide a lot under all the glorification of consumption and huge debt, but it's hard to hide the fact that people are working many more weeks a year than they did twenty-five years ago just to keep incomes from stagnating or declining.

What about state colleges in Massachusetts. What's going on there?

That's much harder in many ways. These are mainly students from poor, urban inner-city or working-class backgrounds, many immigrants, ethnic minorities, and others. Although I think most of them are white working class, who have a chance to get ahead, meaning become a nurse or police officer.

The pressures on them are very tight. They don't have a large margin to maneuver the way you do in an elite school. I think that has a strong disciplinary effect not only on what they do but even on what they think. Also, these colleges are under great pressure.

In what way?

My feeling is that there's an effort on the part of the state authorities to essentially undercut the state schools that do offer these opportunities for poor and working people. What's happening is that they are raising standards for admission to the state colleges, meaning basically poor and working-class schools. They're raising the admissions standards but they're not improving the K–12 public schools. It's easy to predict what happens. If you raise the admissions standards and don't improve the schools, that means fewer people can qualify, so you have reduced admissions.

In fact, the reduction in admissions is quite sharp in the last year or two. If you reduce the admissions, you have to go back to the state legislature and the businessmen who run the place. They say, Cut the staff and faculty, which then reduces the opportunities even more. It introduces labor market flexibility into staff and faculty, meaning they won't have any security either, less commitment to the college.

The long-term tendency, maybe not so long-term, is to diminish or possibly eliminate the public education system that is geared to the poorer and the working people in the state, which will leave the options of not going to college at all or paying $30,000 a year at one of the private colleges.

It's the season of electoral politics. Once again, the question arises about voting and its efficacy. What do you think about that?

I don't think there's a general answer. In my opinion, if there's a general principle at all, and it has so many exceptions I hate to state it, it's probably a decision of low-order significance. The second principle is that it tends to be of more significance at the lower end of the representation system. So it's probably more important to vote for a representative to Congress than for president and similarly down the line. Public pressures are usually greater at the lower end, although private pressures are also greater at the lower end, so it's a mixed story.

Ralph Nader has announced his candidacy for the presidency on the Green Party ticket. Would that be something that would attract you?

It's a very tricky issue. You have to try to calculate extremely unpredictable and kind of low-order choices. A vote for Ralph Nader is going to be a protest vote. Everybody knows that. Is it advantageous to do that or to vote for a marginally better candidate who has a chance to win? The New Party had come up with a very sound proposal for running fusion candidates. You could vote for Nader, the New Party, or the Labor Party, and have the vote counted by whoever you preferred in the actual competitive election, say, a Democrat. But the New Party was defeated at the Supreme Court level, which is very unfortunate and undercuts the possibility of developing a really significant electoral alternative.

Nader says he's giving voters a choice between the usual Tweedledum-Tweedledee options that they have. Isn't that valid?

It's valid at a certain abstract level, except he and everybody else know that he's not going to win the election. So the vote that does express this choice is taken away from somebody. It may be taken away from not voting at all, in which case it's a good idea. If it's taken away from actually voting, you have to calculate the consequences. And those consequences are very hard to judge. It's by no means obvious that it's efficacious to vote for the person who has the rhetoric that you slightly prefer — in fact, often not.

In a New Mexico congressional race, for example, there was the case of the Green Party candidate doing rather well, and it resulted in the election of a right-wing Republican.

Those are the kinds of questions you have to ask all the time. Suppose there had not been a right-wing Republican. What would the difference have been on the national scene? It's hard to predict. Sometimes it's not hard, but sometimes it's a very mixed business.

To go back in time, in 1968 the presidential race was Hubert Humphrey versus Richard Nixon. I could not bring myself to vote for Humphrey. I didn't vote for Nixon. But my feeling at the time, and in retrospect I think it's probably correct, was that a Nixon victory was probably marginally beneficial in winding down the Indochina wars, probably faster than the Democrats would have. It was horrendous, but maybe less horrible than it would have been. And also even domestically, Nixon did a lot of pretty awful things, but he was also essentially the last liberal president.

You often say that to the astonishment of many. Let's move on to the Internet and issues of privacy. Unbeknownst to many Internet users, businesses are collecting profiles and amassing data on people's preferences and interests. What are the implications of that?

The implications could be pretty serious, but in my view they are still secondary to another issue, which is Internet access. The huge mergers that are going on in the media megacorporations carry the threat which is not at all remote that they'll be able to effectively direct access to favored sites, meaning turning the Internet system even more than it is now into a home shopping service rather than information and interaction.

Norman Solomon, a media critic, pointed out in a column that in the early 1990s, while the system was still under government control, the Internet was commonly referred to as an "information superhighway."[16] In the late 1990s, after it was handed over as a gift to private corporations in some manner that nobody knows, it's become e-commerce, not an information superhighway.

The megamergers like AOL and Time Warner offer technical possibilities to ensure that getting on the Internet will draw you into what they want you to see, not what you want to see. That's very dangerous. The Internet is a tremendous tool for information, understanding, organizing, and communication. There is no doubt at all that the business world, which has been given this public gift, intends to turn it into something else. If they're able to do it, that will be a very serious blow to freedom and democracy.

And this is quite independent from what is called the "digital divide," which is access at all.

That's also very critical, but it's not the same issue.

You described the Internet to me once as a "lethal weapon." Someone once wrote an article and put your name on it and circulated it on the Net.

That happened. That article was then picked off the Net and published. A lot of ugly things can happen.

Isn't that going to invite demand for controls and regulation?

That's true, but let's put it into perspective. There's nothing to stop a columnist in the *New York Times* from writing a column attributing to me idiotic and outrageous views with a guarantee that the editors won't allow me to write a letter in response.[17] Is that better?

And all of these things are so marginal as compared to the other things we're talking about. These are personal annoyances. They're unpleasant and bad, and they shouldn't happen in a decent society. But as compared with the problems that most people face, let's be honest, they're not huge.

You're speaking in Albuquerque this Saturday night at a 2,300-seat auditorium. It's completely sold out. People have been calling me from around the country the last couple of days asking me to get them tickets.

I knew you were my agent, but I didn't know you were that prominent. [*Laughs.*]

You're doing a benefit for the Interhemispheric Research Center. They have done very little publicity. In fact, just a mention in a local food co-op newsletter was enough to sell out the Convention Center.

That's publicity the way it ought to be done. They have a terrific record of regular publications that are very informative and useful. They also have a recent book, *Global Focus,* which covers very well many of the topics we've been talking about.[18] That's connected with activism, too. That's the way they ought to be spending their energy, not in advertising a talk.

If you could only develop your jump shot, we'd have the complete package.

My grandson is working on it.

1 Andrew Simms, "Unctad Offers Way Forward for Talks on World Trade," *Guardian Weekly* (Manchester), February 23, 2000, p. 12.

2 Susan Strange, *Mad Money: When Markets Outgrow Governments* (Ann Arbor: University of Michigan Press, 1998), p. 127.

3 See the articles on-line at http://www.twnside.org.sg/unctad.htm and http://www.twnside.org.sg/title/focus15.htm.

4 Martin Wolf, "The Curse of Global Inequality," *Financial Times,* January 26, 2000, p. 23.

5 Thomas L. Friedman, "Senseless in Seattle," *New York Times,* December 1, 1999, p. A23.

6 Doug Henwood, "Miscellany," *Left Business Observer* 91 (August 31, 1999), p. 8. See also http://www.panix.com/~dhenwood/Gini_supplement.html and http://www.panix.com/~dhenwood/Wealth_distrib.html.

7 Patricia Adams, *Odious Debts: Loose Lending, Corruption, and the Third World's Environmental Legacy* (Toronto: Earthscan, 1991). See also Noam Chomsky, *Rogue States: The Rule of Force in World Affairs* (Cambridge: South End Press, 2000), pp. 82–92 and 101–107.

8 Karin Lissakers, *Banks, Borrowers, and the Establishment: A Revisionist Account of the International Debt Crisis* (New York: Basic Books, 1991).

9 Michael Elliott et al., "The New Radicals," *Newsweek,* December 13, 1999, p. 36ff. See sidebar on "The New Anarchism."

10 Lynda Gorov, "Seattle Caught Unprepared for Anarchists," *Boston Globe,* December 3, 1999, p. A11.

11 Interview, Boulder, Colorado, October 3, 1996.

12 Andrew Pollack, "Talks on Biotech Food Today in Montreal Will See U.S. Isolated," *New York Times,* January 24, 2000, p. A10.

13 Edward S. Herman, "Corporate Junk Science in the Media," Z Net. On-line at http://www.zmag.org/ScienceWars/junk3.htm.

14 See Dean Baker, "The High Cost of Protectionism: The Case of Intellectual Property Claims," Economic Policy Institute, September 1996, and Dean Baker, "The Real Drug Crisis," *In These Times,* August 22, 1999, p. 19.

15 See World Bank, *World Development Report 1995: Workers in an Integrating World* (New York: Oxford UP, 1995), p. 109. Cited in Jerome Levinson, "The International Financial System: A Flawed Architecture," *Flectcher Forum* 23: 1 (Winter–Spring 1999), pp. 1–56. Additional *World Development Reports* are on-line at http://www.worldbank.org/wdr/.

16 Norman Solomon, "What Happened to the 'Information Superhighway'?" *Z Magazine* 13: 2 (February 2000), pp. 11–13.

17 See Anthony Lewis, "It Tolls for Thee," *New York Times,* June 23, 1997, p. A15.

18 Martha Honey and Tom Barry, eds., *Global Focus: U.S. Foreign Policy at the Turn of the Millennium* (New York: St. Martin's Press, 2000).

6

Liberating the Mind from Orthodoxies

Lexington, Massachusetts, April 10, 2000

*D*riving out here this morning to Lexington, I was struck by not just the statue of the Minuteman but the names of the streets, like Adams, Pilgrim, and Hancock. Here dwells Noam Chomsky, described as America's leading dissident, in the fortress of Americana.

In a week they're going to have a huge celebration, going on for days, of Patriots Day. It's some anniversary with a round number. They're going to have people retreating from Concord to Boston. Every year they enact the great battle of Lexington Center, where the Minutemen tried to hold off the Redcoats. I think four people were killed, one of those huge massacres. Everybody's dressed up in the right costumes. So if you really want to see some pageantry, come around.

No doubt you'll be the grand marshal of the parade.

We're there at 6 a.m. every April 19. Actually, the kids used to go when they were little.

A lot of people don't know that your given name is actually Avram. When did that switch take place?

Before I was conscious. My parents told me that when I was a couple of months old they didn't want everyone calling me Abie, so they figured they'd switch to the second name.

Is Abie the diminutive of Noam?

No, of Avram. Avram is Abraham.

It is No-am in Hebrew?

Yes. Don't tell anybody — it means "pleasantness."

Surely the irony was noted by your parents. You once told me there was a little bit of gender confusion around your name.

I once had to get my birth certificate for some reason. I wrote a letter to City Hall in Philadelphia. They sent me a copy. The birth certificate had my name crossed off in pencil. Some clerk didn't believe it and changed Noam to Naomi. That's understandable. But they also changed Avram to Avrane. I think the idea is that girls could have crazy names, but boys have to have names like John or Tom. They didn't change M to F, so I was still male.

I've often wondered whether that was the reason why I never got called for the army after I was passed as 1A. I got a couple of weeks deferment to finish a Ph.D., which incidentally I hadn't intended to get until then, but this was the last chance to delay going to Korea for a couple of weeks. Then I never got called. Maybe somebody misread my birth certificate.

You would have been around twenty-two when the Korean War broke out in 1950.

This was 1955.

Ever since that Naomi incident there's been a long series of confusions about your gender.

A lot of the junk mail that comes in often is to "Naomi." It's people's natural misreading.

Tell me a little bit about your dad, William, who was a noted scholar of Hebrew. Did that spark your initial interest in language and linguistics?

I got interested quite young. When I was a kid, about ten or so, I read the proofs of his doctoral dissertation. He wrote it late. He came over as an immigrant, worked in a sweatshop and finally got himself to college. It was a scholarly study of a medieval Hebrew grammarian, David Kimhi. I read that as well as articles of his on the history of the Semitic languages, Hebrew and Arabic.

You also taught Hebrew, didn't you?

First of all, that was part of the life we lived. It was like eating breakfast. By the time I got to college, that's the way we supported ourselves. Both Carol and I lived at home and worked. That wasn't even a question. The work was teaching Hebrew, running Hebrew-speaking organizations, youth groups. We continued after we got married. There was no question of being funded. You worked.

You lived at home with your parents after you got married?

After we got married, we got a little apartment a couple of houses away.

In Philadelphia.

Right. It was a great apartment. I remember that the front door didn't quite close. The floor was at such an angle that at one end it closed, and the other end was about six inches away from the floor. Everything else was more or less like that.

Now you have a number of grandchildren. Have you, as they get older, noticed anything that verifies or even perhaps disproves some of your own notions about language acquisition?

How dare you suggest that anything might disprove it? [*Laughs.*] One set of my grandchildren has an interesting history. I have two grandchildren who live in Nicaragua. Children generally tend to speak the language of their peers, not their parents. So, for example, I don't speak with my father's Russian accent or my mother's New York accent. I speak with the accent from a certain area in northeastern Philadelphia where I grew up.

My grandchildren who live here in Massachusetts don't speak their parents' language. They speak the language of the streets, which is normal. The Nicaraguan story is more complicated. The older of my grandchildren there grew up in a household of two North American women who spoke English to each other. The father wasn't living there at the time. My daughter speaks fluent Nicaraguan Spanish. Over the telephone, people think she's Nicaraguan. The other woman had adopted a Nicaraguan street child — of whom unfortunately there are plenty since the country was restored to the U.S.-dominated system again in 1990 — and this little girl of course spoke only Spanish.

From my grandson's point of view, she was an older sister. My daughter spoke English to him because she wanted him to learn English, but he answered in Spanish. He spoke the Spanish of the "sister" and the kids on the street. For a couple of years, he couldn't understand us. He would try very hard to teach me Spanish, to teach me the words and how to pronounce them properly. He now speaks English fluently, but a kind of bookish English with a Spanish accent.

He now has a younger sister. Both he and his little sister now talk to my daughter in English and to their father in Spanish. They talk to each other in English. Most of the surrounding environment — and of course school — is in Spanish. The little girl speaks English, but she's fully bilingual and even translates back and forth with ease. She'll ask her mother, How do you say such-and-such in Spanish so she can say it to her father and converse with him. She's now two and a half.

It's the normal situation, but in a complicated way. Children do not pick up what their parents speak. Of course their parents have an influence, but they typically speak the language of their peers.

Do these observations confirm your ideas about the brain being hard-wired for language acquisition?

You could say they confirm it. It's just not even a serious question, so yes, they confirm it. But these aren't careful experiments. There is really careful work on these topics.

Let's talk about a theme that we return to periodically, and that is propaganda and indoctrination. As a teacher, how do you get people to think for themselves? Can you in fact impart tools that will enable that?

I think you learn by doing. I'm a Deweyite from way back, from childhood experience and reading. You figure out how to do things by watching other people do them. That's the way you learn to be a good carpenter, for example, and the way you learn to be a good physicist. Nobody can train you how to do physics. You don't teach methodology courses in the natural sciences. So a typical graduate seminar in a science course would be just people working together, not all that different from an artisan picking up a craft and working with someone who's supposedly good at it.

The right way to do things is not to try to persuade people you're right but to challenge them to think it through for themselves. There's nothing in human affairs of which we can speak with very great confidence. Even in the hard natural sciences, that's largely true. In the case of human affairs, international affairs, family relations, whatever it may be, you can compile evidence and you can put things together and look at them from a certain way. The right approach, putting aside what one or another person does, is simply to encourage people to do that.

In particular, you try to show the chasm that separates standard versions of what goes on in the world from what the evidence of the senses and people's inquiries will show them as soon as they start to look at it. A common response that I get is, I can't believe anything you're saying. It's totally in conflict with what I've learned and always believed, and I don't have time to look up all those footnotes. How do I know what you're saying is true? That's a plausible reaction. I tell people it's the right reaction. You shouldn't believe what I say is true. The footnotes are there, so you can find out if you feel like it, but if you don't want to bother, nothing can be done. Nobody is going to pour truth into your brain. It's something you have to find out for yourself.

Another comment I hear in talking about this issue is that people say, I'm no Noam Chomsky. I don't have his resources. I work at Logan Airport from 9 to 5. I've got a mortgage to pay. I don't have the access and the ability. Does it take special brains?

It doesn't take special brains, but it takes special privilege. Those people are right. You have to have special privilege, which we have. It's unfair, but we've got it. To have the resources, training, time, the control over your own life. Maybe I work a hundred hours a week, but it's a hundred I choose. That's a rare luxury. Only a tiny sector of the population can enjoy that, let alone have the resources and the training. It's extremely hard to do it by yourself.

However, we shouldn't exaggerate. Many of the people who do this best are people who lack privilege, for one thing because they have several advantages: not having undergone a good education, not being subjected to the huge flow of indoctrination, which an education largely is, so that you don't internalize it. So there are advantages also to being outside of the system of privilege and domination. But it's true that the person who's working fifty hours a week to put food on the table does not have the luxury we do.

That's why people get together. That's what unions were about — workers' education, which often came out of the unions. These were ways for people to get together to encourage one another, to learn from one another, to find out about the world. Over quite a range, in fact: literature, history, science, mathematics. Some of the great books on science and mathematics for the public were written by left-oriented specialists, and such topics found their way into workers' education.

There are things you can do in groups you can't do by yourself. In fact, that's true of the most advanced sciences. Very little is done individually. It's usually done in groups by collective action and interchange and critique and challenge, with students typically playing an active and often critical role. The same is true here.

Part of the genius of the system of domination and control is to separate people from one another so that doesn't happen. We can't "consult our neighbors," as one of my favorite Wobbly singers once put it back in the 1930s.[1] As long as we can't consult our neighbors, we'll believe that there are good times. It's important to make sure that people don't consult their neighbors.

Who was that singer?

T-Bone Slim.

You were listening to T-Bone Slim?

I read these things. I'm not attuned to the auditory world.

Let's talk in concrete ways about liberating the mind from orthodoxies. Let's say, for example, humanitarian intervention.

Humanitarian intervention is an orthodoxy, and it's taken for granted that if we do it, it's humanitarian. The reason is because our leaders say so. But you can check. For one thing, there's a history of humanitarian intervention. You can look at it. And when you do, you discover that virtually every use of military force is described as humanitarian intervention.

The major recent big academic study of humanitarian intervention is by Sean Murphy.[2] He's now an editor of the *American Journal of International Law*. Murphy points out that before the Second World War, in 1928, the Kellogg-Briand Pact outlawed war. Between the Kellogg-Briand Pact and the U.N. Charter in 1945, he finds three major examples of humanitarian intervention. One was the Japanese invasion of Manchuria and north China. Another was Mussolini's invasion of Ethiopia. And a third was Hitler's takeover of the Sudetenland. They were accompanied by quite exalted and impressive humanitarian rhetoric, which as usual was not entirely false. Even the most vulgar propaganda usually has elements of truth. In fact, the propaganda was similar in its rhetoric to other so-called humanitarian interventions, and about as plausible.

It's interesting to look and see what the U.S. reaction was. Some of it is public, but parts of it are from the internal record, which is now partially declassified. The reaction is commonly called "appeasement." But that's a little misleading, because that makes it seem as if you're groveling before the tyrants. It doesn't convey the fact that the reaction was actually rather supportive. When it was critical, the criticism was on very narrow grounds.

So in the case of the Japanese invasion of Manchuria and north China — these are things I wrote about over thirty years ago, because these were public records — the official U.S. reaction was, We don't like it, but we don't care, really, as long as American interests in China, meaning primarily economic interests, are guaranteed. The U.S. ambassador to Japan, Joseph Grew, who was a very influential figure in the Roosevelt administration, ridiculed the idea that Japan was "a big bully and China the downtrodden victim." By then there had been huge atrocities, including the Nanking massacre. Grew said the only real problem was that the Japanese were not protecting U.S. interests in China. If they did that, it would be OK. At the same time, Roosevelt's secretary of state, Cordell Hull, said that we could reach a modus vivendi with Japan if they would protect U.S. commercial interests in China. If they wanted to massacre a couple of hundred thousand people in Nanking, it's another story.[3]

Same with Mussolini. The State Department hailed Mussolini for his magnificent achievements in Ethiopia and also, incidentally, for his astonishing accomplishments in raising the level of the masses in Italy. This is the late 1930s, several years after the invasion. Roosevelt himself described Mussolini as "that admirable Italian gentleman." In 1939, he praised the fascist experiment in Italy — as did almost everyone, it's not a particular criticism of Roosevelt — and said it had been "corrupted" by Hitler. Other than that, it was a good experiment.[4]

How about Hitler's taking over the Sudetenland in 1938? One of Roosevelt's major advisers was A.A. Berle. He said that there's nothing alarming about the takeover. It was probably necessary for the Austrian Empire to be reconstituted under German rule, so it's all right. The State Department, internally, was much more supportive of Hitler, on interesting grounds: he was a representative of the moderate wing of the Nazi Party, standing between the extremes of right and left. In 1937, the European Division of the State Department held that fascism "must succeed" or the "dissatisfied masses, with the example of the Russian Revolution before them," will "swing to the Left," joined by "the disillusioned middle classes."[5] That would be the real tragedy.

Notice that this is the late 1930s. There's no concern about Russian aggression. That's a typical remark. That's the way every monster is described, a moderate standing between the extremes of right and left, and we have to support him, or too bad. That's a famous remark of John F. Kennedy's about Rafael Trujillo reported by Arthur Schlesinger, the liberal historian and Kennedy aide. Kennedy said something like, We don't like Trujillo. He's a murderous gangster. But unless we can be assured that there won't be a Castro, we'll have to support Trujillo.[6]

We can never be assured that there won't be a Castro. Remember how Castro was regarded at the time. We know that from declassified records. Kennedy was going to focus on Latin America. He had a Latin American mission, including Schlesinger, who transmitted the conclusions of the mission to Kennedy. Of course they discussed Cuba. Schlesinger said the problem of Cuba is "the spread of the Castro idea of taking matters into one's own hands."[7] He later explained that it's an idea that has a lot of appeal to impoverished and oppressed people all over Latin America who face similar difficulties, oppression, and misery and might be inspired by the example of the Cuban revolution. So that's the Cuban threat.

He also mentioned the Soviet threat. He said, "Meanwhile, the Soviet Union hovers in the wings, flourishing large development loans and presenting itself as the model for achieving modernization in a single generation."[8] So that's the Cuban threat and the Soviet threat. You have to stop that. It was the same reason that the State Department gave for supporting Hitler in the 1930s, and in fact just about every other case. Case after case after case. The threat of a good example, or it's sometimes called the virus effect. The virus of independent nationalism might succeed and inspire others. Actually, the war in Vietnam started the same way.

There was a comment attributed to FDR about Somoza in Nicaragua.

He may be an SOB, but he's our SOB. That's falsely attributed, but it's the right idea.[9]

Speaking of Nazi Germany, Joseph Goebbels, its propaganda minister, once said, "It would not be impossible to prove with sufficient repetition and a psychological understanding of the people concerned that a square is in fact a circle. They are mere words, and words can be molded until they clothe ideas in disguise."[10]

It's worth remembering where he got that idea. We ought to come back to humanitarian intervention, because of course the fact that Hitler and Mussolini and the Japanese fascists called it humanitarian intervention is not enough to prove that other cases are not humanitarian intervention. It just raises some questions that a serious person would want to look at.

Goebbels got that idea, as did Hitler, from the practice of the democracies. Hitler was very impressed by the successes of Anglo-American propaganda during World War I and felt, not without reason, that it partly explained why Germany lost the war. Germany couldn't compete with the extensive propaganda efforts of the democracies.

Britain had a Ministry of Information, or some Orwellian term, the purpose of which, as its leaders put it, was to control the thought of the world, and in particular to control the thought of liberal American intellectuals. Remember the circumstances. Britain had to somehow get the United States into the war, or it wasn't going to win. That meant it had to appeal to the educated sectors in the U.S. and get them on its side, and they did.

If you read what John Dewey's circle produced about World War I, I'm sorry to say it's very similar to the chorus of self-adulation that similar circles produced during the bombing of Yugoslavia in 1999, full of praise for their own enlightenment. They were very supportive of Wilson's war, though the population wasn't. Wilson was elected on a kind of pacifist program. His slogan was "Peace without victory," but he immediately tried to turn the country into raving warmongers through propaganda, and succeeded.

But the educated sectors, especially the progressives, took great pride publicly — in the *New Republic,* for example, the main journal of the liberal, educated sector — that this was the first war in history, as they said, that was not due to military conquest or crass economic motives but just for values. It was a new era in human history.

Incidentally, this is the same thing we heard about the war in Yugoslavia. It was the first war ever fought for principles and values. We are an enlightened state. There was a huge chorus of self-praise, very similar to the First World War. At that time, the educated sectors here were transmitting tales about Hun atrocities like tearing arms off Belgian babies. Like most propaganda, there was some element of truth to it, but it turned out that it was mostly fabrication.

In fact the picture wasn't pretty, but it was not what was being presented. One of very few people who resisted was Randolph

Bourne. He had been in Dewey's circle and was more or less thrown out, barred from participation, because he was telling the truth, what later was recognized to be the truth, about what the war was really about and why Wilson was trying to get us into it. That was not acceptable, just as it's not acceptable here, right now. In fact, the similarities are very striking, as is the style, and intellectual and moral level, of the defense of orthodoxy. For people who want to think about humanitarian intervention, it's worth looking at.

So the British had the Ministry of Information. The U.S. had the Committee on Public Information, which was known as the Creel Commission. It included liberals like Walter Lippmann and Edward Bernays. Bernays went on to found the public relations industry. They were very impressed with their success in turning a pacifist population very quickly into raving anti-German fanatics. There was real hysteria about the Germans. The propaganda was very effective.

A number of groups were impressed. One group was the progressive intellectuals. That's the background for the influential social and political theories that developed in the 1920s, mostly from progressive circles. It's part of the founding of modern political science and the public relations industry and the media. The new insight — the new "art of democracy," in Lippmann's phrase — is that we have ways, as Bernays put it, to regiment "the public mind every bit as much as an army regiments the bodies of its soldiers."[11] And we should do it, because we're the good guys and smart guys and they're stupid and dumb, and therefore we have to control them for their own good. And we can do it because we have these marvelous new techniques of propaganda. It was honestly called propaganda in those days. Bernays's book is called *Propaganda.*[12]

Another group that was impressed was business leaders. Their leaders were again pretty frank. We have to impose on people a "philosophy of futility" and ensure that they're focused on "the superficial things of life, like fashionable consumption." They have to try to pursue what were called "fancied wants," invented needs. We create the needs and then get them to focus their attention on it. Then they don't bother us, they're out of our hair. It's not hard to see the consequences years later.

This wasn't new. These ideas start with the Industrial Revolution, but there was a real upsurge in the 1920s and since. These are the huge industries of domination and control. Incidentally, it's not in the least surprising. It should be expected that it's in the democracies that these ideas would develop. Because in a democracy you have to control people's minds. You can't control them by force. There's a limited capacity to control them by force, and since they have to be controlled and marginalized, be "spectators of action," not "participants," as Lippmann put it, you have to resort to propaganda.[13] This was well understood. It was a very reasonable reaction. You can trace it right back to the seventeenth century and the first democratic revolution.

I didn't realize that Dewey was pro-war.

Dewey was very pro-war, and on interesting grounds. He said that the war is an exercise of pragmatic intelligence, and that's what we're good at. We're pragmatists and we're intelligent. We can carry out social control and social management, and we should do it because we're better than the other guys. He was extremely critical of and ridiculed what he called pacifism because it was irrational. It wasn't considering the pragmatic principles. His point was that the use of violence is fine if it achieves good ends. In a sense, that's correct. I don't argue against the principle altogether, but when you look at its application, it's pretty ugly.

The good ends happened to be pursuit of the needs of the British propaganda agencies, who were feeding him and others the nonsense and distortions that they were then believing and using to drive the country into war with quite high-flown rhetoric about their own intelligence and insight. You can debate whether the U.S. should have gone to war or not, but not on the grounds that the educated intellectuals were praising themselves for.

And the praise was remarkable. Very similar to what we've just seen with Yugoslavia. I don't remember a chorus of self-adulation of the kind that occurred last year since that time. There has been plenty, but not at that intensity. Remember, it was last year that Václav Havel was explaining to us that we were for the first time in history fighting for "principles and values." Leading legal scholars, with a good record in human rights issues, I should say, were explaining in *Foreign Affairs* how the "enlightened states," which by definition is us, have to create their new, modern notions of justice and apply them irrespective of the old boring rules, which we can forget about.[14] This is pretty much a repetition of World War I.

So, in both cases, World War I and the bombing of Yugoslavia, liberal intellectuals took a very pro-war stance.

Intellectuals are both the main victims of the propaganda system and also its main architects. That's standard. This bears directly on humanitarian intervention. When you ask whether a certain action is or is not a case of humanitarian intervention, you should at least approach it with a sense of history and an understanding of what's happened in the past. Then of course you have to evaluate the case on its own terms. You have to ask, for example, whether the bombing of Yugoslavia was a case of humanitarian intervention. Was it undertaken with humanitarian intent and with the expectation of benign humanitarian consequences? No matter what the past record is of the state in question, that question has to be asked. Of course, that is not the same as the question whether the action was legitimate — a truism that many Western intellectuals seem unable to grasp — when the motives of their own governments are subjected to the criteria they rightly apply to official enemies.

When you investigate motive and intent, in this case, I think you find quite the opposite of what is declared. The bombing was undertaken with the expectation that it would lead to a very sharp escalation of atrocities and had nothing to do with humanitarian goals. The opposite is very passionately claimed, but with no credible evidence or argument, to my knowledge. It is simply put forth as a doctrine that we must believe.

We can ask the same question about the other main atrocity that was being carried out at the time, namely East Timor. Here the history is already being reshaped in interesting ways by good people. You see the standard line everywhere, from the *American Journal of International Law* over to people on the left. Even if you were opposed to the war in Yugoslavia, there's one good thing about it, at least: it served as a precedent for the intervention in East Timor, and we all agree that this was good. The only trouble is that the facts are totally different. In fact, there never was any intervention in East Timor in any serious sense of the term, so it couldn't have been a humanitarian one. The United States and Britain continued to support the Indonesian army until after the worst atrocities had taken place. It was not until after the Indonesian army withdrew, having been informed by Clinton that the time had come, that they were willing to allow a peacekeeping force to enter. That's not intervention.

How would you explain what happened?

What had happened, in brief, is this. As the U.S. and Britain were planning the bombing of Yugoslavia, Indonesian military reinforcements, led by Kopassus special forces commandos, entered East Timor. The Kopassus units are infamous for their brutality and savagery in East Timor and throughout Indonesia. They were, incidentally, fresh from renewed U.S. training under Clinton's "Iron Balance" program for training the Indonesian military, a program that was kept secret because it was in violation of the intent of congressional legislation. It's still secret in the U.S., by choice. It was prominently reported in England and Canada, and on international news services, but was not in the mainstream here, at least last time I checked. These military forces entered in November 1998. Killings began very soon, and by February 1999 they had initiated "Operation Clean Sweep," which was intended to intimidate and terrorize the population so that they would not call for independence in a referendum, which was likely to come, it seemed clear at the time.[15]

The army, which ran East Timor, wanted to make sure the population didn't vote the wrong way. In early 1999, the atrocities were mounting. They were way beyond the level of Kosovo. The Racak massacre — which is the one big massacre in Kosovo, in January 1999, with forty-five people killed — was quickly surpassed in East Timor by one massacre in a church in Liquiça, which killed about 60 people taking refuge there, perhaps many more, it is now reported by Western investigators on the scene. And that was only one of many, unlike Kosovo, where Racak was an isolated event according to official Western sources.[16]

We now know quite a lot about what was going on in Kosovo in the months before the bombing. A lot of documentation has been released from Western sources, including the State Department, NATO, the OSCE, the Organization for Security and Cooperation in Europe, the Kosovo Verification Mission monitors in Kosovo, and others. I was kind of surprised when I went through these records. If one can believe them, there was a steady but relatively low level of violence, pretty much distributed among Serbs and Albanians, and it did not change in the several months before the bombing, with the single exception of Racak. According to these sources, the standard cycle of violence began with Albanian Kosovar guerrillas — the Kosovo Liberation Army, based in Albania — killing Serb police and civilians. This was done with the expectation — as they openly proclaim — that it would lead to a brutal and well-publicized Serb response, which could be exploited to arouse support in the West for direct military intervention.

The situation was entirely different in East Timor. East Timor was occupied by a foreign army which had no sovereign rights (other than those conferred, implicitly, by support from the U.S. and Britain) and had already slaughtered perhaps one-third of the population, with crucial U.S.-British diplomatic and military support. In contrast, NATO insists for its own reasons that Kosovo is part of Serbia, not the victim of foreign aggression and mass slaughter, in collusion with the U.S. and U.K., along with other industrial democracies.

In East Timor, there was very limited conflict. The small resistance forces were isolated in the mountains, with virtually no outside contacts. The Indonesian army and the militias it organized were murdering defenseless civilians. In the first half of 1999, through July, about 3,000 to 5,000 people were killed, according to the East Timorese church, which has been a reliable source in the past.[17] Those numbers are far beyond Kosovo prior to the NATO bombing — the relevant period — and under very different circumstances, as I've just reviewed.

There were also tens of thousands of people driven from their homes. The Indonesian military had also announced very clearly that if the vote went the wrong way in the referendum planned for August, they would move on to mass murder and destruction — as they did, after the August 30 referendum. They were not quiet about it. It's inconceivable that U.S. intelligence didn't know about this. Australian intelligence certainly did. You could read it in extensive detail in the Australian press, also in the British press. A lot has come out since, but a lot of information was readily available to anyone who chose to know about the crimes for which we share critical responsibility and those that were very likely to come if we continued to ignore what was happening and to continue to support it. That's the first half of 1999.

What happened? The atrocities continued. The referendum came on August 30. To everyone's surprise — mine, too — in an amazing display of courage, despite the atrocities and intimidation and murders and ethnic cleansing, virtually the entire population went to the polls. About 80 percent voted for independence, which is astonishing. A couple of days later, the predictions, the announcements, of the Indonesian military were fulfilled. According to the U.N., they continued the atrocities and drove out about 750,000 people, 85 percent of the population, about a quarter of a million to Indonesian territory, West Timor, where they went into brutal concentration camps, the rest driven up into the mountains, where they were mostly starving. Most of the country was devastated.

If you look at the *Far Eastern Economic Review,* published by Dow Jones — not on the left, and in the past rather solicitous of the sensibilities of Suharto and the military — they had a report saying that children and the elderly, the most vulnerable, are dying at a very high rate from preventable diseases in East Timor because the Indonesians poisoned the wells with dead bodies and chemicals, destroyed the water supplies, in fact destroyed most of the country.[18]

All through this period, what's the U.S. doing? It's saying, Our official position, repeated on September 8, after the worst atrocities, is that it is the responsibility of the government of Indonesia and we don't want to take it away from them. At the same time the Pentagon announced that it had just carried out joint military exercises with Indonesia. They ended on August 25, five days before the referendum. They were aimed at training the Indonesians in human rights and humanitarian exercises. That's kind of mind-boggling.

Remember that this is against the background of endless atroci-

ties resulting in the killing of maybe a third or a quarter of the population in earlier years, with crucial U.S. support all the way through.
We're just talking about the tail end of it. What happened? The U.S.
position was, as they put it, rather elegantly, "We don't have a dog
running in the East Timor race." By September 10, they recognized,
as they also put it, "We do have a very big dog running down there,"
namely Australia.[19]

The Australians did send troops into East Timor.

The Australian population was furious and was forcing the Australian government to do something, pleading with the United States
to get involved. Clinton finally made some mild gesture of disap-
proval and for a while they suspended relations with the Indonesian
military and stopped sending arms. The U.S. government was sending arms all through this. It's striking what happened. The Indonesian generals immediately reversed course, 180 degrees. They were
saying, Nobody's going to ever get into East Timor. We're going to
run the place. A day later they were saying, Good-bye. We're getting
out. That tells you what the latent power was all along.

After the Indonesians announced they were withdrawing, a
peacekeeping force was allowed to enter. This is after everything
had happened. And then the U.S. did nothing. There were a half a
million people starving in the mountains. No air drops. There were
Australian air drops, but nothing from the U.S. Air Force, which is
certainly capable of it. They can carry out pinpoint bombing of civil-
ian targets and anti-Milosevic opposition centers like Novi Sad, but
they can't drop food in the mountains to people who are starving
and have been driven there through our fault.

Interestingly, there was no call for air drops from the liberal intellectuals who were just euphoric about their own magnificence
during the chorus of self-praise of the preceding six months. I
couldn't find a word saying, Why don't we drop food to people
starving in the mountains in East Timor, whom we've driven there?
Hundreds of thousands were kept in the camps in West Timor,
which is Indonesian territory. According to the United Nations
High Commissioner for Refugees, the refugee organization, it's the
only place in the world where they didn't have free access to the ref-

ugee camps. When they or the Red Cross did occasionally get in, they reported awful conditions, people dying. The U.S. made a couple of statements, but it didn't do anything about it. It's still doing nothing. We ought to be paying huge reparations. This is one of the major atrocities of the last part of the awful century that's just over, and we're directly responsible, from the beginning in 1975 right through mid-September 1999.

So there was no intervention in any meaningful sense of term, and no humanitarian intervention, though there were humanitarian motives on the part of the Australian people, who compelled their government to react. On the part of the U.S. and Britain, the major culprits — the leaders of the enlightened states as they are depicted by responsible intellectuals — there was simply support for Indonesia while it was carrying out the atrocities, from the beginning and again through the worst atrocities. It tells us quite a lot about humanitarian intervention, and about the operative principles and values, for anyone who really cares about the matter.

There's a striking contrast between how the situations in Kosovo and East Timor were handled.

The sharp contrast between Kosovo and East Timor goes even further. In Kosovo, as soon as the fighting was over, NATO forces entered, actually in violation of the peace accord, but let's put that aside. As soon as they entered and took over, the place was flooded with forensics experts, probably thousands of them, trying to dig up anything they could to show Serb atrocities, which is kind of an interesting logic. If you think it through, the worse the atrocities, the greater the crime of NATO.

Suppose nobody had been killed. Then you could give an argument for the bombing. You could say that it prevented likely atrocities. On the other hand, if, say, a million people were killed, you have to say that the NATO bombing was a huge crime and led to enormous atrocities. But, because of the effectiveness of propaganda, the logic is the other way around.

In this case, the propaganda line is that if there were atrocities following the NATO bombing and obviously elicited by it, then that gives retrospective justification to the bombing. It's an astonishing thesis, but it's almost universally accepted. So the advocates of the war are trying to show the highest numbers of atrocities, and opponents of the war are trying to show the lowest numbers. It's a strange picture, unless one accepts the principle that if we do something with the anticipation that it's going to lead to an escalation of atrocities, it's justified by the fact that the atrocities took place. It's an amazing propaganda assumption.

In Kosovo, the place is flooded with forensic experts trying to find anything they can. Take a look at East Timor. The U.N. mission was pleading for forensics experts. They weren't sent. They were withheld. Some came in with the Australian forces, but virtually none. The U.N. and everyone continued to point out, If you delay sending forensics experts until the rainy season, November, everything's going to be wiped out. It's the tropics. East Timor is a poor country. It's all happening in little villages. Nothing's going to be left if you wait until the rainy season. But they withheld them.

Forensics experts were supposed to be coming in late January. Whether they actually did or not, I don't know, because the coverage is so bad. But it was planned to send them in late January. I hadn't heard that they arrived. Even if they did, it doesn't make any difference. It's all over. In East Timor it was extremely important not to know what happened. There's a good reason for that. In this case the logic is impeccable. If you find out what happened, somebody's going to figure out who's responsible. And that goes right back to Washington and London.

What about the issue of war crimes tribunals? Have any been proposed for those responsible for the massacres in East Timor?

That's quite interesting. In the case of Serbia, the U.S. and Britain demanded an indictment right in the midst of the bombing, and they got it, of course. So in May 1999, the International Court issued an indictment against Slobodan Milosevic and other gangsters. Of course the indictment is accurate, probably very accurate. For the first time ever, the court was given U.S. and British intelligence, which had been withheld prior to that. In this case, they were so eager to get an indictment that they provided intelligence information. If you look over the declassified intelligence information, it often is accurate. In fact, in this case it actually undermines the NATO case if you look at it prior to the bombing. But I assume it's accurate.

It's kind of interesting. If you read the indictment, with marginal exceptions, it's about crimes committed *after* the bombings started. The same is true of the State Department documentation to justify the war, and in fact everything we have. But there was an indictment, using high-level British and U.S. intelligence given to the court. That's right in the middle of the bombing. It was necessary to support the propaganda effort.

What about East Timor? The U.N. mission called for an international tribunal. It was very quickly scotched. Remember, it's Indonesia's responsibility, and we don't want to take it away from them. That line persisted. So there can be an Indonesian tribunal.

In fact, there's a pretty honest Indonesian prosecutor and civil rights organization that tried to organize a tribunal. What was reported here is that the Indonesian tribunal will only look at events after the referendum. That's not quite true. It said it would look at events earlier. But here in the press it was reported that way and that's the way it'll probably be, or be reported at least. You can predict with fair confidence that if there is an Indonesian tribunal, it will overwhelmingly keep to events after the referendum — not to the atrocities that were going on earlier in the year, which were well beyond Kosovo pre-bombing, and certainly not to what went on for the twenty-five years before. It will be very carefully contained. Also, if it's an Indonesian tribunal, however honest the prosecutor may be, the chances of getting very far are not particularly high.

In fact, the president of the country has already given a preemptive pardon to General Wiranto, the general in charge. So if he's ever indicted, he's already been pardoned. Just as, incidentally, Suharto got a pardon in advance of a potential investigation. So there will probably be an Indonesian tribunal run by honest people, but the chances of their doing anything are slight. It will be focused on the post-referendum atrocities, which is important from the U.S. point of view. Then you can argue — falsely, but not absurdly — that there wasn't much time to do anything. In fact, if you look before August 30, there was clearly plenty of time. They knew what was going on and what the Indonesian generals were announcing about their plans, and kept supporting it.

In fact, as a side comment, just two weeks ago an Indonesian general was invited here by the State Department, one of the generals from East Timor who was involved in the atrocities. It was supposed to be a festive occasion. But it was spoiled by the annoying activists from the Center for Constitutional Rights. He was served a subpoena for crimes committed in East Timor. That can be done now under the Alien Tort Claims Act, which is centuries old but is now being used for such cases.[20]

Nothing has been reported here, but it's been reported in Indonesia. The State Department apologized profusely for this gross indecency. I presume he'll flee the country, which is what usually happens in such cases, and he may even be tried and indicted, which has happened a couple of times. But this isn't the right kind of exciting event, so we don't have it on the front pages, or even in small print.

So there may be a tribunal, but if so, focused narrowly, or at least reported that way. It will avoid the higher-ups. It will certainly avoid the leading culprits, the U.S. and Britain. The chances that they'll be brought in approach zero, just as their role has been ignored, to quite an astonishing extent, in the United States for twenty-five years, right to the present. The most that is said is that we "looked away," or "didn't do enough" to stop the terror in which we were enthusiastically participating. Maybe because we were so exhausted by the terrible experience of Vietnam, or for "Cold War" reasons, an excuse that can be trotted out for every occasion, no matter how remote the connection.

It's quite different in Yugoslavia. There, it's now fashionable to blame all the horrors of the Balkan wars on Milosevic. It's the other fellow's crimes that arouse horror and indignation, not those for which we share responsibility and which we could therefore terminate or mitigate. These must be marginalized or suppressed, a crucial requirement of any well-functioning doctrinal system and a prime responsibility of responsible public intellectuals.

Is the U.S. or NATO doing anything to clean up the mess they left behind in the Balkans? The war caused enormous environmental and infrastructural damage, in addition to its immediate toll.

Both in Kosovo and East Timor the U.S. is refusing to undertake constructive efforts, with marginal exceptions. Alongside the radical differences — of a systematic character, as any honest inquiry will show — there are also some important similarities between the East Timor and Kosovo cases.

In Kosovo, for example, they won't clear the unexploded cluster bombs that are all over the place. That's a war crime. Serbs are being tried at an international tribunal for that crime, for using missiles with cluster bombs. People have been tried and convicted for that. Not NATO, of course. And the U.S. won't clear them. It's giving very little assistance to Kosovo. It's somebody else's responsibility. We bomb, but we don't help.

The same is true in East Timor. The U.S. has only provided trivial amounts of aid. Clinton called for a reduction of the small U.N. peacekeeping force that might be helping to overcome our crimes. All of this passes without comment. And this is supposed to be the era of humanitarian intervention, the era in which our principles and values are opening up a new world. These are things that people should look at if they're interested in humanitarian intervention.

Let's talk about what is happening in northern Iraq and in Turkey right now, where the Turkish government is involved in ethnic cleansing of the Kurds.

On April 1 of this year, the Turkish army initiated new ground sweeps in southeastern Turkey, in one of the regions which has been most devastated by U.S.-backed ethnic cleansing and other atrocities in the Clinton period. There have been huge atrocities, with 3,500 Kurdish villages destroyed and a couple of million refugees. Turkey has an annual spring offensive. They have another one going on right now. They also invaded northern Iraq to kill more Kurds.

Almost at the moment, to the minute, practically, that the Turkish offensive was beginning, Defense Secretary Cohen was giving a talk to the American Turkish Council, with a lot of laughter and applause, praising Turkey for its contributions to preventing ethnic cleansing by bombing Yugoslavia with F-16s that are either sent them by the U.S. or coproduced with the U.S. in Turkey and are, incidentally, used to carry out massive ethnic cleansing inside NATO. Turkey is a member of NATO. All this is inside NATO, not across its borders, with a huge flow of American arms. Cohen praised Turkey for its contributions to preventing terror and stopping ethnic cleansing by participating in the humanitarian bombing of Yugoslavia.[21] This is mind-boggling.

The Turkish case is a real monstrosity. In northern Iraq, Turkey is following the U.S.-backed Israeli model. For twenty-two years, Israel has occupied parts of southern Lebanon in violation of Security Council orders. Because the U.S. authorized it, it's OK. In that time, they killed maybe 45,000 Lebanese and Palestinian civilians and repeatedly drove hundreds of thousands of people out of their homes.

Cohen went on to announce — this is the first announcement — that Turkey would be participating in the development of a new, advanced fighter bomber, the strike bomber project that is expected to cost hundreds of billions of dollars. It will be coproduced in Turkey as a reward for their stellar record defending the world against terror and ethnic cleansing. There was not a word reported about any of this, though it is certainly known in the newsrooms. Again, these are questions that one should think about when asking about humanitarian intervention.

Can you think of any positive examples of humanitarian intervention?

When you look at the historical record honestly, it's extremely hard to find any examples of use of military force undertaken for genuine humanitarian aims. In fact, a possible thesis is that the category is empty. Maybe you can find an example, but it's not going to be easy.

If you look at the big casebooks of international law, humanitarian law, they offer some cases. The case they usually fall back on is French intervention in the Levant in 1860 to protect Christians who were being killed by Muslims. When you look into that in any detail, you find that this is not what was happening. That was part of the game that was being played between the Ottoman Empire and the French and the British to see who was going to control the area. It's true that some Christians were being killed, but that wasn't the reason for the intervention.

In every case you look at that I know of, it pretty quickly falls apart. States are not moral agents. They do not engage in the use of force for humanitarian ends, although that's always claimed. Maybe there are some authentic cases.

There are interventions that have had humanitarian consequences. Getting rid of Hitler was a humanitarian consequence, although incidentally it wasn't an intervention. The U.S. got into the war when it was attacked. Germany declared war on the United States, not the other way around. But the military action was one that I did support as a kid and would support now.

In the post–Second World War period, there were a few cases, two that I know of, that are genuine: the Vietnamese invasion of Cambodia, which got rid of Pol Pot, and the Indian invasion of what is now Bangladesh, which stopped a huge atrocity. They were not undertaken with humanitarian intent, so they're not humanitarian interventions, but they did have humanitarian consequences. For those who are interested in our principles and values and humanitarian intervention, it's worth looking at the reaction.

In both cases, and these are the only convincing cases that I know of in the postwar period, the U.S. reaction was total fury. So Vietnam had to be punished severely for getting rid of Pol Pot, and it was. The U.S. imposed extremely harsh sanctions. The U.S. supported a Chinese invasion to teach them a lesson. And the U.S. turned to open diplomatic support of Pol Pot.

In the case of India, the same thing applies. The Seventh Fleet was mobilized, and there were threats of war. India had to be punished. Again there was a China connection. Kissinger at that time was planning a secret trip to China that was going to open up Sino-American relations and he was going to go through Pakistan. That was apparently the main reason for the hysteria about the India action. It might spoil some surprising and exciting photo ops in Beijing. So therefore a couple million more people have to be murdered. That's about what it amounts to.

Notice that there was a China connection in both cases. In between the two came Indonesia's invasion of East Timor, which we had to support, it was claimed, because of the threat of China. It gives some insight into the flexibility of Cold War pretexts. Those are the two clearest cases of intervention that had humanitarian consequences.

There were others, but they're more dubious, like the Tanzanian intervention to overthrow Idi Amin. Getting rid of Idi Amin was fine, but the trouble was that Milton Obote, who came in, was as bad or worse. So the humanitarian consequences are not easy to detect. Incidentally, Idi Amin had been getting Western support, but that's another story.

I want to come back to the idea of what individuals can do in overcoming orthodoxies. Steve Biko, the South African activist who was murdered by the Apartheid regime while he was in custody, once said that "the most potent weapon of the oppressor is the mind of the oppressed." [22]

That's quite accurate. Most oppression succeeds because its legitimacy is internalized. That's true of the most extreme cases. Take, say, slavery. It wasn't easy to revolt if you were a slave, by any means. But if you look over the history of slavery, it was in some sense just recognized as the way things are. We'll do the best we can under this regime.

Another example is women's rights. There the oppression is extensively internalized and accepted as legitimate and proper. It's still true today, but it's been true throughout history. That's true in case after case.

Or take working people. At one time in the United States, in the mid-nineteenth century, working for wage labor was considered not very different from chattel slavery. That was not an unusual position. That was the slogan of the Republican Party, the banner under which Northern workers fought in the Civil War. We're against chattel slavery and wage slavery. Free people do not rent themselves to others. Maybe you're forced to do it temporarily, but that's only on the way to becoming a free person, or "free man," to put it in the rhetoric of the day. You become a free man when you're not compelled to take orders from others. That's an Enlightenment ideal.

Incidentally, this was not coming from European radicalism. These were workers in Lowell, Massachusetts, a couple of miles from where we are. You could even read editorials in the *New York Times* saying this around that time. It took a long time to drive into people's heads the idea that it is legitimate to rent yourself. Now that's unfortunately pretty much accepted. So that's internalizing oppression. Anyone who thinks it's legitimate to be a wage laborer is internalizing oppression in a way which would have seemed intolerable to people in the mills, let's say, 150 years ago. So that's again internalizing oppression, and it's an achievement.

Just as Biko says, it's a tremendous achievement of the oppressors to instill their assumptions as the perspective from which you look at the world. Sometimes it's done extremely consciously, like the public relations industry. Sometimes it's just kind of routine, the way you live. To liberate yourselves from those preconceptions and perspectives is to take a long step toward overcoming oppression.

Let's discuss the role of intellectuals in this equation. There's a lot of talk today about public intellectuals. Does that term mean anything to you?

That's an old idea. Public intellectuals are the ones who are supposed to present the values and principles and understanding. They're the ones who took pride in driving the U.S. into war during World War I. They were public intellectuals.

On the other hand, Eugene Debs wasn't a public intellectual. In fact, he was in jail. A very vindictive Woodrow Wilson refused to grant him amnesty when everyone else was getting Christmas amnesty. Why wasn't Eugene Debs a public intellectual? The reason is that he was an intellectual who happened to be on the side of poor people and working people. He was the leading figure in the U.S. labor movement. He was a presidential candidate. Despite the fact that he was running outside the main political system, he got plenty of votes. He was telling the truth about the First World War, which is why he was thrown into jail.

Look back at what he was saying, it's quite accurate. So he was thrown into jail and wasn't a public intellectual. Public intellectuals are the ones who are acceptable within some mainstream spectrum as presenting ideas, as standing up for values. Sometimes what they do is not bad, maybe even very good. But again, take a look at humanitarian intervention. The people who do not accept the principles, the assumptions, rarely qualify as public intellectuals, no matter how famous they are.

Take Bertrand Russell, who by any standard is one of the leading intellectual figures of the twentieth century. He was one of the very few leading intellectuals who opposed World War I. He was vilified, and in fact ended up in jail, like his counterparts in Germany. From the 1950s, particularly in the United States, he was bitterly denounced and attacked as a crazy old man who was anti-American. Why? Because he was standing up for the principles that other intellectuals also accepted, but he was doing something about it.

For example, Bertrand Russell and Albert Einstein, to take another leading intellectual, essentially agreed on things like nuclear weapons. They thought nuclear weapons might well destroy the species. They signed similar statements, I think even joint statements. But then they reacted differently. Einstein went back to his office in the Institute for Advanced Studies at Princeton and worked on unified field theories. Russell, on the other hand, went out in the streets. He was part of the demonstrations against nuclear weapons. He became quite active in opposing the Vietnam War early on, at a time when there was virtually no public opposition. He also tried to do something about that, including demonstrations and organizing a tribunal. So he was bitterly denounced.

On the other hand, Einstein was a saintly figure. They essentially had the same positions, but Einstein didn't rattle too many cages. That's pretty common. Russell was viciously attacked in the *New York Times* and by Secretary of State Dean Rusk and others in the 1960s. He wasn't counted as a public intellectual, just a crazy old man. There's a good book on this called *Bertrand Russell's America.*[23]

You make yourself available for various groups all over the country. You made that choice pretty early on. Why don't other intellectuals, other privileged people in your position, get engaged politically?

Individuals have their own reasons. Presumably the reason most don't is because they think they're doing the right thing. That is, I'm sure that overwhelmingly people who are supportive of atrocious acts of power and privilege do believe and convince themselves that it was the right thing to do, which is extremely easy.

In fact, a standard technique of belief formation is to do something in your own interest and then to construct a framework in which that's the right thing to do. We all know this from our own experience. Nobody's saintly enough that they haven't illegitimately done that any number of times, from when you stole a toy from your younger brother when you were seven years old until the present.

We always manage to construct our own framework that says, Yes, that was the right thing to do and it's going to be good. Sometimes the conclusions are accurate. It's not always self-deception. But it's very easy to fall into self-deception when it's advantageous. It's not surprising.

And when you have the culture and the media celebrating...

It is advantageous. If you convince yourself, or just maybe cynically decide to play the game by the official rules, you benefit, a lot. On the other hand, if you don't play the game by those rules and you, say, follow Bertrand Russell's path, you're a target. In some states you may get killed. If it's a U.S. client state, you may get killed.

We've just passed the twentieth anniversary of the assassination of Oscar Romero, a conservative archbishop who tried to be a "voice for the voiceless" in El Salvador. So he was assassinated by U.S.-backed forces. The anniversary of his assassination just passed, incidentally, but there was virtually nothing in the mainstream national press about it. Practically the only place where the assassination was reported was Los Angeles. The *Los Angeles Times* had an article.[24] Los Angeles happens to have the biggest Salvadoran community in the country, and Archbishop Romero is kind of a saint there, so they had a piece. But basically the media ignored it.

A few months earlier, last November, was the tenth anniversary of the murder of six leading Latin American Jesuit intellectuals in El Salvador by the forces armed and trained by the United States. This was part of a large-scale massacre, but they happened to be murdered with particular brutality.

If, say, Václav Havel and half a dozen other Czech intellectuals had their brains blown out by Russian-run forces ten years ago, the anniversary would have been noted, and people would know their names. In this case, again, there was essentially nothing. Their names were literally not mentioned in the U.S. press.

In addition to the six Jesuit intellectuals, their housekeeper and her fifteen-year-old daughter were murdered.

And hundreds of other people were killed whose names you never heard of. It is intriguing, instructive, that no one knows the names of the assassinated Salvadoran intellectuals. If you ask well-educated public intellectuals or your well-educated friends, Can you name any of the Salvadoran intellectuals who were murdered by U.S.-run forces, it's very rare that anyone will know a name.

These were distinguished people. One was the rector of the leading university. Some people who were involved in Central American solidarity work know about them. But everybody knows the names of the East European dissidents and reads their books and praises them. They suffered repression. But in the post-Stalin period nothing remotely like the treatment regularly meted out to dissidents in the Western domains. It's a very enlightening reaction.

Actually, the story gets worse. Right after they were murdered, in 1990, Václav Havel came to Washington and gave a rousing address to a joint session of Congress in which he praised the "defenders of freedom," in his words, who were responsible for just murdering six of his counterparts.[25] That led to a euphoric reaction, rapture in the U.S., and editorials in the *Washington Post* asking, Why can't we have magnificent intellectuals like that who come and praise us as defenders of freedom? Anthony Lewis wrote about how "we live in a romantic age."[26] That's quite interesting.

What happens if you're a dissident intellectual in our domains? In the rich societies like the U.S. and England, you don't get murdered. If you're a black leader, you might get murdered, but for relatively privileged people you're secure from violent repression. On the other hand, there are other reactions that plenty of people don't like. In fact, about the only way to continue to do it is not to care. For example, if you have contempt for the mainstream intellectual community and you really don't care, then you're safe.

On the other hand, if you want to be accepted by them, if you want to be praised and have your books reviewed and told how brilliant you are and get great jobs, it's not advisable to be a dissident. It's not impossible, and in fact the system has enough looseness in it so that it can be done, but it is not easy. Both of us can name plenty of people who were simply cut out of the system because their work was too honest. That blocks access. It's not like having your brains blown out or being thrown in jail, but it's not nice.

One activist scholar whom you knew was Eqbal Ahmad. He died in Pakistan in May 1999. You spoke at a tribute in his honor at Hampshire College. He told me once that after he had been released from jail, you flew to Chicago and spent some time with him. Do you remember that?

I've done such things so often I don't know. Yes, probably.

It was very important to him. He didn't know you very well then. This was in the early 1970s.

I do remember flying to Chicago a couple of times. One of the trips that is very clear in my memory is going to Fred Hampton's funeral. That was another case of a person who should have been a public intellectual, a very important figure, in this case from the black community, who was murdered. It was a straight Gestapo-style assassination set up by the FBI. That is exactly what it was. We don't have to debate the facts. They were all conceded in court.

How many people remember Fred Hampton? In fact, he was assassinated by the Nixon administration. It never came up in Watergate. You want to assassinate a black leader, that's fine. So when I said you're secure from repression if you're relatively privileged — that doesn't apply if you're not privileged.

Eqbal Ahmad also told me that he did suffer rather serious consequences for his militancy. He had difficulties at Cornell. He couldn't get a job in the academy. Finally, little Hampshire College in Amherst gave him a job in 1982.

He was a person who was doing quite impressive academic work. That's a case in point, in fact. There are others who were treated much more badly.

What's your assessment of Ahmad and your memory of him?

First of all, in his personal life he was a very dedicated and honorable activist. He was right in the middle of everything. Also, his writings alone were quite important. He was giving a critical, analytic account of international affairs, the U.S. role in them, and the problems of oppressed peoples all over the world, from North Africa to the Middle East to Indochina. He was a student of revolution and imperialism, and a very good one. That was serious and important work. He did manage to get published now and then in the major journals. Not often, but sometimes.

Let's talk about the situation in South Asia, an area that Eqbal Ahmad was very concerned with, particularly in his later years, when he resettled in Pakistan. Clinton was there in mid-March, and he called it "the most dangerous place in the world." [27]

Most dangerous, I don't know. But it's dangerous. The nuclear testing in India and then Pakistan significantly increases the threat of a nuclear war. There's a big conflict over Kashmir which has been going on for a long time, and India and Pakistan have had several wars in which both of them were armed by the West. And there could be another one.

For Clinton to say that takes a slight touch of hypocrisy. Part of the reason that India developed nuclear weapons is as a deterrent against the United States. That's understood in the mainstream. John Mearsheimer, a political scientist at the University of Chicago, had an op-ed in the *New York Times* about nuclear issues in South Asia. [28] He mentions that part of the reason why India felt impelled to develop nuclear weapons was the U.S.-led wars in the Gulf and in the Balkans. That's quite generally understood around the world, though public intellectuals in Europe and the United States don't talk about it.

You mean, they tested again in the late 1990s.

They had developed nuclear weapons, but carrying out the tests, which is a big step, was apparently in part because like many other countries, they feel that they need a deterrent against the U.S., a rogue state that is unconstrained. That was a very broad reaction to the Balkans war. Even in client states like Israel, leading military analysts pointed out that the U.S. is becoming a danger to the world and other countries are going to have to develop weapons of mass destruction simply to defend themselves. They pointed out that if Serbia had owned nuclear or chemical and biological weapons, the West wouldn't have been so quick to bomb them. Everybody can understand that. That was part of the reason why India proceeded to carry out testing of nuclear weapons. That's part of the reason. There are others.

Clinton criticized India for violating the Nonproliferation Treaty. But the United States regularly violates it. For one thing, the U.S. Congress — this isn't Clinton's fault — refused to pass the Comprehensive Test Ban Treaty. But the Nonproliferation Treaty itself is violated by the U.S. The treaty calls for good-faith efforts to reduce nuclear weapons on the part of the nuclear states. The United States and other nuclear powers succeeded in keeping out of the treaty a call for eliminating nuclear weapons. It's only other people who shouldn't have them. That's all the nuclear states. But part of it is a call for good-faith efforts to reduce them.

The U.S. has certainly not done that. In fact, it's going in the opposite direction. Just a couple of days ago they announced that they were going to add 6,000 additional nuclear weapons, rehabilitating old ones, over and above the levels permitted by the Strategic Arms Reduction Talks treaty. The missile defense system that's now being advocated by the Clinton administration, Star Wars Lite, is recognized throughout the world, and in fact by most military analysts right here, to be a step toward increasing the threat of nuclear war. There are many who are very critical of it. The last issue of the *Bulletin of the Atomic Scientists* was full of discussion about this.[29]

In India and other countries, it's understood that this is a weapon against them. A national missile defense system is in effect a first-strike weapon. It means that you can protect yourself against a retaliatory strike by a country with limited nuclear power, not against Russia, but against China. Or India. It neutralizes the deterrent and therefore compels China or India to move to higher levels of destructive capacity. Just a couple of days ago, I got an article from an Indian general discussing it. Furthermore, even if China alone reacts, as it presumably would, that would lead to Indian moves to deter China, and Pakistani moves in response, and Israeli moves, and so on. It's no big secret. These are steps toward increasing the danger of nuclear war.

Furthermore, it is well understood that this national missile defense system, the weak missile defense system, is a threat against major nuclear powers, too, like Russia, because it can quickly be escalated. It probably won't work, but forgetting that, these things don't have to work. People only need to think there's a possibility that they might work, that will lead to development of weapons of mass destruction as a stronger deterrent.

And it is understood that once in place, even a weak system can quickly be strengthened to pose a first-strike threat even to a major military power. So it will lead, very likely, as predicted, to a proliferation of nuclear weapons, just as the bombing of Yugoslavia apparently did, as had been predicted by strategic analysts. All of this is part of the background against which we have to listen to Clinton lecturing India on what in fact is a criminal act. To test nuclear weapons in this day and age, or anytime, is criminal.

I don't know if you noticed, but actually at a state dinner, the president of India, K.R. Narayanan, lectured him back.

I did read that. He is not a nice person, incidentally, and comes from an awful political party, but that's a separate issue. If you look at the debate over nuclear testing in India, these were the issues that were raised. India was extremely critical of the Balkans war, in part for these reasons. Throughout most of the world, outside of Europe and the English-speaking countries, the war was just regarded as gunboat diplomacy. Here are the imperial powers again beating up somebody who's in the way.

Pakistan today is routinely described as bankrupt and corrupt. In October there was a military coup that brought General Pervez Musharraf to power, overthrowing Nawaz Sharif. Pakistan was very useful to the U.S. during the Cold War in the Middle East, as well as South Asia. One retired Pakistani general told the writer Tariq Ali that Pakistan was "the condom that the Americans needed to enter Afghanistan."[30]

That's true, and in fact the Taliban were trained, and Tariq Ali has pointed this out, in Pakistani religious schools and turned into real maniacs. With Pakistani army support they've taken over Afghanistan and turned it into a horror chamber and are now aiming to do the same in Pakistan, and may. It's not clear. It's part of what Eqbal Ahmad was struggling against in the last years of his life.

It was not just Afghanistan. Pakistan was part of the system by which the U.S. controlled the Middle East. The Saudi Royal Guard protecting the Saudi royal family from its own population, not from anybody else, was Pakistani for a long time. It was part of the system of peripheral states, like Israel and Turkey, and Iran under the Shah, that was used to protect the monarchies in the oil-producing regions against the threat of their own populations.

Pakistan was part of that. Now it's not so pliable, and the U.S. is unhappy with the way it's going. It's sort of out of control. Clinton signaled that pretty clearly by his brief stop in Pakistan after a long visit to their major enemy.

He spent five days in India and five hours in Pakistan.

It was a very clear signal. Everyone understood it. In fact, he's trying to reconstruct relations with India. India is carrying out what are called reforms, so it's now moving itself into the U.S.-dominated system, which it hadn't done before, with interesting effects on the country. Here it's regarded by good economists, and not totally falsely, as a great success.

Reforms were instituted in 1990 and 1991. "Reforms" means liberalization and opening the country up to foreign investment, subordinating the country to the corporate-dominated globalization system. So naturally we're in favor of that. India's macroeconomic statistics are not bad, so there's been growth and great praise for India, despite objections that it is moving too slowly. It didn't liberalize finance, as South Korea did under U.S. pressure. This is part of the reason, it is widely assumed, that South Korea was hit so hard by the Asian financial crisis while India, like China, stayed more or less immune. There's a fair amount of U.S. and other foreign investment coming in, a lot of buying up of the country. But there's more to it, as usual.

India, unlike the United States and like practically every other industrial country outside the U.S., keeps regular social statistics. The U.S. is maybe the only industrial country that doesn't do this. India has a regular publication of social indicators. The central statistical office does sample studies every year and big studies every five years. Those are interesting. India is mostly a rural country, so the interesting question is, What's happening to the rural population? They study poverty, per capita consumption, and per capita production in the rural areas. Pre-reform, up until 1990, rural poverty was sharply decreasing. Both per capita consumption and per capita production were going up in the rural areas, including non-agricultural production, because they were putting money into non-agricultural production.

In 1990, all those figures reverse. Rural poverty stagnates or gets worse. Consumption again stagnates or declines, and production decreases in 1991, not by accident. That's when the reforms were instituted, and the reforms have a lot of effects. For one thing, they opened the country up to subsidized foreign agricultural imports, which undercut poor farmers. Public spending declines under "reforms," which also require reducing resources for rural development. And it shows. That's the other side, not the side you read about unless you're reading the Indian press. And that's very typical, incidentally.

In the United States, unlike other industrial countries, there's no national government review of social statistics, but there are private reviews. The main one is done at Fordham University, a Jesuit university in New York, which has an institute that publishes regular annual measures of social indicators like child abuse, hunger, illiteracy, and average wages. They also have a composite measure. The results are interesting. They just came out with their latest volume.[31] From about, say, 1960 up until the mid-1970s, social indicators improved. Indicators tracked GDP, gross domestic product. GDP is a kind of mixed measure. It doesn't measure economic health in any reasonable sense, but it measures something.

So with the growth of the economy by this gross measure, social indicators improved. The line was practically the same line. It tracks it closely. In the mid-1970s the two curves separate. GDP continues to go up, social indicators start to go down, not just stagnate. And they've been going down since the mid-1970s, with a slight upturn in the late 1990s. They're now at a level of about 1959, when the study started.

What happened in the mid-1970s? The U.S. started undergoing reforms, not unlike the structural adjustment programs designed for the poor countries. And with the usual consequences. Here's the leading democracy of the South and the leading democracy of the North showing very much the same pattern. The Fordham investigators called this a "social recession" in the United States. It's one part of the story which is not shown in the applause for the wonderful new era we're in.

In fact, there's another side of the story which is known to economists but is barely reported. That is that even the major economic indicators have deteriorated since the reforms began worldwide. A couple of years ago there was a Bretton Woods commission headed by Paul Volcker, the former head of the Federal Reserve Board, and a very respectable figure in the profession. Their report came out about five years ago.[32] They studied what had happened to the global economy and the U.S. economy since the so-called reforms were instituted in the early 1970s, when the post–World War II Bretton Woods system was dismantled. Their conclusion was that in the industrial countries economic growth had declined by half. It was still growth, but half the rate of the previous period. Other studies make it about two-thirds. A significant decline in growth. That's only one thing.

There has also been a decline in capital investment. There's been a productivity decline. There's been a sharp increase in interest rates, which slows the economy. There have been repeated financial crises, increase of the volatility of financial markets. In the U.S., strikingly, there has been a stagnation of wages, which is extremely unusual in economic history. Usually wages go up as economic growth goes up, and that has not happened in the last decades. In the last couple of years in the U.S. that's changing a little bit, but it still hasn't affected the general picture. There has also been a very sharp increase in working hours, now higher in the U.S. than in any other industrial country. The general picture is quite striking.

What's been happening to growth rates outside the industrialized countries? Are those also declining?

UNCTAD just came out with its annual trade and development report. They found the same thing for the so-called developing countries. They report a sharp decline in growth rates, on average, in the past twenty years, since "reforms" were instituted, and deterioration in other macroeconomic indicators as well.[33]

The president of the World Bank, James Wolfensohn, pointed out that in Latin America the situation is like it was in the 1970s. He said Latin America's economy has been stagnant for twenty years, despite the reforms.[34] The word "despite" draws a conclusion based on weak theoretical and empirical grounds — and deeply held ideological convictions — which have to at least be recognized and evaluated.

That's pretty much the picture for the whole world. If you take a close look, things are different here and there, particularly for Asian countries that didn't follow the rules, but it's a very general picture. That's just macroeconomic statistics. When you look at social indicators, meaning what matters for people's lives, then you find, fairly generally, a picture similar to India and the United States. For a sector, for the Silicon Valley millionaires, it's great. If you look at the people who are writing the articles about the fairy tale economy, it's fine for them. They, like me, come from the small sector of the population that's benefiting enormously from the relatively slow growth that has been going on. Most of the population is not. They're like those people we were talking about before, working day and night to try to keep food on the table. Same in India, same in the U.S., same worldwide.

So we have two phenomena that coincide pretty closely with the reforms, so closely that many very fine international economists — David Felix, who is an emeritus professor of economics at Washington University in St. Louis, for one — do not hesitate to conclude that they are related.[35] Particularly with regard to one component of the reforms, financial liberalization, it's fairly widely accepted. The Volcker Commission lent qualified support to that conclusion.

One phenomenon is a decline in general economic health. Not an absolute decline, but slower growth, slower improvement. Economic health is supposed to improve constantly. GDP should generally be going up all the time, even under poor conditions. But the major estimates of economic health are slowing. And there's also a split. For the majority of the population and most of the world, things are either stagnating or declining in terms of quality of life, and that's true of both of the two major democracies, of the North and the South. These are important things about the world. That's what the protests here and in other countries were about.

Going back to your earlier point about learning about this, it's not made easy for you. You have to work to find out what's happening to the rural population in India and what's happening to the majority of the population in the U.S. That's not the picture that's presented. That's quite different. You can find it out, but not without resources.

Just to return briefly to the situation in India, the country is the locus of tremendous resistance to globalization. Why is there this level of resistance in India? Does it have anything to do with the legacy of Gandhi?

First of all, India has a very rich and complex history. If you go back to the eighteenth century, India was the commercial and industrial center of the world. In the early nineteenth century, book publication in Bengal was probably higher per capita than in England, but India was severely harmed by the British occupation. The country was deindustrialized and turned into an impoverished rural society, though one maintaining a rich cultural tradition and a rich tradition of resistance.

The Gandhian legacy is there, but remember, there was a revolution that threw out the British. This included the Congress Party. There was a national movement and so on. And that remains. It's remained a vibrant, complex society.

After the British were thrown out, economic development resumed. It had stagnated for a couple hundred years, but it began again in a serious way. Also, in a very mixed fashion. India developed heavy industry and advanced technology.

On the other hand, the poverty is perhaps beyond that of anywhere in the world. It's like Central Africa, if you take a look at the quality of life — not just numbers, because it's a huge country, but averages. Take a look at the quality of life measures published by the U.N. *Human Development Report*.[36] South Asia is among the worst by most measures.

There's some very interesting work on this by Amartya Sen, who won the Nobel Prize in economics. Part of the major work that he did for which he got the prize was comparisons of India and China.[37] They're quite interesting. I looked carefully when he got the prize, and the subject was never mentioned. India and China are a good comparison. As Sen points out, they were at approximately the same level of development in the late 1940s, when the colonial period ended. They followed different courses. India followed the course of capitalist democracy. Here it's called socialist, but that's a joke. It's a state capitalist democracy, like all other capitalist democracies. China went through a Maoist period up until 1979 and then has moved on to "reform" in a complicated way. So these are interesting comparisons.

One comparison Sen makes is quite famous. It's been all over the *New York Times* and everywhere in the last couple of weeks. A book came out called *The Black Book of Communism,* which is about the huge crimes of communism.[38] We have to have the courage at last to face these crimes, previously ignored, as the new millennium opens; that's the general drift, with only slight exaggeration. The *Black Book* gives the shocking figure of 100 million deaths attributable to communism. Let's say it's right. Let's not argue about the numbers.

The worst example of the killing, the biggest component of this alleged 100 million, is the Chinese famine around 1958 to 1960. It's prominently discussed in the first issue of the *New York Times Review of Books* for the millennium and another one a couple of weeks later.[39] Maybe thirty million died in the famine. Sen studied that, and he points out that although India used to have plenty of famines under the British, it hasn't had famines like that since independence. So there was never a famine in India since the early 1950s in which huge numbers of people died as they did in China. Sen gives plausible reasons for it. He says this is related to India's specific forms of socioeconomic, political, and ideological development.

India is more or less democratic. It has a free press. Information comes back from the bottom to the top, and if there are signs of a famine, the central authorities will know about it and there will be protest about it. In China, which is a totalitarian state, no information gets back to the center, and any protest will be smashed, so you get huge famines. These are crimes of communism, traceable to the nature of the system.

That's half of what Sen says. The other half of his inquiry, which somehow escapes notice, has to do with another comparison. He says China in the late 1940s began to institute rural public health and educational programs, as well as other programs oriented toward the mass of the population. India, on the other hand, plays the game by our rules, and it didn't do any of this. And there are consequences, for example, in mortality rates. These started to decline sharply in China from around 1950 until 1979. Then they stopped declining, and started going up slightly. That was the period of the reforms. During the totalitarian period, from 1950 to about 1979, mortality rates declined. They declined in India, too, but much more slowly than in China up to 1979.

Sen then says, suppose you measure the number of extra deaths in India resulting annually from not carrying out these Maoist-style programs or others for the benefit of the population, what you would call reforms if the term wasn't so ideological. He estimates close to four million extra deaths every year in India, which means that, as he puts it, every eight years in India the number of skeletons in the closet is the same as in China's moment of shame, the famine. If you look at the whole period, it's about 100 million extra deaths in India alone after the democratic capitalist period enters.

This is the work that Sen has done in collaboration with Jean Drèze?

This is Amartya Sen in the books he's written together with his colleague, Jean Drèze.[40] This is no big secret. They're well-known books. This is right in the mainstream. Sen won the Nobel Prize in economics, after all, and publishes in the journal of the American Academy of Arts and Sciences. It's not easy to miss.

Suppose you were to undertake the same calculations that are used quite correctly to count up the crimes of communism. It turns out that in the leading democratic capitalist country of the South, in fact of the world, if you count population, that country alone just up until about 1980 has produced about 100 million dead, the same number that's attributed to all the communist countries of the twentieth century in the world. And that's of course only the beginning.

Suppose we carry out the same calculation on the same grounds elsewhere in the domains that are dominated by Western power. You're going to get astronomical figures. But this is not an acceptable topic. There can be no *Black Book* detailing such facts, just as there can be no realistic comparison of the utterly hideous Soviet record with the record of comparable countries that remained under Western domination, for example Brazil, taken over as a "testing area for modern scientific methods of industrial development" based solidly on capitalism, according to celebratory and respected scholarship, with consequences for the vast majority of the population that are hardly much to celebrate.[41]

So that's another part of India. It did develop in important, constructive ways, but also in very destructive ways, as Sen and Drèze point out, as part of the ideological, political, and social system that was instituted. It's as much a consequence as the Chinese famine is a consequence of Chinese totalitarianism.

The point becomes even clearer when we consider other cases that Sen, Drèze, and their colleagues investigate. One of the poorest states in India is Kerala, which is rather like Cuba in that though very poor, it has health and other quality-of-life standards far beyond the rest of India, more or less comparable to the rich developed countries in important respects. The reasons are again traceable to the use of resources — for health, literacy, women's education, and the like — instituted and maintained under Communist Party governance, incidentally, and maintained even by other governments because of the popularity of the programs.

In the case of China, the improvement in mortality rates stops around 1979 and in fact probably deteriorates. There's another part of the story, and that is that it's not unlike what we were discussing in the post-reform period in India, when things start getting worse for most of the population after not as much of an improvement as in China, but an improvement before the so-called pre-reform period. These are all things that ought to be studied and understood — which may, incidentally, not be so straightforward. In any system as complex as a human society, there are many intricate and interwoven factors. But the general picture, as Sen and Drèze point out, is rather striking. One should know the whole story, not just the half that supports Western power and the preferred self-image of Western elites.

This isn't exactly something you read about in the mainstream media

When I said I never saw a comment about this, it's not entirely true. I had an interview with an Indian economist after Sen won the prize. He asked me what I thought about it, and I mentioned the part of Sen's work that had mysteriously disappeared. He knew it in the back of his mind, but said he hadn't planned to write about it. He did, though. In the story that he wrote in India, this was included. I presume it's not the only case, but it's the only one I came across where this part of the story was included in the publicity about the Nobel Prize. This has never been mentioned in the studies of *Black Book*, as far as I've seen.

The commentary on the *Black Book* rightly condemns the horrifying and unspeakable crimes of communism, alleging absurdly that these condemnations are somehow new. It describes communism as a system of unique evil, with no redeeming features, with crimes that simply cannot be imagined — the worst being the Chinese famine. Surely the crimes cannot be comprehended by civilized people like us. We only gaze at them with awe and horror. As for crimes of the West, crimes of capitalism and democracies, maybe there are some minor flaws here and there, a failure to act promptly enough to respond to crimes of others, that sort of thing.

It's the same story as with the tribunals for Yugoslavia and East Timor that we talked about before.[42] On the most elementary moral principles, the reaction should be quite the opposite, if only because we can quite easily do something about our crimes. But to bring up such truisms commonly elicits fury, or else a blank stare of incomprehension.

There's an organization in India called the Narmada Bachao Andolan, the Movement to Save the Narmada, to stop some of the big dam projects. There are some very prominent activists involved, like Vandana Shiva, Arundhati Roy, Mehda Patkar and others, interestingly all women.

India is a complicated case. For a sector of the population, it's a rich and vibrant culture. The people you mentioned are figures of international renown. Roy is a well-known novelist and essayist. She wrote a novel, *The God of Small Things*, and many important essays, including "The Cost of Living." Activists there are carrying on a very important campaign against the dam and many other things.[43] The issues go well beyond World Bank development projects. They reach to the core of the form of "globalization" that has been instituted by Western power and the investor-rights agreements that are mislabeled "free trade agreements."

There was significant protest about these issues in India, huge demonstrations with hundreds of thousands of people. In fact, there was so much protest that the Indian Parliament couldn't pass the agreement with the World Trade Organization and it had to be kind of rammed through over their heads.

It's kind of interesting to see what's happened since. It hasn't been well studied, so I'm not confident about what I'm saying, but from what I can figure out, it's the following: The Indian pharmaceutical industry is no longer complaining about this. In fact, they're cheering for the new patent regime which prevents them from producing cheap pharmaceuticals.

Why are they doing that? Putting together the little I've been able to find, and this is a guess, what seems to have happened is that the pharmaceutical corporations have consolidated. A lot of them disappeared, a few of them got huge, and the directors realized that they could benefit from this. They have a very well-educated, highly trained, skilled labor force which is extremely cheap, just like software programmers. So they have very good scientists trained in a high-class educational system for the elites, and they pay them very little. So they can in fact develop new products, probably not the super-fancy ones that Merck will produce, but things that will make money, and then they can enjoy the monopoly rights that are given by the patent regime. So they can make plenty of money by exploiting the fact that they have a cheap, highly trained labor force, and then they can get into the act, too. That means the mass of the population isn't going to get cheap pharmaceuticals anymore, but that's somebody else's problem.

The economy as you describe it, particularly in the Nehru period, from 1947 to 1964, was a little bit more mixed than state capitalist, as you describe it. For example, the Indian Institutes of Technology are state-funded technical universities. Wasn't there a larger state sector in the economy?

Larger than what? Let's take a look at the United States, starting with me. I happen to work at a private university, MIT. So it's not the state sector, except take a look at where the funding comes from. I happened to be on a faculty-student committee looking at the university's funding in the middle of the student protests in 1969. I don't remember the figures exactly, but roughly about half the budget of this private university was devoted to running two secret military laboratories, one for advanced guidance systems for missiles and the other for electronics connected with the military. That's half the budget. What about the academic budget? At the time I think about 90 percent of it came from the Pentagon. Now that percentage is lower, but that mostly means more is coming from the National Institutes of Health (NIH) or the National Science Foundation. So it's overwhelmingly a government institution.

By now, there's corporate funding as well, which is harmful for the most part, although not entirely, to any institution. Sometimes it's for real research. But corporate funding tends to be more applied and also more secret. Pentagon funding is not secret. When you're working for the Pentagon, as I was, in fact, there were no constraints. You can do anything you like. If you're working on a project for a pharmaceutical corporation, it's likely to be an applied project for something they can profit from, soon; for them, not for their competitors, or for the society generally. That tends to lead to secrecy. They can't demand it formally, but they can make it clear that you're not going to be funded unless you meet secrecy conditions. So it imposes secrecy. There was even a case last year at MIT that made it to the *Wall Street Journal* when a student refused to answer a question on a test, though he said he knew the answer, because he was working with another professor in the same department who wanted the information kept secret because he was planning a startup.[44] This became a pretty big scandal. But those are the kinds of consequences you expect with corporate funding.

But for the most part MIT is publicly funded. The same is true of a good part of the R&D system, particularly the more exploratory and risky parts, with no short-term payoff. The more risky exploratory parts are overwhelmingly publicly funded. Of course India was not the same as the U.S. and the U.S. is not the same as Japan. Every two state capitalist countries are different if you look closely. The differences are not small. Nevertheless, there are very striking similarities that run through all of them, particularly with regard to socialization of cost and risk.

When you said that you were working for the Pentagon, do you mean that literally or figuratively?

I meant I was working for the Pentagon in a bookkeeping sense. I was working in a laboratory that happened to be 100 percent funded by the three armed services. But if I was in the music department, I'd also be funded by the Pentagon, although it wouldn't look that way in the bookkeeping. The reason is quite simple. If the electrical engineering department doesn't have enough funding, they're not going to have a music department. If the electrical engineering department gets ample funding, there's a little spillover for things like the music department. So somebody in the music department may think they're not being funded by the Pentagon, but that's a bookkeeping trick. We should recognize it.

Incidentally, to say you're funded by the Pentagon is misleading. That means you're funded by the taxpayer, who doesn't know anything about it. The reason why the Pentagon doesn't care what you do — and they didn't, they've been the best funder there was — is because they're not under congressional surveillance and the generals understood that their domestic function is to be part of the method by which the costs and risks are transferred to the general population. Costs and risks are socialized, and the profit is privatized. That's called capitalism. And the Pentagon is one component of this. The same with the NIH.

Returning to Amartya Sen, I remember reading something he wrote about the infamous 1943 Bengal famine. Bengal at the time was a major rice-producing area.[45]

In fact, quite commonly during periods of even the most extreme famines there's plenty of food. The famines have to do with access. And that has to do with socioeconomic arrangements. The same is true in the U.S. As I mentioned before, the statistics are not good, but a rough estimate seems to be that about 30 million people are hungry in the U.S., and among children the percentage is higher. That's not because of a shortage of food. In fact, last year the U.S. spent $24 billion or so to subsidize farmers to keep prices up because there's too much food.

Talk about evolving U.S. policy in Colombia. The Interhemispheric Resource Center in Albuquerque has just issued a statement: "U.S. Policy in Colombia: Towards a Vietnam Quagmire." Do you think that's an appropriate analogy? The New York Times *writes in an editorial titled "Dangerous Plans for Colombia" that the aid to Colombia "risks dragging the United States into a costly counterinsurgency war."* [46]

I don't like the phrase "Vietnam quagmire" for Vietnam or Colombia. Were the Russians caught in a quagmire in Afghanistan? They shouldn't have invaded. The problem with the Afghan war is not that the Russians got caught in a quagmire. It's that they shouldn't have invaded the country. The same is true of the U.S. and Vietnam. The fact that it became costly to the U.S., which is what a quagmire means, is irrelevant. The U.S. invaded South Vietnam and destroyed it, along with much of the rest of Indochina. So I think we ought to keep away from the phrase.

Interestingly, the IRC is an alternative organization.

They do wonderful work, but the problem in Colombia is not whether the U.S. will get dragged into a war. That's a minor issue. The major issue is what this is all about. Take a look at today's *New York Times* and *Boston Globe*. Both papers happen to have articles about this issue, although I'm not sure they entirely realize the connection. The *Times* has an article on Bolivia, where farmers are staging big protests.[47] One background reason is that there are farmers who have been compelled to grow coca because there are no other options. The U.S. has come in with crop destruction programs and counterinsurgency operations which have destroyed their coca crops, and now they're starving. So they're among those who are protesting, though the immediate causes are different.

Bolivia is one of the poorest countries of the world. So first they are driven to coca production by the "Washington consensus" and IMF/World Bank programs which say, You've got to open your country up to agriculture and other imports and you have to be a rational peasant producing for the agro-export market trying to maximize profit. You put those conditions together and it spells c-o-c-a. A rational peasant producing for the agro-export market when the country is being flooded by subsidized Western agricultural production is going to be producing coca. Then the West comes in and violently wipes it out, and they end up with peasants protesting in the streets. That's part of what is going on in Bolivia.

The *Boston Globe* has a good article on Colombia by a reporter in one of the areas that's targeted for the new program where the United States is planning to come in to destroy the crops.[48] That's actually a cover for eliminating the guerrillas. These are areas that are under guerrilla control and have been for a long time.

This is the FARC.

There's another guerrilla organization, the ELN, but it's mainly FARC. Those are the areas that are targeted by the new program. The paramilitaries are up to their neck — as is the military — in narco-trafficking, but they're not targeted by the program. So the military program happens to be concentrated in the areas of guerrilla control and not the areas of military and paramilitary control, although it's well known that they're deep into narco-trafficking in pretty much the same way the guerrillas are, namely the paramilitaries tax production, just like the guerrillas. In fact, the involvement of the guerrillas in coca production is just that they tax everything. So they tax coca production, too. There may be some other involvement nobody knows about, but that's basically it.

What does the *Boston Globe* article on Colombia say? Colombia peasants are terrified because there are rumors going around that the U.S.-Colombian program is going to start fumigating. If they fumigate, it's going to be like Bolivia. That will destroy their crops. In fact, they'll destroy not only the coca crops but maybe other crops.

The chemical and biological warfare that the U.S. carries out, and that's what it is, may say it's going after coca, but it has unknown consequences for the rest of the ecology. It's an experiment, after all, and these are third world people. You just carry out experiments. You don't know what's going to happen. If it destroys the forests, too bad, we'll change the mix next time. So Colombians are terrified that the programs are going to wipe out their livelihoods. They probably don't know about Bolivia, but then they'll be like Bolivian peasants whose protests are described in the *New York Times*.

These are two *New York Times*–owned newspapers, incidentally, so we're talking about two branches of the *New York Times* discussing different aspects of the policy as it affects the poor people, the peasants.

Here we're getting to the issues, not the quagmire. Whether the U.S. manages to keep troops out of it and lets the Colombian army do the dirty work or not is not the issue. The policies are not nicer if the Colombian military and its paramilitary associates carry out the policies under U.S. direction, funding, and pressure. The Colombian government is dragging its feet, not very happy, apparently, about the U.S. insistence on destruction and counterinsurgency rather than, say, funding of alternative crops. The U.S. isn't opposed to that, but it's a concern for others, perhaps Europe.

The U.S. will support the military and hence, indirectly, the paramilitaries. It is not disputed, not controversial, that they are responsible for the overwhelming mass of the atrocities. They're mostly attributed to the paramilitaries, but the paramilitaries who are very closely linked to the military. Human Rights Watch has a report that documents the ties between high military authorities and the paramilitaries.[49] Farming out atrocities to paramilitaries is standard operating procedure. Serbia in Kosovo and Indonesia in East Timor are two recent examples.

Almost paralleling Central America, would you say?

In many ways. There are different mixtures in different countries. So the U.S. war against Nicaragua had to use U.S.-run paramilitaries, the contras, because the usual repressive force, the army, wasn't available, and the U.S. public wouldn't tolerate direct invasion, like the Kennedy-Johnson attack against South Vietnam. But in El Salvador, they just used the army.

And affiliated death squads.

They're kind of like paramilitaries. Often they are straight military officers. In Colombia, the resort to paramilitaries actually traces back to the Kennedy administration. It had been a very violent place with a hideous history. In 1962, the Kennedy administration sent a team to Colombia headed by General William Yarborough of Special Forces. He advised the Colombian military on how they should deal with their domestic problems. His recommendations, which were then implemented, with joint training and so on, were that the security forces were to be trained to "as necessary execute paramilitary, sabotage and/or terrorist activities against known communist proponents."[50] This means union leaders and peasant organizers, priests and teachers and human rights activists. That's understood. The Kennedy administration proposal, then implemented, was to use military and paramilitary terror against that sector of the population, and that led to a change in the violence. It got a lot worse, which is recognized by Colombian human rights activists.

Then comes the period of mostly U.S. influence on the system, and it has been pretty awful. Just in the 1990s there have been at least a million and a half refugees forced out. The political killings run around ten a day, mostly by paramilitaries and military. Colombia is potentially a very rich country, but there's a huge amount of poverty, suffering, and starvation. That's the basis for the guerrilla movements, which are quite strong by now. The U.S. is now moving in to try to destroy them.

That's the background, and that's what ought to be discussed — not whether this is a Vietnam quagmire, or whether it will be too costly to us, as in the *New York Times* editorial.

Incidentally, there's another question that ought to be raised. What right do we have to do anything in Colombia? There happens to be a lethal drug produced in the United States that is killing far more people than cocaine. The Supreme Court just described it as the major health hazard in the United States — tobacco. We force that on other countries of the world. Countries in, say, East Asia not only have to accept our lethal drugs but they have to accept advertising for them, advertising aimed at vulnerable populations, like women and children.

These issues came up at the same time that President Bush was announcing the latest phase of the drug war with great fanfare. With virtually no media coverage, the U.S. Trade representative conducted hearings on the refusal of Thailand to accept advertising for U.S. lethal drugs. They were threatened with trade sanctions, which are murderous for them, if they don't accept U.S.-produced drugs, which in reality means advertising, too, whatever the words may be.

In effect, it's as if the Colombian cartel could insist that we import cocaine and allow them to post billboards in Times Square showing how cool it is for kids to use it. Suppose China, where millions of people are being killed by our lethal drug, would say, OK, we're going to go into North Carolina and carry out counter-insurgency operations and chemical and biological warfare to destroy the drugs that you are forcing on us. You've even forced advertising on us. Do they have a right to do that? If they don't have that right, how do we have a right to do anything in Colombia?

That's the most elementary question that ought to be asked. That is never raised. At least I can't find it. Even the critics of the new program don't go that far. But that's not going far.

We recognize that China doesn't have that right. If China tried to claim such a right, we'd probably nuke them. But we're supposed to have that right. Again, going back to the beginning of our discussion, these are the kinds of things that people ought to be asking themselves. And they're not profound. It's not like quantum physics. It is right on the surface that we have absolutely no right to do a thing in Colombia.

If we have a problem with drugs, that problem is here. And it's known how to deal with it. So when this new appropriation was passed, there was an amendment proposed by Nancy Pelosi, a representative from California, that some of the money be used for rehabilitation programs here. It was voted down. The Clinton administration has also rejected any emphasis on such programs, though it is well known that they are much more effective than criminalizing drugs, and far more than source-country control, the

U.S. Plan Colombia. A famous Rand Corporation study found that rehabilitation programs are seven times as cost-effective as criminalization, eleven times as effective as border interdiction, and twenty-three times as effective as source-country control.[51] But that's not what's wanted. Policymakers want harsh punitive measures at home, and military helicopters and crop destruction abroad.

If we have a problem here, deal with it here, not only with rehabilitation and education but also with looking at the socioeconomic basis of it. There are reasons why people turn to self-destructive drugs, so take a look at those. These are all problems within the United States. They give us no justification for carrying out chemical and biological warfare and military action in other countries, whether that military action is done by proxy or not. These are the real questions, but invoking "Vietnam quagmires" leads elsewhere, to the side issue of whether the U.S. might get trapped into something costly to itself — a side issue in the case of Vietnam, too, or Russia in Afghanistan.

You've said that war tribunals are for people who lose wars. In response to an audience question at the "Right of Return" conference at Boston University, you quoted something very interesting about war tribunals. What's the citation?

A spokesman for the International Relations Committee of the House of Representatives was asked a question about whether the war crimes tribunal would go after NATO for its war crimes, which have certainly been committed in Yugoslavia. He says, "You're more likely to see the U.N. building dismantled brick-by-brick and thrown into the Atlantic than to see NATO pilots go before a U.N. tribunal."[52] Which is correct. They know better than to go after NATO.

Jamie Shea, who was the official NATO spokesman during the war, was asked a similar question last May. He discounted the threat of NATO liability for war crimes. He said, NATO is the friend of the tribunal. NATO countries are those that have provided the finances to set up the tribunal. NATO countries have established the tribunals, fund them, and support their activities on a daily basis. Therefore he is certain that the prosecutor would only indict people from Yugoslavia. I'm quoting from a very good paper by Robert

Hayden, a very good East European specialist at the University of Pittsburgh, on the way the tribunals work, how they handle the same war crimes when they're conducted by NATO and when they're conducted by one or another party in Yugoslavia, mostly Serbs. His paper is called "Biased Justice."[53] It's excellent.

How did you get it?

He sent it to me.

Again, going back to that guy who works at Logan Airport — Robert Hayden doesn't know who I am. I can't get hold of it.

I asked Hayden for it. It's a long story, but I had gotten in touch with him recently because of common interests. I was interested in some of the work he was doing, so I asked him to send me his paper. But it's available now on the Internet.

In your presentation at the "Right of Return" conference, you gave an over-view of U.S. Mideast policy in the 1990s. You concluded with the following, speaking of U.S. policy: "These are not laws of nature. They can be changed. The most important changes will have to take place right here. Unless they take place within the U.S., it's not going to matter much what happens elsewhere."[54] It seems like you're taking agency and autonomy away from groups and movements outside the U.S. Is that your intention?

It's not my intention, and it's not true. There's an interplay between what happens elsewhere and what happens here. But say, Arundhati Roy's protest against dam projects in India is likely to have only limited effect unless it sparks protests here, because here is where the policies of the World Bank and the international agencies are going to be determined. It's not that what goes on in India is irrelevant. Of course it's not irrelevant. Even a totalitarian state is affected by what people do. But the primary agency is going to be here, just because of distribution of power.

Things get stimulated here by what happens abroad. Take, say, genetically modified organisms. The protest has been very strong abroad, in India, Europe. It began to have a big effect when it flew over the Atlantic. And it came over the Atlantic as a result of protests elsewhere, which have something like the feared "virus effect" of independent development.

It wasn't that it had been absent here, but it was significantly stimulated by protests elsewhere. Then it happened here, and pretty soon you had Monsanto backing off publicly. We should not disregard the facts about the way power is distributed. That means the primary responsibility is here on most issues, not on everything, but on most issues, just because this is the richest and by far the most powerful country in the world.

When you talk about the Middle East, a topic that's been close to you and that you have been addressing for decades, I sense a certain weariness in your voice and body language when you go through the record, the recitation of facts. You do liven up during the questions and answers? Is that a fair assessment?

I can't judge that. You have to. But if it's true, I can understand why. It is kind of frustrating after twenty-five years to discover, not that it's a big surprise, that the most elementary facts cannot enter the public record. I'm not talking about arcane facts, but the most elementary ones that I talked about at Boston University: the diplomatic record, U.N. Resolution 242 and what the Oslo framework meant when it was instituted. It was quite clear. Anyone who knew the facts about what had happened could tell it. I wouldn't change anything that I wrote on the topic.

But those facts are not only not in the media, they're mostly not even in the scholarly record. They've been wiped out. You have to look really hard to find out what the U.S. did and what Israel did in January 1976, when the Security Council debated a proposal for a two-state settlement, including U.N. 242. It was blocked by a U.S. veto. These are important things. You'll also have to figure out what U.N. 242 means. It's on the record, but you're going to have a hard time finding it. Many of the major scholarly books don't even include it, or else distort it.

You shared a panel at that conference with Ilan Pappé of Haifa University. He's one of what is called the "new historians" in Israel, along with Benny Morris, Avi Shlaim, Tom Segev, and Zeev Sternhell. Do they represent something important in Israel?

Ilan Pappé in particular, and others as well, are doing extremely good historical work. He's helped to reconstruct the self-image of educated Israelis, and it's even working its way into the school curriculums. Sure, that's important, just like it's important when as a result of the 1960s in the U.S. it became for the first time really possible to take a minimally honest look at our own history with regard to the indigenous population.

Until the 1960s that was almost impossible. But work — incidentally, work that began outside the academy, by Francis Jennings and others, using the fact that there was a tremendous amount of popular mobilization at the time — was able to bring about a recognition of the parts of the actual history which is now seeping into public consciousness. Not seeping very far, I should say. We still name our military helicopter gunships after victims of genocide. Nobody bats an eyelash about that: Blackhawk. Apache. And Comanche. If the Luftwaffe named its military helicopters Jew and Gypsy, I suppose people would notice. Or the mockery of mascots for sports teams. It's very ugly. But still, it's a change.

A front-page New York Times *story says Israel's use of torture on Palestinian suspects has now been banned, and the practice of stripping Palestinians of their residence rights, particularly in East Jerusalem, has all but ended. In a landmark ruling, the equal right of Arabs to land allocated by the state has been affirmed, and for the first time in Israel's history, a part of a Jewish town that had been taken away by the state may now be returned to its Arab citizens. Natan Sharansky, the minister of the interior, is quoted as saying, "If you want to have a stable, normal, democratic Zionist society, you have to give minimal rights, at the least."* [55]

These developments are important, but are not terribly exciting. Sharansky himself has a shocking record of opposition to elementary civil rights. He refused to sign a statement supporting a Palestinian editor who had come under attack because he didn't feel it was his business to support the civil rights of Arabs. But these are all changes. On the other hand, let's be a little careful how we respond. For example, when the Israeli Supreme Court finally declared that torture should not be legal, Anthony Lewis had an article called "A Light Unto the Nations" saying that now Israel is a light unto the nations because it joined the nations who need its illumination in saying that you shouldn't carry out torture.[56] It would be nice if they stopped torturing people routinely, but it doesn't make them a light unto the nations.

The Supreme Court decision on the lands was a pretty startling case. Up until now, about 90 percent of the land has been essentially barred from non-Jewish citizens. Western commentators have denied this. They've described Israel as a wonderful democracy, a leading light, and simply denied these facts. The fact that the courts made a dent in that system, we have to see what it means, but they made a dent. They allowed one Arab family to move to land run by the agencies that are fixed by law to serve only interests of Jewish people — not citizens, incidentally, but Jewish people in the diaspora, too. I can have access to those lands, but not the people who live there. If that's changed, that's good, but I'm not going to have a parade about it.

As for Sharansky's comment about returning the land to the village — I think it's mentioned in the article — this is Kafr Kassem, not just any old village. That's the scene of one of the worst massacres in Israel's history. Soldiers simply massacred forty-nine Palestinians who hadn't heard of a curfew that had been announced when Israel was invading Egypt in 1956. They just killed them. The officer in charge was sentenced and had to pay the equivalent of a penny, and some lower people got a couple of years in jail, kind of like the My Lai massacre in Vietnam. So it's not just any old land. Then after that, much more of their land was taken away, even after the massacre. So this is nice if some of their land goes back, but I'm not cheering, exactly.

Do you think the Times *is reporting on the massacre now because the game is essentially over?*

They've probably mentioned it before and may have reported it at the time. But at the time the *Times* was not a pro-Israel paper. It was kind of non-Zionist. So it's quite possible that they reported it accurately at the time. In recent decades, the *Times* has been a highly pro-Israel paper. Even this report is extremely misleading. For example, if I remember correctly, it gives the impression that settlement expansion is being reduced in the territories under Ehud Barak, and it's the opposite. Settlement is going up. If you see the Hebrew press, you read it every day.

The same day as the conference, the Boston Globe *ran two op-eds, one by Hussein Ibish of the American-Arab Anti-Discrimination Committee, and one by the Israeli novelist and journalist A.B. Yehoshua.[57] You describe Yehoshua as kind of on the liberal left.*

I asked Ilan Pappé about him. In fact, I thought he was probably a supporter of Meretz, the left wing of the political establishment. I think he said yes, but I'm not sure. Anyway, he's on the liberal left part of the spectrum. The *Globe* ran it in connection with the conference. That's mentioned if you look closely.

Yehoshua's article is disgraceful. His argument is that there aren't any refugees. You guys are mistaken. These are just displaced people, not refugees. Kind of like I moved from Cambridge to Lexington. I'm not a refugee. If I had been forced to move from Cambridge to Lexington, I would be a displaced person, not a refugee. They just moved from one part of their homeland to another. If you're an Arab, you don't care where you live. It's here or there or somewhere else. So there aren't any refugees anyway. Their calling themselves refugees is just part of their effort to try to kill all the Jews. He didn't say that, but that's the hidden statement right underneath it.

His picture of the history is quite different from that of the historians. So for example he says, correctly, that Israel lost 6,000 people during the 1948 war and you can't give them back to us, implying and saying that it was just an attack by the Arabs against the Jews. He knows better than that. He's literate, and he probably remembers it.

It started as a civil war within the Palestinian British mandate in which the Jewish population, which was much better armed and organized, had by far the best of it. There were plenty of atrocities on both sides. By the time the state was declared, six months after the civil war broke out, about 300,000 Palestinians had already been expelled or fled under threat.

After that, after the state was established, the Arab states did enter. There was maybe a week in which the outcome was uncertain, but after about a week or ten days it was pretty clear that Israel was by far more powerful. There was only one serious Arab army, the Transjordan army, but it was under British control. They had a sort of tacit arrangement with Israel that they'd kind of leave each other alone. The best scholarly study of this is by one of the "new historians" you mentioned, Avi Shlaim.[58]

So that army was out of it since it was under British control. Virtually all the fighting took place in the area designated for the Palestinian state. There were plenty of massacres. One of Ilan Pappé's students, Teddy Katz, has a dissertation coming out as a book on a new massacre that was discovered in Tantura in late May 1948.[59] It has already been discussed in the Hebrew press. Yehoshua knows all this. He can't fail to know it.

So the picture is by no means the way he describes it. The effort to claim that the Palestinians are not refugees, just displaced people and therefore there's nothing to talk about, is miserable apologetics. It's as if we were to say, and maybe people do say, that the Cherokees have no real complaints. After all, they moved from one part of their homeland to another. What do they care?

1   T-Bone Slim, *Juice Is Stranger Than Friction: Selected Writings of T-Bone Slim,* ed.
     Franklin Rosemont (Chicago: Charles H. Kerr Publishing, 1992).

2   Sean D. Murphy, *Humanitarian Intervention: The United Nations in an Evolving
     World Order* (Philadelphia: University of Pennsylvania Press, 1996).

3   See Noam Chomsky, *American Power and the New Mandarins* (New York:
     Pantheon, 1969), Chapter 2.

4   David Schmitz, *The United States and Fascist Italy, 1922–1940* (Chapel Hill:
     University of North Carolina Press, 1988); Schmitz, *Thank God They're On
     Our Side: The United States and Right-Wing Dictatorships, 1921–1965* (Chapel
     Hill: University of North Carolina Press, 1999); John P. Diggins, *Mussolini
     and Fascism: The View from America* (Princeton: Princeton UP, 1972). See also
     Noam Chomsky, *World Orders Old and New,* expanded edition (New York:
     Columbia UP, 1996), pp. 37–44.

5   See references from note 4 above.

6   See Noam Chomsky, *Deterring Democracy,* expanded edition (New York: Hill
     and Wang, 1992), pp. 37–45.

7   *Foreign Relations of the United States, 1961–63: American Republics,* vol. 12
     (Washington, DC: Government Printing Office, 1997).

8   *Foreign Relations of the United States, 1961–63.* See also Noam Chomsky, *Profit
     Over People: Neoliberalism and Global Order* (New York: Seven Stories Press,
     1999), pp. 63–87.

9   No source has ever been found for this quote, which first appeared in *Time,*
     November 15, 1948, and has often been repeated since, sometimes
     referring to Somoza, sometimes to Trujillo. See Schmitz, *Thank God They're
     On Our Side,* p. 313.

10   Cited in *New Internationalist* 314 (July 1999).

11   See Alex Carey, *Taking the Risk Out of Democracy: Corporate Propaganda Versus
     Freedom and Liberty,* ed. Andrew Lohrey (Urbana: University of Illinois
     Press, 1997); Noam Chomsky, "Intellectuals and the State," reprinted in
     Noam Chomsky, *Towards a New Cold War: Essays on the Current Crisis and How
     We Got There* (New York: Pantheon, 1981), pp. 60–85; Chomsky, *Deterring
     Democracy,* Chapter 12; and Chomsky, *Profit Over People,* Chapter 4.

12   Edward L. Bernays, *Propaganda* (New York: H. Liveright, 1928).

13   Walter Lippmann, *The Essential Lippmann: A Political Philosophy for Liberal
     Democracy,* ed. Clinton Rossiter and James Lare (New York: Random House,
     1963).

14   Michael J. Glennon, "The New Interventionism: The Search for a Just
     International Law," *Foreign Affairs* 78: 3 (May–June 1999), pp. 2–7.

15   Noam Chomsky, *A New Generation Draws the Line: Kosovo, East Timor, and the
     Standards of the West* (New York: Verso, 2001), pp. 48–93.

16   Chomsky, *A New Generation Draws the Line,* pp. 94–147, especially 109–12.

17   See references in Chapter 4, note 3.

18   Jan Mayman, "Ethnic Conflict — Fighting for Survival," *Far Eastern
     Economic Review,* February 24, 2000, p. 34.

19   Peter Hartcher, "The ABC of Winning US Support," *Australian Financial Review,* September 13, 1999.

20   John M. Miller, "Indonesian General Sued in U.S. Court," *East Timor Estafeta* 6: 1 (Spring 2000), p. 3. *Estafeta* is published by East Timor Action Network and is on-line at http://www.etan.org.

21   William Cohen, "Turkey's Importance to 21st Century International Security," Department of Defense Briefing, Washington, DC, March 31, 2000, Federal News Service. See Chomsky, *A New Generation Draws the Line,* p. 16.

22   See Steve Biko, *I Write What I Like: A Selection of His Writings,* ed. Aelred Stubbs (Randburg, South Africa: Ravan Press, 1996).

23   Barry Feinberg and Ronald Kasrils, *Betrand Russell's America 1945–1970,* vol. 2 (Boston: South End Press, 1983).

24   Margaret Ramirez, "Salvadorans Honor Slain Archbishop," *Los Angeles Times,* March 19, 2000, p. B3.

25   Václav Havel, "Upheaval in the East," *New York Times,* February 22, 1990, p. A14.

26   Anthony Lewis, "Out of This Nettle," *New York Times,* March 2, 1990, p. A33.

27   Barry Bearak, "Pakistanis Are Uneasy Over Clinton's Visit," *New York Times,* March 25, 2000, p. A4.

28   John J. Mearsheimer, "India Needs the Bomb," *New York Times,* March 24, 2000, p. A21.

29   See *The Bulletin of the Atomic Scientists* 56: 2 (March–April 2000), pp. 22–41.

30   Tariq Ali, "The Panic Button," *Guardian,* October 14, 1999, p. 21.

31   Marc L. Miringoff and Marque-Luisa Miringoff, *The Social Health of the Nation: How America Is Really Doing* (New York: Oxford UP, 1999).

32   Bretton Woods Commission, *Bretton Woods: Looking into the Future* (Washington, DC: Bretton Woods Commisssion, 1994). See Martin Wolf, "Bretton Woods at an Awkward Age," *Financial Times,* October 7, 1994, p. 19, and Michael Prowse, "IMF and World Bank 'Must Adapt to New Global Financial Landscape,'" *Financial Times,* July 7, 1994, p. 5.

33   UNCTAD, *Trade and Development Report, 1999* (Geneva: UNCTAD, 1999). For a review, see Chakravarthi Raghavan, *Third World Economics,* November 1–15, 1999. See also John Eatwell and Lance Taylor, *Global Finance at Risk: The Case for International Regulation* (New York: New Press, 2000), p. 295, estimating a decline of growth rates to two-thirds below the pre-reform period.

34   Henry Tricks, "Latin America No Better Off Now, Says World Bank," *Financial Times,* February 4, 2000, p. 5. See also Richard Lapper, "Policymakers Focus on the Region's Poor," *Financial Times,* Latin American Finance Survey, March 24, 2000, p. 2.

35   See David Felix, "Asia and the Crisis of Financial Liberalization," in Dean Baker, Gerald A. Epstein, and Robert Pollin, eds., *Globalization and*

Progressive Economic Policy (Cambridge: Cambridge UP, 1998); and Felix, "IMF Bailouts and Global Financial Flows," *Foreign Policy In Focus* 3: 5 (April 1998). See also Eatwell and Taylor, *Global Finance at Risk.*

36   United Nations Development Program, *United Nations Human Development Report 2000: Human Rights and Human Development* (Oxford: Oxford UP, 2000). On-line at http://www.undp.org/hdro/.

37   Amartya Sen, "Indian Development: Lessons and Non-Lessons," *Daedalus: Proceedings of the American Academy of Arts and Sciences* 118: 4 (Fall 1989), pp. 369–92. Jean Drèze and Amartya Sen, *Hunger and Public Action* (New York: Oxford UP, 1989); Jean Drèze and Amartya Sen, eds., *The Amartya Sen and Jean Drèze Omnibus: Comprising Poverty and Famines, Hunger and Public Action, and India: Economic Development and Social Opportunity* (New York: Oxford UP, 1999); Jean Drèze, Amartya Sen, and Athar Hussain, eds., *The Political Economy of Hunger: Selected Essays* (New York: Oxford UP, 1995); and references in Noam Chomsky, *Rogue States: The Rule of Force in World Affairs* (Cambridge: South End Press, 2000), pp. 237–38 n4–12.

38   Stéphane Courtois et al., *The Black Book of Communism: Crimes, Terror, Repression,* trans. Jonathan Murphy (Cambridge: Harvard UP, 1999).

39   Alan Ryan, "The Evil Empire," *New York Times Book Review,* January 2, 2000, p. 7: 12. John F. Burns, "Methods of the Great Leader," *New York Times Book Review,* February 27, 2000, p. 7: 6.

40   See books cited in note 37 above.

41   Gerald K. Haines, *The Americanization of Brazil: A Study of U.S. Cold War Diplomacy in the Third World, 1945–1954* (Wilmington, DE: Scholarly Resources Books, 1989). See also Chomsky, *Deterring Democracy,* Chapter 7.

42   See pp. 80–81 and 159–62 above.

43   Arundhati Roy, *The God of Small Things* (New York: Random House, 1997), and Arundhati Roy, *The Cost of Living* (New York: Modern Library, 1999).

44   Amy Dockser Marcus, "Class Struggle: MIT Students, Lured to New Tech Firms, Get Caught in a Bind," *Wall Street Journal,* June 24, 1999, p. A1.

45   Amartya Sen, *Development as Freedom* (New York: Knopf, 1999).

46   Interhemispheric Resource Center and Institute for Policy Studies, Press Release, "U.S. Policy in Colombia: Towards a Vietnam Quagmire," March 7, 2000. Editorial, "Dangerous Plans for Colombia," *New York Times,* February 13, 2000, p. 4: 16.

47   Associated Press, "5 More Die in Bolivia Protests After Emergency Is Declared," *New York Times,* April 10, 2000, p. A3. For specific circumstances, see Chomsky, *Rogue States,* pp. 77–78.

48   Kirk Semple, "Antidrug Efforts Sowing Fear in Colombia," *Boston Globe,* April 10, 2000, p. A1.

49   Human Rights Watch, "The Ties That Bind: Colombia and Military-Paramilitary Links," *Human Rights Watch* 12: 1 (February 2000).

50   Michael McClintock, "American Doctrine and Counterinsurgent State Terror," in *Western State Terrorism,* ed. Alexander George (New York

Routledge, 1991), p. 139, and Michael McClintock, *Instruments of Statecraft: U.S. Guerrilla Warfare, Counterinsurgency, and Counter-terrorism, 1940–1990* (New York: Pantheon Books, 1992), p. 222. See also Chomsky, *Rogue States,* pp. 62–81.

51   See Derrick Z. Jackson, "Study Strikes a Blow Against Mandatory Sentencing for Drug Crimes," *Boston Globe,* May 14, 1997, p. A15, and John Donnelly, "Narcotics Bill Reopens Drug War Debate," *Boston Globe,* April 1, 2000, p. A2.

52   See John Robson, "Tell It to the Judge ... If He Doesn't Eat You First," *Ottowa Citizen,* June 2, 1999, p. A17.

53   Robert M. Hayden, "Biased 'Justice,' Humanrightism and the International Criminal Tribunal for the Former Yugoslavia," *Cleveland State Law Review* 47: 4 (1999), pp. 549–74. A version of the report is also available on-line at http://wwics.si.edu/ees/reports/2000/191hay.htm.

54   See Naseer H. Aruri, ed., *Palestinian Refugees: The Right of Return* (London: Pluto Press, 2001). The "Right of Return" conference was held on April 8, 2000, at Boston University, Boston, Massachusetts. More information on the conference is available on-line at http://www.tari.org/.

55   Deborah Sontag, "Israel Is Slowly Shedding Harsh Treatment of Arabs," *New York Times,* April 7, 2000, p. A1.

56   Anthony Lewis, "A Light Unto the Nations," *New York Times,* September 14, 1999, p. A23.

57   Hussein Ibish, "They Still Have Their Rights," *Boston Globe,* April 8, 2000, p. A11. A.B. Yehoshua, "They Exiled Themselves," *Boston Globe,* April 8, 2000, p. A11.

58   Avi Shlaim, *Collusion Across the Jordan: King Abdullah, the Zionist Movement, and the Partition of Palestine* (New York: Columbia UP, 1988).

59   See Phil Reeves, "Teddy Katz, Justice Campaigner: The Man, the Massacre, and Israel's Secrets," *Independent* (London), January 29, 2000, p. 19. Katz was later sued for libel and retracted his charges, under duress, he claimed. He was denied the right to reaffirm them in court. Detailed forthcoming work by Ilan Pappé provides strong confirming evidence about the massacre, based on direct testimony from Israeli army and Palestinian sources.

7

Solidarity

Woods Hole, Massachusetts, June 12, 2000

*S*ince the last time we talked, honorary degrees have been literally showering *on you. You got two in Canada a couple of weeks ago, and last week you were given one by your alma mater, Harvard. There was a little distinction between Canada and Harvard.*

The degree from Harvard didn't mention anything connected with any of my political activities, which is the first time that's happened in my memory. But so be it.

You were given degrees by the University of Toronto and the University of Western Ontario. A couple of weeks before that, there was a very critical op-ed on you in the Globe and Mail. *I compared that with a similar op-ed that appeared about a year before in the* Wall Street Journal, *also just about the time you were going to get a degree from Columbia University.[1] Did you notice any similarities?*

They were very similar. The *Wall Street Journal* article was timed for the day of the Columbia University graduation. I don't know if the editors will be too happy about this, but it had been copied by the president, who was handing it around at the celebratory luncheon afterward, because people found it amusing, I guess.

In our last interview, you actually surprised me by mentioning a song by T-Bone Slim.[2] Apparently you had read about it in some book. Are there any other musical references in your writing?

It just shows you really haven't read what I've written carefully. [*Laughs.*] I actually quoted that in print — but I'll leave it to you to find out where. I read it in a collection of T-Bone Slim's songs which was put out by one of the anarchist publishers a couple of years ago.[3] I kind of liked that one.

Going back to the thirties and forties and that whole period of Woody Guthrie and the Weavers, were you ever connected to any of that music?

Not much. I used to listen to Leadbelly years ago. I heard it but I was not much part of it.

Some music groups today take inspiration from you, like Rage Against the Machine, U2, Chumbawamba, and Bad Religion, with whom you've actually recorded. Are they in touch with you?

Just for interviews now and then. I had an interview with a musician from Rage Against the Machine a couple of weeks ago. I hear about it now and then, but I honestly don't know anything about it.

Talk a little bit about linguistics. In layman's terms, could you explain your theory of language?

First of all, theories aren't personal. Nobody owns them. So there is an approach to language of which I'm one of the participants in studying it and there are contributors from lots of sources and plenty of interaction. It starts from the fact, and it's not a very controversial fact, that the capacity for language is a species-specific property. That is, every normal human being has that capacity. As far as we know, it's biologically isolated.

A capacity isn't one thing. It has many strands. So for example, the fact that I'm using my tongue when I speak is not biologically isolated. Other organisms have tongues, like cats. And undoubtedly there are many other aspects of it that are shared by primates or mammals or maybe all of life.

But some particular crucial aspects of language do appear to be biologically quite isolated with properties that we don't find elsewhere in the biological world. There's nothing homologous, meaning same origins, or analogous, meaning roughly the same structure, among other species. So it's some kind of unique aspect of human intelligence that may have developed in many hominid lines, but only one has survived, namely us.

The one that survived apparently came from a pretty small breeding group, maybe tens of thousands of people, maybe a hundred or two hundred thousand years ago, something in that range. Since that time, there has been essentially no time for evolutionary effects to have become detectable and, as far as is known, there's extremely little genetic variation among existing humans as compared with other species. So we're a very homogenous species, and the language faculty in particular seems to be essentially shared. What that means is that if your kids grow up in East Africa they'll learn to speak Swahili as perfectly as anyone there. If their kids grow up in Boulder, Colorado, they'll speak the Boulder dialect of English as well as anyone there.

These characteristics seem to be a shared and specific part of our genetic endowment. We want to find out what they are. What they are, wherever they are, they allow an infant, maybe even pre-birth, there's evidence for that, but certainly very early on, to do some pretty astonishing things. First the infant has to pick out of the environment, which is a lot of undifferentiated noise and activity, the child has to somehow select out of that massive confusion the parts that are language. Nobody knows how to do that.

There are similar problems faced by other organisms. Insects, which seem to be more similar to humans in this respect than any other known organism — no relevant evolutionary relationship, obviously — a bee, for example, has to be able to pick out of all the activity that it observes just the parts which are what are called the "waggle dance," the dance of the bees that's used to communicate distance and the quality of the flower. Exactly how that's done, nobody knows. When we look at bees dancing around, we don't see it. You have to be a bee to see it. In fact, to discover it is sophisticated enough a trick that you can get a Nobel Prize for it.

A human has a much more complicated task to pick out a language, and no other organism will do that. If you raise an ape in the same environment as a child without special training, and even with special training, the ape won't pick out the linguistic activities as a category distinct from anything else. It's just a mass of things happening. But somehow a human infant is designed to do exactly that.

The infant has some sort of mental faculty, some special component of the whole intellectual system, call it the language faculty, and that faculty picks out the stuff that's linguistic, that's language-related, and then passes through various transitions and gets to the point where you and I are, where you use this system of knowledge freely and productively to talk about new circumstances in ways that are not caused by the circumstances in which you are nor caused by your inner state but are somehow appropriate to the circumstances and coherent. Those are the rough facts about language, which have been observed for hundreds of years.

The next question is, How is it done? What's the nature of the initial state of the language faculty, the shared initial state, the genetically determined initial state? What are its properties? How do these get refined and shaped and modified in one way or another through interaction with the environment to lead to the mature state of what we call having a language? That's the topic.

In order to investigate it, there are some upper and lower bounds that have to be satisfied by the theory of the initial state. It has to be at least rich enough to account for the fact that a child does — on the basis of the scattered evidence around it — arrive at a state of knowledge which is highly specific, very articulated, extremely detailed, productive, applies to new circumstances, and does so in a very rich and complex way, as you can demonstrate.

So the initial state has to be at least rich enough to account for that transition. But it can't be so rich as to exclude some of the options. So you can't, for example, say, The initial state is my dialect of English. It can't be that rich, because that won't account for your dialect of English, or somebody speaking Japanese. So the upper bound that you can't go beyond is as much complexity and richness as would rule out possible languages, not just actual ones, but possible ones that could be attained. The lower bound is that it has to be at least rich enough to account for the fact that in every linguistic community a normal child will acquire a rich, complex understanding and capacity to use the language of that community.

In between those bounds lies the truth about the initial state.

You study it by looking basically at those two problems. What principles must it have in order to be able to be articulated as a particular complex system? The study of languages of widely different typology puts a constraint on whether you are going too far in imposing internal structure. That's where the subject is.

You've written more recently about what you call a "minimalist program."
Can you explain what that is about?

In the last twenty years or so, there has been a huge explosion of research which has dealt with typologically quite varied languages. We can suspect, and more or less know in advance, that they're all going to be more or less alike. Otherwise you couldn't learn any of them. The basic structure of them, including the meanings of words and the nature of sentences, just has to come from inside. You don't have enough information to have all that richness of knowledge.

If it comes from inside, it's going to be shared. So we would predict that, say, a Martian looking at humans the way we look at other organisms would see them as all basically identical, with minor variations from one another. We have to discover just what that Martian would be seeing, what's the mold that they're all cast to and how does experience lead to slight variations.

A lot's been learned about that. It's also opened new questions which happen to interest me particularly. That is what's sometimes called the minimalist program, a program of research, not a set of answers, which asks questions that really couldn't be asked before.[4]

Maybe they're premature now, but it may be possible that we know enough about language to be able to raise these questions. These are questions about how well the system is designed. There are certain conditions that language simply must meet in order to be usable at all. For example, it has to be accessible to the sensorimotor system. If it's not, you might have it but nobody would know it. It has to be accessible to systems of thought. Otherwise you yourself couldn't use it. You could be sitting there and you couldn't use it to think or articulate your thoughts. Those are minimal conditions that the system must meet.

So you can ask, at least in theory, the question, How close does language come to being an optimal solution to the problem of satis-

fying those external conditions, what are called "interface conditions"? That's led to quite interesting and surprising work, which
suggests that in unexpected ways there is some important nontrivial
element of optimal design in the system — which is intriguing if true.

*Have you thought about the differences in script and how they're acquired?
For example, Hebrew, Urdu, Armenian, Korean, Chinese, and Hindi are all
radically different scripts.*

They can't really be radically different. We know that. Furthermore, they're a superficial aspect of language.

What I meant is they can't be used interchangeably.

But we can be quite certain that they're very similar. They're a
representation of very similar objects, namely human languages.
When I say that they're superficial, it's extremely recent in human
history that they even exist. Even today, they exist only for part of
the human population. They are definitely secondary, despite what's
claimed sometimes in postmodern discourse. They are a secondary
reflection of the language capacity. Its products can be represented
in a number of different ways, and these are some of the examples.
You can have syllabic scripts or in a few cases alphabetic scripts. Not
many possibilities.

Much more interesting than that in my opinion is the study of
sign systems. It has only recently, in the last couple of decades, been
discovered that the signing systems that are used by non-hearing
language users are very similar to spoken languages and apparently
acquired in very similar ways by infants going through the same
stages and probably even neurally represented in the same or similar
parts of the brain. So they appear right now to be just another expression of the same language faculty using a different modality.
That's extremely interesting. That wouldn't have been guessed thirty
or forty years ago.

*You took a transatlantic voyage in 1953. Something of interest in terms of
your insight into language happened.*

I was extremely seasick, and that seasickness was made worse
by the fact that everyone around me was talking about what a calm

voyage it was. They said the ocean was like a lake. So I felt doubly seasick. It was also an interesting ship. This was just a couple of years after the war. My wife, Carol, and I were taking our graduate student trip overseas, bumming around. We looked for the cheapest possible liner, which happened to be Canadian Pacific. We went from Montreal. Shortly before we were to go, the ship that we were supposed to go on sank or something. It wasn't available. They had to quickly get another ship. So they dredged up one that was sunk by the Germans in Rotterdam harbor. They washed it off. It wasn't completely seaworthy. It tilted at a funny angle. When you looked off one side you saw the water and when you looked off the other side you saw the sky. When we got off at Liverpool we could tell very quickly who had been on that ship because they were all walking at an angle.

It was a complicated voyage. During the course of it, to get to your point, I had for some years been working on two topics in linguistics. One of them was the approach that I had been taught, which was called procedural. The idea was that linguistics was essentially the study of how to take a corpus of linguistic materials and present them in an organized, simplified form in such a way that they could be used for various purposes, a kind of reduction of a collection of texts to some organized, structured form. That's what I assumed was the right thing, and I was working on that.

Independently of that, I was working on something else, what turned out later to be generative grammar, the topic I was just describing to you. I was thinking about it and trying to work on it on my own. I thought it was kind of crazy. I didn't know at the time that it had a tradition going back to the Indian grammarians in 500 B.C. I was totally unaware of that and only learned it much later.

I was working on these two parallel paths, assuming that the one I was trained in must be correct and that the one I was doing as a hobby must be weird. But the weird hobby seemed to be getting interesting results. My efforts to try to sharpen up and formalize and improve the analytic techniques that were being taught were leading mostly to dead ends. I could publish articles in the *Journal of Symbolic Logic,* but it didn't seem to be going anywhere. In the midst of this bout of seasickness on this tilting ship, I came to the realization that maybe the hobby was really the right way to proceed and the other one was a dead end. I managed to convince myself of that and from then on worked on the hobby.

Talk about the power of language to shape and control political discussion. For example, the IMF's much-criticized "structural adjustment program" has now been renamed "poverty reduction and growth facility." The School of Americas, the notorious training facility for the Latin American military at Fort Benning, Georgia, is now called the Western Hemisphere Institute for Security Cooperation.

Let me just make clear, this has absolutely nothing to do with linguistics. There's no insight into this topic that comes from having studied language. This is all obvious on the face of it to anybody who looks. This is the topic that Orwell satirized, and of course it goes way back. If you have a war between two countries, they're both fighting in self-defense. Nobody is ever the aggressor. Furthermore, they're both fighting for exalted humanitarian objectives. To take some of Orwell's examples, if you're trying to control a population by violence and terror, it's "pacification."[5]

There's plenty of this. The U.S. has a deterrence strategy. Other countries, enemies, don't have a deterrence strategy. Maybe the one real success of deterrence in the postwar period has been the Russian deterrence of a U.S. attack on Cuba, but that's not called deterrence, because it would imply that we attack them. We don't attack. We only defend. This is as old as the hills. I presume you can find this in Genghis Khan's records.

On the other hand, in the past few years it has become comical. I think this is mainly since the early 1990s. My impression is it comes along with the Newt Gingrich Congress, roughly, which was highly sensitive to public relations issues, much more so than its predecessors. It was never missing before, but I think it took a quantum leap at that point. If you look at the Contract with America and the acts of Congress that followed, they're laughable. Orwell would have been in hysterics.

And it's very conscious. The Republicans' chief polling person, Frank Luntz, for example, was asked during the health debate, How do you decide how to formulate the programs for the parties? He said, We form focus groups and do tests on them. We asked them to react to different ways of formulating the same point. When we find that certain ways of formulating it bring out nice vibes and other ones turn people off, we modify the terminology in which we describe it. We present the same policies in these terms and gradually you craft phrases which will sound good.[6]

They're the opposite of what the program actually is, but that doesn't matter. By now they are largely the opposite. The Africa Growth and Opportunity Act is a non-growth and non-opportunity act. They had a wonderful phrase for ending welfare. It was called the Responsibility and Work Opportunity Act. Another was the Freedom to Farm Act, which was going to, as Gingrich put it, end the East German socialist or communist system that we had of forcing farmers to do this and that by government orders and providing subsidies which distorted the market. We were going to free up farmers. The next year, or shortly thereafter, federal subsidies tripled. But it's still the Freedom to Farm Act.

This goes on in case after case, including the ones you mentioned. It very quickly became comical. By now it's just a poor joke. Structural adjustment is just a case in point. I presume they're all using the same PR advisers. It's Orwell's point.

We're all sensitive to criticism and it seems that when it comes from friends and allies it's particularly difficult to deal with. Robert Fisk, a respected Middle East correspondent for The Independent, *spoke at the "Right of Return" conference. He delivered a rather scathing attack on Arab-American organizations. My perception was that it wasn't taken well. Some people were really offended. How do you deliver criticism so that it can be effective?*

I don't think there's any problem in delivering criticism. If you want to deliver criticisms, you have to first make sure they're accurate. He's a terrific reporter and has done great things, but in that case he just wasn't accurate. I don't think he knew the people he was talking to. Many of those people have been doing for years very actively and very courageously exactly the things he says were never done. Yes, they took it pretty negatively.

On the other hand, I was sitting on the platform, there was a lot of applause, mostly from young people, who I think were not unhappy to hear their elders criticized. Dump it on my father. Whether accurately or not. There is something to what he was saying, and all the activists in the audience not only know it, but have been struggling against it for years. It is in fact true that the more or less official Arab organizations have been quite quiescent and to a large extent subordinated to power and that the Arab communities have been also kind of quiet and not interested in being active. However, I think that the kind of criticism he was giving is not only inaccurate but also somewhat unfair. There are reasons for the quiescence.

I can remember very well from my own childhood when Jewish communities were not dissimilar. Right after the Second World War, there were plenty of people dying in displaced persons camps. The Jewish community made virtually no effort to try to have them admitted to the United States. There was one particular Jewish group that was quite active, the American Council for Judaism, which is off the main spectrum and was anti-Zionist. But the major Jewish organizations didn't do much. In fact, they did very little, and very few Holocaust victims made it to the U.S. We don't know exactly where they wanted to go. You can't believe what is reported from the camps because they were under tight control from Zionist organizations.

They couldn't really express themselves freely. But there's very little doubt that most of them would have wanted to come to the U.S. There's been research done on this — in Hebrew only, unfortunately, so far — by Yosef Grodzinsky, a very interesting study called *Good Human Material*.[7] Almost anybody in Europe would have been happy to come to the U.S. at that point. Certainly people coming out of death camps and concentration camps. But they didn't.

It's an interesting story in itself. One of the reasons they didn't is that there was very little effort to bring them here. The communities were quiet. This was right after the Holocaust. Here are the victims, and you could save them, but the communities were quiet. Part of the reason was that they didn't want to be visible. Anti-Semitism wasn't like racism, but it was real.

I remember it as a child and I remember it at Harvard University when I was there, not that long ago. People simply didn't want to be too visible. They were working their way into a society, and there are a lot of problems when you do that. Anti-Arab racism is the last officially tolerated form of racism. The kinds of things that are said about Arabs, publicly in the mainstream, you can't say about any other group now. People are aware of that. They are aware that they are a minority which is regarded with suspicion, sometimes hatred, condemned, vilified.

To put yourself forward in public is an act of some degree of courage. It's not courage like standing up before a death squad, but it's courage. And it's not surprising if people tend to adopt a low posture and try to become accepted. It's not terribly admirable, but it's not surprising. Coming from the outside and condemning them for that was out of place, particularly because the specific criticisms regarding the people in the audience were really incorrect. Many of those people have taken a very strong activist stand on exactly these things and have done so for years and don't like being told they never did it before.

How do you give criticism? Accurately. The right way to do it, whether you can handle it or not, is not in an adversarial fashion but just accurately. I've said things like what I've just said to Arab audiences for years. One of the first articles I wrote happened to be a talk, over thirty years ago, to an Arab audience in which I very harshly condemned the Arab organizations and the Palestinians for acts which — if I recall, the words were "intolerable to civilized opinion," actually stronger words than I've used in criticizing Israel and Jewish groups. They knew what I was talking about.

There was a lot of disagreement. Some of the disagreement later surfaced. I was extremely critical in particular of the PLO and their programs for a democratic secular state which in my view were a fraud. They were not talking about a democratic secular state. They were talking about an Arab state with Jews tolerated as a religion, which is not a secular state. I wrote about this and spoke about it. There was an interchange in one of the left journals which at that time was called *Socialist Revolution*. It's now called *Socialist Review*.[8]

The person who wrote the criticism of what I wrote is a personal friend who was writing under a pseudonym. We both knew it. Nothing hidden between us. We had an interchange about this. It's in print. There are also pieces of it in some books. This was over twenty-five years ago. But I don't find that difficult. I don't think it led to any antagonism. We remain friends. We happen to disagree about this. These are parts of living together. You give and hear criticism and you expect to.

What do you think about striking tactical alliances with groups or individuals that you ordinarily wouldn't be caught in the same room with?

I don't see anything wrong with issue-oriented alliances, up to a limit. I wouldn't want to join with a Nazi organization. But certainly many alliances bring together people who differ very sharply on other issues. For example, for years the only journal I could publish in as long as it existed was a right-wing libertarian journal, *Inquiry*. I think it was supported by the Cato Institute. We had a lot of beliefs and interests in common. The editor is a personal friend. But we also differed very sharply on many things. But that didn't make me feel I shouldn't publish there. We're not a cult, after all. If we're serious, we know we could be wrong. Anyone who's too confident about their beliefs on topics like this is in serious trouble. So where there are differences of opinion, there may well be reason for self-questioning, too. You just make your choices. There's no formula for it.

So you wouldn't subscribe to the criticisms of Ralph Nader for joining with Pat Buchanan in opposing the WTO or the China trade bill?

I wouldn't. If it was being on the same platform, what do you mean joining with him?

Rhetorically...

That's irrelevant. That's a point that Trotsky made years ago when he was accused of being a fascist because he was criticizing Stalinism in the same terms that the fascists were. If somebody else happens to use the same criticisms you do, and they are accurate, that's not a reason to give them up. That kind of joining doesn't make any difference at all. If you mean forming the same organization, then further questions arise.

Let's move on to education. Paulo Freire was a noted Brazilian educator. The thirtieth anniversary of his important book The Pedagogy of the Oppressed *is coming up. Freire once said, "Washing one's hands of the conflict be-*

tween the powerful and the powerless means to side with the powerful, not to be neutral." [9]

I certainly agree with that and would hope that it would be regarded as a kind of truism, which is what it is. Freire's a very important figure. He was writing at approximately the same time at which the Brazilian church and the church in Latin America generally was rethinking its entire past and turning to what came to be called "the preferential option for the poor," recognizing that in the past the church had been the church of the oppressors but it would not be enough just to stand back and be neutral. They had to become engaged in the struggles and efforts of the huge majority of the population who are poor and oppressed.

Part of that was consciousness-raising of the kind that Freire discussed in interesting ways in the educational setting. Priests and nuns or lay workers were forming base communities, reading the Gospels, and rethinking what they meant about their own situation. And they were organizing. All of this was very much in the same spirit, and is exactly on the right track, I think.

There's a major political battle going on today in the U.S. in education. The word "reform" is often attached to it.

"Reform" is one of those words you should watch out for. Changes are called reforms if the powerful are in favor of them. For example, Pol Pot changed a lot of things in Cambodia, but we don't call those reforms. "Reforms" is an Orwellian term. You use it for the changes that you're supposed to support. What are called educational reforms should be evaluated on their own terms, but not on the assumption that because they're called reforms they're necessarily positive. Many are quite destructive.

Alfie Kohn wrote a book called No Contest: The Case Against Competition.[10] *You wrote a favorable blurb for it. Football coach Vince Lombardi once said, "Winning isn't everything. It's the only thing." What kind of societal consequences result from that kind of thinking?*

If anyone were to take that seriously, if you do it on the sports field, it's just obscene. If you do it in the general society, it's outrageous. It happens. I see it with children's sports. Let me give you a personal experience. One of my grandchildren is a sports fanatic. He was describing to me with disappointment a game that was called off. Seven-year-old kids playing baseball, they're all organized into teams, which is OK. You want to play teams, that's fine. They had a game scheduled with another team. The other team didn't have enough players. Some kid didn't come that day. My grandson's team had more than enough players. So they had to call off the game.

The kids were all disappointed. They couldn't have their game. There was an obvious solution. Let some of the kids on his team play on the other team. In fact, you could have one team and still have a game, the kids that are in the field could be the kids at bat, just intermingle. Then they all would have had fun. But then it wouldn't have been a game in which the team with one color won and the team with the other color lost. This way they all had to be disappointed. This isn't a huge problem, but it's carrying the cult of competition to childish absurdity.

When it enters into the rest of life, it's extremely harmful. Any decent human existence is going to be based on sympathy, solidarity, and mutual support. If we push it to the limit, the idea that the only thing to do is win, then in a family the strongest person would take all the food. This is just inhuman. It's just as inhuman when you generalize.

What do you say to the argument that competition is intrinsic to human nature — and not only that, it builds character?

It builds a certain kind of character, namely the kind of character that wants to beat other people down. Is it intrinsic to human nature? First of all, anyone who says anything about what's intrinsic to human nature is automatically talking nonsense, because we don't know very much. But it's a plausible guess that all kinds of characteristics are intrinsic to human nature.

I presume that every one of us could be a torturer under certain circumstances and a saint under different circumstances. All of these things are part of human nature. We don't know any reason to believe that people are fundamentally different in these respects. So, many of the characteristics that emerge are a reflection in part of the kind of people we are but in part of the kind of circumstances in which we grow up and develop. I'm sure you can create social circumstances in which competition governs human nature.

But that takes work. It takes something like, say, market systems. These are held to be intrinsic to human nature, but as Karl Polanyi pointed out in his classic work almost sixty years ago, these are not only not common in human societies, but they have to be driven home almost by force.[11]

Much of the educational system is built around a system of rewards based on grades, beating other students in tests, and then coming to the front of the classroom and being praised by the teacher.

It is, and that's a particular kind of training. It's training in extremely antisocial behavior that is also very harmful to the person. It's certainly not necessary for education.

In what way is it harmful to a person?

It turns them into the kind of people who do not enjoy the achievements of others but want to see others beaten down and suppressed. It's as if I see a great violinist and instead of enjoying the fact that he's a great violinist and I'm not, I try to figure out a way I can break his violin. It's turning people into monsters. This is certainly not necessary for education. I think it's harmful to it. I have my own personal experiences with this, but I think they generalize.

How you deal with day-to-day situations is a complicated matter. But as far as schooling was concerned, it just happens that I went to a school up to about age twelve where there was no competition. I didn't know I was a good student until I got to high school. I knew I had skipped a class and the other kids hadn't, but it never occurred to me that it meant anything. It was just the way it was. Everyone was encouraged to do their best and to help others do their best. You applauded them if they did. If they fell short of their own standards you tried to help them meet them. I didn't really know about the idea of competition for grades until I got into an academic city high school. And the educational level declined at that point.

Incidentally, going on to my last forty-five years of educational experience, which happens to be at MIT, it is not a competitive environment. In a graduate scientific department, technically you have to give grades because there's some formalism that requires it. But people are working together. You don't try to do better than the next guy. You have a common goal. You want to understand this stuff. Let's work on it. It's certainly the most positive way for an educational or a research experience to proceed.

If you've internalized a sense of competition, being number one, getting ahead, while you're a student going through the educational system, by the time you get into the workplace it seems to be almost irreversible.

Maybe. If it is, that's too bad. People ought to be working together in the workplace. For example, again, at least in the kind of graduate scientific research programs I've been aware of and seen, when this happens, as it does, it is indeed destructive. In the better ones, it just doesn't happen. People on the contrary work together because they have a common aim. You're not trying to make the other person's experiment fail.

Let's say in a different kind of environment, like an auto factory, the boss tells you, If you work an extra eight hours this week, I'll increase your pay by $100 and I'll give you an extra week's vacation.

That's a different question. That has nothing to do with harming other people and being first and making sure they're second. That's a question of how you want to react to an inhuman system in which you're forced to exist. You're compelled because of lack of other choices to exist in a system in which some human being can control you, which shouldn't happen in a decent society, and you have to ask, How do I adjust to that? It's like being in prison. If a guard says, If you do such-and-such you'll be punished, and if you do such-and-such you'll get a little extra freedom, you may make choices, and one of them may be to avoid the punishment and accept the reward. But you should do that with an internal understanding of what you're doing. That has nothing to do with competition. On the other hand, if the boss says, Look, if you work harder, I'll punish him, that's a different issue. If you're human, you don't do it.

Let me ask you about your research. You rely somewhat on official declassi-

fied government documents. The New York Times *published excerpts of a CIA report on the 1953 agency coup in Iran which overthrew the elected government of Mohammed Mossadegh and restored the Shah to power.*[12] *When you look at these declassified documents, what kinds of precautions or allowances do you make for omissions, distortions, and outright fabrications?*

If there are fabrications, they would be the kind that appear typically within bureaucracies, when people say things to please the ones at the next higher level because they know that's what they want to hear. That happens all the time. So you have to always compensate for that. If you look at cases where we can follow the chain of evidence from the field up to the executive, we see that. That's one reason why the executive branch of the U.S. government during the Vietnam War never knew what was going on. The field reports, it turns out, were quite accurate. As they moved up the chain of command they were being modified and adjusted to conform to what the next person up wanted to hear. It's a natural way to act if you're a subordinate. By the time they got to the center, they often had no relation to what was going on.

In this case, you would also want to qualify for that. I doubt that there would be conscious distortion of other kinds. It would be unlikely. Also, you have to recognize a very high degree of unconscious ideological control coming from the belief system. Again, we see remarkable examples of this in the declassified record. The most amazing one I know is from the Vietnam War, which has an extremely rich record because of the Pentagon Papers. These were not intended for release. This was not an example of normal government declassification. The Pentagon Papers were more like conquering some country and getting its archives. It led to a release of a flood of other documents, which gave us an unusually rich record. That gives you a lot of insight into how these things work.

Maybe the most interesting part of the Pentagon Papers, and strikingly it's never discussed, is simply the intelligence record and the question of how it reflects ideological preferences at the command center, meaning Washington.

I've written about it in detail, but the brief story is this. In the late 1940s, the United States hadn't quite decided whether to support Vietnamese nationalism, and it had no doubt whatsoever that this meant supporting Ho Chi Minh. They said so straight out. Either support Vietnamese nationalism or support the French. Those were the choices. Around 1950, they decided to support the French. Intelligence was essentially given the task at that point of showing that what we now call the enemy — no longer called nationalist, but just communist — was an agent of either China or Russia. They didn't care which. One or the other.

For several years, the intelligence agencies attempted to fulfill this task. The attempts are kind of comical. Somebody found a copy of *Pravda* in the Bangkok embassy of Vietnam. They concluded after several years that they couldn't do it. This seemed to be the only country, the only movement in Southeast Asia, that didn't seem to have connections either to China or to Russia.

At that point, the decision was made in Washington that this proved that Ho Chi Minh was such a loyal slave of Moscow and Beijing that they didn't even have to send him orders. He was just a superloyal slave. That establishes the point. From that point on, there is literally no discussion in intelligence circles of what is an obvious truth, that the Vietnamese had their own national interests. Even if they were slaves to Moscow and Beijing, they still had their own national interests. That point is never raised, or to be precise, it's brought up in exactly one staff paper which was not submitted.

This is the intelligence records of the CIA, the Defense Intelligence Agency, the State Department. Nobody allowed themselves to perceive something that was obvious on the surface, that the Vietnamese were following their national interests, not simply taking orders and acting as agents of a foreign power. This is a level of self-deception that would be shocking, practically psychotic, and this is right in the middle of an intelligence agency whose task is not to tell pleasant truths to the people at the top but to try to give them an accurate picture of the world. That's maybe an extreme example, but it's not the only one. When you're looking at internal documents, you have to qualify for the ideological distortion that comes from the framework of thought that they're forced into from their educational system or whatever.

And getting into another aspect, you have plenty to suppress. A striking case which fooled me was when the documents finally were released about the 1958 uprising in Indonesia. It was a kind of military effort to strip off the outer islands. I had assumed the United States had to be involved in this, and there was some evidence that it was. An American pilot was shot down. When I read the official documents that came out, I sort of changed my mind. Apparently the U.S. wasn't much involved, to my surprise. Then George Kahin, the founder of Southeast Asian scholarship, and Audrey Kahin came out with a book called *Subversion as Foreign Policy*.[13] They did their own research. They had their own connections with the Indonesian military and they discovered that not only was the U.S. involved but this was probably the major clandestine effort of the postwar period. But the documents had mostly been suppressed in the publicly released materials.

Going back to Iran, that's something to be very much concerned about. The Reagan administration, which would have been the time to release the Iran and Guatemala documents from the early 1950s, suppressed them and probably destroyed them.

That's conceded in the Times *report on Iran, as well.*

It was public. It was so outrageous that the State Department historians, the board of academic historians from the universities, a pretty conservative lot, who supervise the declassification, actually resigned in public protest over the Reagan administration's destruction of documents from the early 1950s. That means we're not getting a lot of what happened at that time and never will. The purpose was to prevent any knowledge of what happened.

There's also a book on Guatemala by a CIA historian, Nick Cullather, who comments on this, as well.[14] He was given what he thought was full access to CIA records when he was inside the CIA as a CIA historian and later discovered he didn't have access. So that material, a lot of it we'll never find out. It's just gone, purposely destroyed. Hence the Iran documents are very partial. Furthermore, they were not very revealing. I saved them just out of curiosity, but I didn't learn anything much from them.

One of the things people ask me about you is, How does he remember all those facts? We've just been talking here impromptu and you've been citing things from memory. How do you do it?

The personal agony is that I don't do it. I'm in agony over the things I forget. When I read things I've written twenty or thirty years ago, I say, My God, how did I forget all of that? I have quite the opposite picture.

What are your plans in terms of MIT and the Boston Red Sox.

I'll be out at the Red Sox park soon with my grandson for our annual breakout into the real world. The other thing, I don't know.

You're not thinking about retirement?

I'm thinking about it.

1 Eli Schuster, "Noam Chomsky: A Degree Too Far," *Globe and Mail,* April 18, 2000, p. A17. Peter Hellman, "A Dishonorable Honorary Degree," *Wall Street Journal,* May 19, 1999, p. A22.

2 See Chapter 6.

3 T-Bone Slim, *Juice Is Stranger Than Friction: Selected Writings of T-Bone Slim,* ed. Franklin Rosemont (Chicago: Charles H. Kerr Publishing, 1992).

4 See Noam Chomsky, *The Minimalist Program* (Cambridge: MIT Press, 1995) and *New Horizons in the Study of Language and Mind* (Cambridge: Cambridge UP, 2000).

5 George Orwell, "Politics and the English Language," in *Collected Essays* (London: Secker and Warburg, 1961), pp. 353–67, especially p. 363.

6 Michael Weisskopf and David Maraniss, "Republican Leaders Win Battle by Defining Terms of Combat," *Washington Post,* October 29, 1995, p. A1. Knight-Ridder/Tribune, "GOP Pollster Never Measured Popularity of 'Contract,' Only Slogans," *Chicago Tribune,* November 12, 1995, p. 11. See also Elizabeth Kolbert, "Shifting Public Opinion by the Turn of a Phrase," *New York Times,* June 5, 1995, p. A1, and "On the Other Hand: Framing the Question," graph, p. B6.

7 Yosef Grodzinsky, *Chomer Enoshi Tov [Good Human Material]* (Tel Aviv, Israel: Hed Artzi, 1998).

8 See Noam Chomsky, "Israel and the Palestinians," *Socialist Revolution* 24 (June 1975), pp. 45–86 and 133–141. See also the Introduction, pp. 4–6.

9 Paulo Freire, *The Politics of Education: Culture, Power, and Liberation,* trans. Donaldo Macedo (South Hadley, MA: Bergin and Garvey, 1985), p. 102. See also Paulo Freire, *The Pedagogy of the Oppressed,* trans. Myra Bergman Ramos, 30th anniversary edition (New York: Continuum, 2000).

10 Alfie Kohn, *No Contest: The Case Against Competition,* revised edition (Boston: Houghton Mifflin, 1992).

11 Karl Polanyi, *The Great Transformation* (Boston: Beacon Press, 1957).

12 James Risen, "Secrets of History: The C.I.A. in Iran—A Special Report," *New York Times,* April 16, 2000, p. 1: 3.

13 Audrey R. and George McT. Kahin, *Subversion as Foreign Policy: The Secret Eisenhower and Dulles Debacle in Indonesia* (New York: New Press, 1995).

14 Nick Cullather, *Secret History: The CIA's Classified Account of its Operations in Guatemala, 1952–1954* (Stanford: Stanford UP, 1999).

Appendix

Some Resources for Further Information

ORGANIZATIONS

Black Radical Congress
PO Box 250791
New York NY 10025-1509
Phone: (212) 969-0348
E-mail: blackradicalcongress@email.com
http://blackradicalcongress.org

Colombia Support Network
PO Box 1505
Madison WI 53701-1505
Phone: (608) 257-8753
Fax: (608) 255-6621
E-mail: csn@igc.org
http://www.colombiasupport.net/

Critical Resistance
1212 Broadway
Suite 1400
Oakland CA 94612-1816
Phone: (510) 444-0484
Fax: (510) 444-2177
E-mail: critresist@aol.com
http://www.criticalresistance.org/

Direct Action Network
PO Box 1485
Asheville NC 28802-1485
E-mail: dan-com@riseup.net
http://www.directactionnetwork.org

East Timor Action Network
PO Box 1182
White Plains NY 10602-1182
Phone: (914) 428-7299
Fax: (914) 428-7383
E-mail: charlie@etan.org
http://www.etan.org/

Global Exchange
2017 Mission Street
Suite 303
San Francisco CA 94110-1296
Phone: (415) 255-7296
Fax: (415) 255-7498
E-mail: info@globalexchange.org
http://www.globalexchange.org

Indonesia Human Rights Network
1101 Pennsylvania Avenue SE
Washington DC 20003-2229
Phone: (202) 546-0044
E-mail: ihrn@etan.org

Food First
Institute for Food and Development Policy
398 60th Street
Oakland CA 94618-1212
Phone: (510) 654-4400
Fax: (510) 654-4551
E-mail: foodfirst@foodfirst.org
http://www.foodfirst.org

Institute for Agricultural Trade Policy
2105 First Avenue South
Minneapolis MN 55404-2505
Phone: (612) 870-0453
Fax: (612) 870-4846
http://www.iatp.org/

International Forum on Globalization
1009 General Kennedy Avenue #2
San Francisco CA 94129-1700
Phone: (415) 561-7650
Fax: (415) 561-7651
E-mail: ifg@ifg.org
http://www.ifg.org/

Interhemispheric Resource Center
PO Box 4506
Albuquerque NM 87196-4506
Phone: (505) 842-8288
Fax: (505) 246-1601
E-mail: irc@irc-online.org
http://www.irc-online.org/

National Labor Committee
275 Seventh Avenue
15th Floor
New York NY 10001-6708
Phone: (212) 242-3002
Fax: (212) 242-3821
E-mail: nlc@nlcnet.org
http://www.nlcnet.org/

Partners in Health
643 Huntington Avenue
Boston MA 02115-6019
Phone: (617) 432-5256
Fax: (617) 432-5300
E-mail: info@pih.org
http://www.pih.org/

Peace Action
1819 H Street NW
Suite 420
Washington DC 20006-3603
Phone: (202) 862-9740
Fax: (202) 862-9762
E-mail: span@peace-action.org
http://www.peace-action.org/

Public Citizen's Global Trade Watch
215 Pennsylvania Avenue SE
Washington DC 20003-1188
Phone: (202) 546-4996
Fax: (202) 547-7392
E-mail: gtwinfo@citizen.org
http://www.tradewatch.org

Rocky Mountain Peace and Justice Center
PO Box 1156
Boulder CO 80306-1156
Phone: (303) 444-6981
http://www.rmpjc.org

School of the Americas Watch
PO Box 4566
Washington DC 20017-4566
Phone: (202) 234-3440
Fax: (202) 636-4505
E-mail: info@soaw.org
http://www.soaw.org/

Student Environmental Action Coalition
PO Box 31909
Philadelphia, PA 19104-0609
Phone: (215) 222-4711
Fax: (215) 222-2896
E-mail: seac@seac.org
http://www.seac.org

Third World Network
http://www.twnside.org.sg/

United for a Fair Economy
37 Temple Place
Boston MA 02111-1308
Phone: (617) 423-2148
Fax: (617) 423-0191
E-mail: info@ufenet.org
http://www.ufenet.org

United Students Against Sweatshops
1413 K Street NW
9th Floor
Washington DC 20005-3400
Phone: (202) 667-9328
Fax: (202) 393-5886
E-mail: kandrewtaylor@hotmail.com
http://www.usasnet.org

Voices in the Wilderness
1460 West Carmen Avenue
Chicago IL 60640-2813
Phone: (773) 784-8065
Fax: (773) 784-8837
E-mail: kkelly@igc.org
http://www.vitw.org/

INFORMATION RESOURCES

Alternative Radio
David Barsamian
PO Box 551
Boulder CO 80306-0551
Phone: (800) 444-1977
Fax: (303) 545-5763
E-mail: ar@orci.com
http://www.alternativeradio.org

Common Courage Press
PO Box 702
Monroe ME 04951-0702
Phone: (207) 525-0900
Fax: (207) 525-3068
http:// www.commoncouragepress.com

Common Dreams Newscenter
PO Box 443
Portland ME 04112-0443
Phone: (207) 799-2185
Fax: (435) 807-0044
E-mail: editor@commondreams.org
http://www.commondreams.org/

Corporate Crime Reporter
1209 National Press Building
Washington DC 20045-2200
Phone: (202) 737-1680

CounterPunch
3220 N Street NW
Suite 346
Washington DC 20007-2896
Phone: (800) 840-3683
Fax: (800) 967-3620
E-mail: counterpunch@counterpunch.org
http://www.counterpunch.org/

Democracy Now!
http://www.democracynow.org/

Dollars and Sense
740 Cambridge Street
Cambridge MA 02141-1401
Phone: (617) 876-2434
Fax: (617) 876-0008
E-mail: dollars@igc.org
http://www.dollarsandsense.org

Fairness and Accuracy in Reporting (FAIR)
130 West 25th Street
Eighth Floor
New York NY 10001-7406
Phone: (212) 633-6700
Fax: (212) 727-7668
E-mail: fair@fair.org
http://www.fair.org/

Foreign Policy in Focus
Institute for Policy Studies
733 15th Street NW
Suite 1020
Washington DC 20005-2112
Phone: (202) 234-9382
Fax: (202) 387-7915
E-mail: leaverfpif@igc.org
http://www.foreignpolicy-infocus.org

FreeSpeech TV
PO Box 6060
Boulder CO 80306-6060
E-mail: director@freespeech.org
http://www.freespeech.org

Independent Media Center
E-mail: general@indymedia.org
http://www.indymedia.org

Institute for Public Accuracy
915 National Press Building
Washington DC 20045
Phone: (202) 347-0020
Fax: (202) 347-0290
E-mail: dcinstitute@igc.org
http://www.accuracy.org/

In These Times
2040 North Milwaukee Avenue
Second Floor
Chicago IL 60647-4002
Phone: (773) 772-0164
Fax: (773) 772-4180
E-mail: itt@inthesetimes.com
http://www.inthesetimes.com/

Labor Notes
7435 Michigan Avenue
Detroit MI 48210-2200
Phone: (313) 842-6262
Fax: (313) 842-0227
E-mail: labornotes@labornotes.org
http://www.labornotes.org

Making Contact
National Radio Project
1714 Franklin Street
Suite #100-251
Oakland CA 94612-3409
Phone: (510) 251-1501
Fax: (510) 251-1342
E-mail: makingcontact@radioproject.org
http://www.radioproject.org

MediaChannel.org
1600 Broadway
Suite 700
New York NY 10019-7413
Phone: (212) 246-0202
Fax: (212) 246-2677
E-mail: editor@mediachannel.org
http://www.mediachannel.org

Multinational Monitor
PO Box 19405
Washington DC 20036-9405
Phone: (202) 387-8030
Fax: (202) 234-5176
E-mail: monitor@essential.org
http://www.essential.org/monitor

New Internationalist
1011 Bloor Street West
Toronto ON M6H 1M1
Canada
Phone: (416) 588-6478
Fax: (416) 537-6435
E-mail: ni@newint.org
http://www.newint.org/

The Progressive
409 East Main Street
Madison WI 53703-2863
Phone: (608) 257-4626
Fax: (608) 257-3373
E-mail: circ@progressive.org
http://www.progressive.org/

PR Watch
Center for Media and Democracy
520 University Avenue
Suite 310
Madison WI 53703-4916
Phone: (608) 260-9713
Fax: (608) 260-9714
E-mail: editor@prwatch.org

Radio for Change
E-mail: info@radioforchange.com
http://www.workingforchange.com/

Weekly News Update on the Americas
339 Lafayette Street
New York NY 10012-9911
Phone: (212) 674-9499
Fax: (212) 674-9139
E-mail: wnu@igc.org

Z Magazine and Z Net
18 Millfield Street
Woods Hole MA 02543-1122
Phone: (508) 548-9063
Fax: (508) 457-0626
E-mail: lydia.sargent@zmag.org
http://www.zmag.org

Index

law: Alien Tort Claims Act, 161;
    international, 35–38, 42, 126,
    163; and torture, 49, 89. *See also*
    International Court of Justice
Leadbelly, 204
Lebanon, 48–49, 163
Left Business Observer, 33, 124
left wing: in foreign countries, 34,
    114, 148; in U.S., 28–29, 30, 73,
    128–29, 153, 213
Lehman Brothers, 102
Levant, 163
Lewis, Anthony, 169, 194
liberalism: in economics, 17, 61,
    65–67, 69, 174–78; of
    intellectuals, 36, 150–51, 153,
    157
liberation theology, 70–72, 215
Libya, 31–32, 35, 41, 89
linguistics, 142–43, 143–44, 204–10
Lippmann, Walter, 20, 151, 152
Lissakers, Karin, 126
literature, 79–80
Lithuania, 132
Lombardi, Vince, 215
Los Angeles Times, 55, 168
Luntz, Frank, 210–11

M

Maclean's, 3
madman theory, 52
Madre, 127
Maimonides, 85
MAI (Multilateral Agreement on
    Investment), 2–5, 8–10, 108, 122
Malaysia, 16, 123
Manchuria. *See* China
manufacturing, 11, 17–19, 67
Manufacturing Consent (Herman and
    Chomsky), 7, 81

Marx, Karl, 20
Massachusetts: public education
    in, 134–35
Massachusetts Institute of
    Technology. *See* MIT
massacres: in Cambodia, 81; in
    China, by Japanese, 148; in
    East Pakistan (Bangladesh),
    164; in East Timor, 48, 114–19,
    154–55, 159; in El Salvador,
    168; in Indonesia, 48, 113–14;
    during Iraqi rebellion, 31; of
    Palestinians, by Israel, 195, 197,
    201n59. *See also* bombing; war
McCarthy, Joseph, 55
McChesney, Robert, 20
Mearsheimer, John, 171
media: alternative, 2, 59, 64,
    108–9, 204; democracy and,
    179; distortion and, 32, 36, 40,
    168; on economics, 3–4, 10–12;
    on Indonesia, 114, 154, 156,
    161; on Iraq bombing, 26,
    38–39, 56; in Israel, 54, 56, 93;
    journals, 26, 59, 93, 213, 214;
    on Laos, 63, 64; on Libya
    bombing, 41; in Thailand, 38,
    47, 55, 56; UNESCO and, 40;
    on U.S. domestic affairs,
    10–12, 28–30, 94, 101–2. *See
    also* censorship; *specific
    publications*
Medicare, 102, 105, 130
Mennonites, 63
Mexico, 64, 68, 70, 93
Miami Herald, 3
Middle East, 15–16, 46–47, 51–53,
    86, 163, 173–74. *See also specific
    countries*

About the Authors

Noam Chomsky, Institute Professor at the Massachusetts Institute of Technology, is a world-renowned linguist, philosopher, and political analyst. He writes extensively and lectures around the world on international affairs, media, U.S. foreign policy, and human rights. He has published nine books with Pluto Press, including *Fateful Triangle, Necessary Illusions,* and *Rogue States.*

David Barsamian lives in Boulder, Colorado, and is the producer of the award-winning syndicated radio program Alternative Radio. A regular contributor to *The Progressive* and *Z* Magazine, his most recent interview books include *Eqbal Ahmad: Confronting Empire* (Pluto Press) and *The Future of History: Interviews with Howard Zinn* (Common Courage). Barsamian has published several other collections of interviews with Noam Chomsky and is the author of the forthcoming *Decline and Fall of Public Broadcasting: Creating Alternatives to Corporate Media* (South End Press, Fall 2001).

Noam Chomsky (left) and David Barsamian (right) at the Harvard Trade Union Program, 2001. Photo by Martin Voelker.

AR's Noam Chomsky Audio Archive

Alternative Radio maintains the largest collection of tapes by Noam Chomsky in the world. For program descriptions and a complete list of Chomsky recordings, visit http://www.alternativeradio.org. Or order toll-free by calling (800) 444-1977. U.S. funds only. Outside the United States, add $1 per tape for shipping and handling (add $1.50 per tape in Australia and Japan). Or write to: AR, P.O. Box 551, Boulder, Colorado, 80306-0551 USA. E-mail: ar@orci.com.

Propaganda and the Public Mind Special Offers

Six-Pack of Chomsky ($60, shipping within U.S. included):

Propaganda and Control of the Public Mind, Cambridge, MA, February 7, 1997. Talk. Two tapes.

Robbing People Blind: US Economic Policy, Cambridge, MA, October 31 and November 3, 1995. Interview. Two tapes.

Class War: The Attack on Working People, Cambridge, MA, May 9, 1995. Talk.

Manufacturing Consent: Media and Propaganda, Cambridge, MA, January 22, 1993. Talk.

Twelve-Pack of Chomsky ($112, shipping within U.S. included):

Globalization: The New Face of Capitalism, Chestnut Hill, MA, October 7, 1999. Talk.

Lessons from Yugoslavia and East Timor, Lawrence, KS, September 20, 1999. Talk.

Kosovo and Iraq, Cambridge, MA, April 21, 1999. Talk.

U.S. Middle East Policy, with Edward Said, Columbia University, New York, NY, April 9, 1999. Talk. Two tapes.

Dialogue with Trade Unionists, Cambridge, MA, February 2, 1999. Talk. Two tapes.

U.S. to World: Get Out of the Way, Lexington, MA, February 1 and February 2, 1999. Interview. Four tapes.

U.S. Human Rights Policy: Rhetoric and Practice, Longmont, CO, May 10, 1998. Talk.

From the following recordings, choose from 23 tapes. Any eight tapes for $77, shipping within U.S. included. All 23 tapes for $200.

It Takes a Lot of Discipline, Cambridge, MA, February 9, 2001. Talk. Two tapes.

At Columbia School of Journalism, New York, NY, April 30, 2000. Talk. Two tapes.

The Cape Cod Interview, Woods Hole, MA, June 12, 2000.

At Z Media Institute 2000, Woods Hole, MA, June 12, 2000. Talk. Five tapes.

U.S. Colombia Policy, Boston, MA, May 12, 2000. Talk.

The Right of Return, Boston, MA, April 8, 2000. Talk. Two tapes.

Liberating the Mind from Orthodoxies, Lexington, MA, April 10, 2000. Interview. Three tapes.

Taking Control of Our Lives, Albuquerque, NM, February 26, 2000. Talk. Two tapes.

The Meaning of Seattle, Boulder, CO, February 23, 2000. Interview.

At the 2000 Harvard Trade Union Program, Cambridge, MA, February 4, 2000. Talk. Two tapes.

Language: Continuity and Innovation, Winona, MN, April 20, 1998. Talk. Two tapes.